SAP® xApps and the Composite Application Framework

 PRESS

SAP PRESS and the SAP NetWeaver Essentials are issued by
Bernhard Hochlehnert, SAP AG

Steffen Karch, Loren Heilig
SAP NetWeaver Roadmap
2005, 312 pp., ISBN 1-59229-041-8

Jens Stumpe, Joachim Orb
SAP Exchange Infrastructure
2005, 270 pp., ISBN 1-59229-037-X

Karl Kessler et al.
Java Programming with the
SAP Web Application Server
2005, 514 pp., ISBN 1-59229-020-5

Chris Whealy
Inside Web Dynpro for Java
A Guide to the Principles of Programming in
SAP's Web Dynpro
2005, 336 pp., ISBN 1-59229-038-8

Jo Weilbach, Mario Herger

SAP® xApps

and the Composite Application Framework

SAP PRESS

© 2005 by Galileo Press
SAP PRESS is an imprint of Galileo Press,
Boston (MA), USA
Bonn, Germany
German Edition first published 2005 by
Galileo Press.

Translation Lemoine International, Inc.,
Salt Lake City, UT
Copy Editor John Parker, UCG, Inc., Boston,
MA
Cover Design department, Cologne, Germany
Printed in Germany

ISBN 978-1-59229-048-2
1st edition 2005, 1st reprint 2007

Contents

4 Implementation Examples 191

5 Outlook: Applications and Application Development   257

A Appendix   267

B Glossary   277

C Sources and Further Reading   283

The Authors   287

Index   289

Preface

In 2003, SAP introduced a revolutionary vision for the future of business applications: Enterprise Services Architecture (ESA). Many of the world's top-performing enterprises adopted ESA in the first year after it was announced, reducing the cost of IT maintenance, and freeing up resources for innovation.

ESA is a radical shift in technology architecture. The last decade was dominated by the client/server-and-database approach to systems, an innovation also pioneered by SAP with the introduction of SAP R/3 in the early 1990s. ESA is based on a service-oriented approach to applications. By eliminating much of the "impedance mismatch" between systems and business processes, ESA can yield much greater business agility while simultaneously achieving substantial reductions in total cost of ownership (TCO).

At the heart of ESA is a new platform. The platform of the 1990s was the client operating system, server operating system, and relational database. Applications were each designed around their own information needs, often with complicated and expensive point-to-point integration across databases. This approach to application integration resulted in integration costs that consumed between 70 % and 90 % of the IT budget of typical enterprises, according to leading analysts such as Gartner Group.

Client/server applications are designed with a dedicated client and server, each server used by a single application, and with integration performed by point-to-point data synchronization. ESA applications are designed with shared servers (called "components") used by many applications (called "composites"). The components expose a standard set of services, understandable to enterprise business processes. These standard services, such as "create purchase requisition" or "order goods from inventory," are called enterprise services.

To realize this ESA vision, SAP introduced SAP NetWeaver in 2003. A breakthrough platform based around the concept of integration, SAP NetWeaver has had the fastest ramp-up of any platform in history, having been adopted by well over 1,500 of the world's leading enterprises by the time this book went to press. By building integration capabilities into each component of the SAP NetWeaver platform, SAP can dramatically reduce TCO. The resources saved can be invested in innovation, used to catch up on the application backlog, or returned to the business. Adopting SAP NetWeaver was the first step on the road to ESA for many SAP customers.

One of the most unique capabilities of SAP NetWeaver is called "Composite Application Framework" (CAF), designed to reduce the cost of developing and deploying composite applications. CAF is the basis on which SAP develops and delivers composite applications, including SAP xApps™. SAP xApps are "packaged-innovation" solutions that deliver next-generation business practices with rapid implementation, very low TCO, and competitive differentiation. SAP xApps are all designed using ESA, and are all "powered by SAP NetWeaver."

This book captures SAP's experiences in developing both composite-application products and custom composite-application projects. The authors designed, developed, and implemented these applications at customer sites. You'll learn everything you need to know about composite applications and SAP xApps in this book, from the greatest experts in the field.

We hope you will enjoy reading this book as much as we enjoyed creating this technology and writing this book. If you'd like to learn more about the topics covered in this book, please visit SAP Developer Network at *http://sdn.sap.com/* you'll have access to the latest information, technologies, and special offers to help you on your journey to composite applications.

Dennis Moore
Senior Vice President, xApps
SAP Labs LLC

Acknowledgements

Although only two people are named on the cover of this book as its authors, it would never have been possible for us to write it without support from and many discussions with our colleagues, partners, customers, and friends. This support went far above and beyond the call of duty, especially since the long distances between the people involved (Palo Alto in California, Sofia in Bulgaria, and Walldorf in Germany) and the resulting time-zone differences meant that telephone conversations had to be held either very early in the morning or very late at night.

It would be impossible to name everybody who contributed to the success of this book. Therefore, we would like to mention just a few individuals and to acknowledge them in gratitude and respect. They are:

Rituparna Reddi, who, despite her already tight schedule, spent many long nights in Walldorf describing user interfaces, helped us to understand the material, and thus regularly missed her last bus home.

Malte Kaufmann, who, without grumbling, provided detailed answers to dozens of e-mails containing modeling questions, and, in several telephone conversations, supplied information and answers to questions regarding functionality, technology, and application.

Jörg Schleiwies, who, without blinking, answered our toughest questions about integrating unstructured information in CAF, and explained all the relevant aspects in detail.

Frank Rakowitz, master of services.

Kalin Komitski, who answered and commented on our modeling questions promptly, in detail, and with Bulgarian flair.

Tim Bussiek, **Steffen Kübler**, **Thomas Anton**, **Jürgen Kremer** and **Werner Algner**, who gave up some of their scarce free time to proofread this book and give extensive, valuable feedback, and in particular, helped us to see the CAF tree in the SAP NetWeaver forest.

Jürgen Hagedorn and **Katharina Rock**, who gave us the freedom to write this book and were always ready with help and advice.

Gunther Piller and **Andreas Henke**, who always knew the answers to our SAP xPD questions.

Martin Botschek: a quick code example? Martin was always ready. Need a quick test environment? He just seemed to pull it out of a hat.

Stephan Böcker, who was always there for us with answers to our questions about the SAP xApps Partner Program.

Yury Golovenchik, Alexander Efimchik, Alayxey Palayzhay and **Ihar Lakhadynau**, who fell in love with the xFlights demo.

Natasha and **Katrin**, who kept us motivated, and always provided comfort and encouraging words when writer's block set in.

... And of course, everyone else from the world of CAF and xApps, without whom we would have had nothing to write about.

Mario Herger and **Jo Weilbach**

Introduction

Today more than ever, enterprises face increasing and ever-changing competition. To survive long-term in the market, they therefore have to adapt themselves flexibly and quickly to changing market conditions, and to continually develop innovative business processes. While the information, data, and processes required to do this do exist in most companies, they are often hard to find among the seemingly countless systems and applications of a heterogeneous IT landscape and are thus accessed only with great difficulty—if they can be accessed at all—by the decision-makers who require them.

Enterprises today also come under increasing pressure to reduce costs. As a result, replacing live systems with new total solutions is often regarded as simply not cost-efficient. The key to continuing success in this environment is the flexibility to use existing infrastructures within the framework of new solutions.

Flexibility is the key

But what technological approach can use heterogeneous system landscapes in innovative business scenarios in a cost-efficient and flexible way? The word on everyone's lips in this context is Web services. These services make the functionality of applications available to external entities, even across system boundaries, and are regarded as the interface technology of the future. They form the basis of the vision of centralized access to enterprise data and functions through a service-oriented architecture.

SAP AG has responded to this vision with its *Enterprise Services Architecture*, the aim of which is to implement a service-oriented system architecture. SAP's market-leading integration and technology platform, *SAP NetWeaver*, is its first step in achieving this aim. With the implementation and use of *Composite Applications*, which are based on SAP NetWeaver and its components, enterprises can generate additional benefit from their existing IT infrastructure. They can thus present data and functionalities from both SAP and non-SAP systems in an innovative and completely new context. Likewise, system architects and application developers can now combine components from existing enterprise applications to form Composite Applications, which, as "applications on applications," implement consistent business processes across the entire organization. SAP calls this new generation of applications *SAP xApps*.

Enterprise Services Architecture

Figure Enterprise Services Architecture

ESA platform SAP xApps are based on objects, services, and processes in the ESA platform. An ESA platform implemented using SAP NetWeaver extends and provides flexible and unified access to the wide-ranging functionality of the heterogeneous system landscapes in enterprises. Generally speaking, the Enterprise Services Architecture comprises the above-mentioned levels of the SAP xApps, the ESA platform, and the heterogeneous system landscapes.

CAF In order to unify and speed up the creation, adaptation, and expansion of SAP xApps, a new addition was made to SAP NetWeaver: the *SAP Composite Application Framework* (CAF). The CAF is a unified development platform that provides extensive tools, patterns, methodologies, and services, and enables developers to create SAP xApps quickly and easily on the basis of modeling and source-code generation.

Aim and structure of this book The aim of this book is to give readers a detailed introduction to the subject of SAP xApps and, based on this, to clearly explain the SAP xApps architecture and how development is ideally carried out using CAF. The book also describes the tools used by SAP and the relevant SAP NetWeaver components, plus real-world examples of solutions and their implementation. After reading this book, IT decision-makers, architects, consultants and developers should understand the philosophy of SAP xApps and be able to implement it in their work.

Basics **Chapter 1**, *SAP xApps—Basic Principles*, deals with the fundamentals of SAP xApps by formulating a definition and describing the attributes of SAP xApps, based on an explanation of the composite application market and the evolution of business applications. It goes on to identify those, apart from SAP itself, who are developing SAP xApps. In this chapter, we also present a typical ideal methodology for developing an SAP xApp and describe the current solution portfolio of SAP and its partners.

Chapter 2, *The Architecture of SAP xApps*, explains the fundamentals of SAP NetWeaver and its components, and the structure and functionality of the SAP CAF in particular. Based on this, this chapter then presents a general model for creating SAP xApps.

In **Chapter 3**, *The SAP Composite Application Framework*, a description of the development of a sample xApp is used to present and describe in detail the tools of the CAF and a typical ideal implementation process of an SAP xApp, from modeling the scenario to delivering the solution.

Chapter 4, *Implementation Examples*, documents the ease of implementation and the benefits of the new generation of applications by describing in detail the following solutions implemented by SAP: SAP xApp Product Definition, and SAP xApp Cost and Quotation Management.

Chapter 5, *Outlook: Applications and Application Development*, takes a look at strategies and concepts for developing the applications of the future.

The **Appendix** provides an overview of the CORE objects of the CAF 1.0, operation types, user interface links, tables and property rules for attributes, a glossary that explains the most important terms used in this book, a directory of sources for further reading, and an index that makes it easier for readers to search for specific content and topics in this book by means of keywords.

The CD for this book, which you can order free of charge using the attached voucher, contains all the relevant code (the metadata that is used to generate code and tables), and the compiled, ready-to-run version of the example application created using CAF in Chapter 3.

Architecture

CAF

Examples

Future prospects

Appendix

CD

1   SAP xApps—Basic Principles

In this chapter you will learn the philosophy behind SAP xApps and gain a general understanding of their market, history and definition. You will be given a step-by-step description of the ideal development process and the current SAP xApps portfolio of this new generation of applications.

1.1   Market Situation and Opportunities

The system landscapes of companies are very often heterogeneous and inflexible. Organizational changes caused by mergers, takeovers, changes to laws, or the temporary resolution of functional problems through department-specific solutions often lead to the use of dozens or even hundreds of systems from different manufacturers. These systems are linked with each other by expensive point-to-point connections which quite often use proprietary communication protocols.

Business pain points

If you move away from the technical perspective and consider the realities of the marketplace, it becomes immediately clear that market participants should not be content with just continuously improving on an operational level. They must be innovative in order to remain successful in the face of competitive pressure. An analysis of the Standard & Poor (S&P) listing underlines this statement.[1] On average, companies are listed there for increasingly shorter amounts of time. Of those that do hold out longer, only a few become top performers in the market. To illustrate: The S&P 500 created in 1957 only contained 74 of these companies at the turn of the century. Out of these, only 12 went strong in the market. The top performers were only able to achieve their above-average results by taking radical strategic measures every three to seven years.

The dilemma in which many companies find themselves today is that the existing IT infrastructures not only fail to support fast, flexible and cost-effective adaptation to required new business strategies and processes, they even impede such adaptation. Thus, the challenge lies in implementing software-based mapping and support of business processes across departmental, organizational, and country boundaries as well as functional limitations.

IT as a stumbling block

---

1   The Standish Group's CHAOS 2001 Research. *www.standishgroup.com.*

Goal The goal of today's applications must therefore be based on quickly, flexibly and efficiently supporting the strategic decisions of a company.

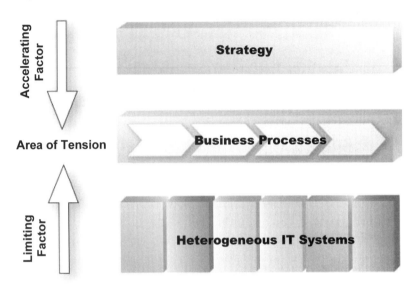

Figure 1.1 Constant Tension between Strategy and IT Infrastructure

Market opportunities Because packaged composite applications (PCAs) are recognized as having the potential to resolve the tension between existing system landscapes and the market-compatible strategies of a company, these applications are expected to create enormous market opportunity. PCAs are composite applications offered as stand-alone solutions. SAP xApps are PCAs that have been developed and marketed by SAP since 2002, and they clearly demonstrate the power of this concept for reaching business goals.

If you bear in mind that PCAs only mark the beginning of this application generation, and that in the future all enterprise applications should be based on the composite application concept, the enormous potential of this still young market becomes obvious. SAP, for instance, is aiming to have all its business solutions compatible with ESA by the year 2007 and is thus pursuing a concrete roadmap for the step-by-step implementation of scenarios based on services (see Figure 1.2).[2]

And SAP delivers on its promises. At Sapphire 2005 in Copenhagen, SAP has unveiled the ESA Preview System to provide customers, partners and developers the opportunity to gain experience with enterprise services

---

2 Details on SAP's ESA Roadmap can be found at *http://sdn.sap.com*.

2004

→ **Service-enablement efforts for this year are focused on enhancing user productivity and collaboration. In addition, SAP is also carrying out a systematic inventory and prioritization on enterprise services, based on the enterprise business scenarios featured in the new industry solution maps.**

2005

→ **SAP will publish an inventory of its enterprise services – available for planning purposes for customers and partners. This list of enterprise services can be leveraged in customers' and partners' composite applications and for long-term road-map planning. Additional service-enabled scenarios will be made available, focusing on business process flexibility and anticipating the needs of new composite applications.**

2006

→ **An enterprise services repository will be published in 2006, based on the next release of SAP NetWeaver. All relevant enterprise services will be actively available from the repository for use by selected partners and customers.**

2007

→ **SAP applications, including mySAP Business Suite, will now fully reflect the Enterprise Services Architecture paradigm. (For example, all enterprise services will be described in a central repository and created and managed by SAP NetWeaver.)**

Figure 1.2 SAP's ESA Roadmap

and to make ESA more tangible and accessible. The Enterprise Services of the ESA Preview System are also delivered off-line via the SAP Solution Composer, which is an ideal tool for planning, defining, documenting, and communicating of business solution requirements.[3]

Concerning the market development of composite applications, Forrester Research, Inc., has made the following forecasts that emphasize the vast potential of this market:[4]

- Market development in two phases, beginning with a revenue total of 100 million to 150 million US$ in the year 2003.
- Phase 1 from 2004 to 2006: annual PCA growth rates of approximately 20 %

---

3 More information on the ESA Preview System, including registration and Feedback Forum, can be found at *http://sdn.sap.com*.

4 Kinikin, Erin; Ramos, Laura (2004): *Packaged Composite Applications Emerge—Slowly*. Forrester Research, Inc., January 2004. See also Donough, Brian (2004): *Worldwide Packaged Composite Applications 2004–2008 Forecast: A First Look at an Emerging Market*. #31280, Vol.1, May 2004, or Abrams, Charles (2003): *Service-Oriented Business Applications: Process Revolution or Next-Wave Hype*. Gartner, Presentation at the Web Services & Application Integration Conference 2003, Baltimore.

► Transition to Phase 2 due to the entry into the PCA market of large, more established vendors of enterprise software and the related availability of open, stable and integrated, service-oriented architectures.

► Phase 2 from 2007 to 2010: Market volume of composite applications which are based on these infrastructures of approximately 1 billion to 1.5 billion US$.

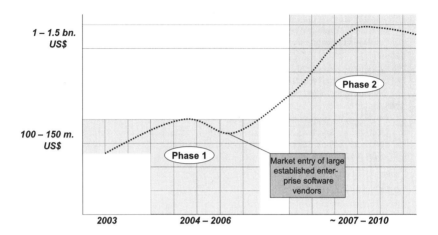

Expected revenues for software licenses, maintenance and installation

Figure 1.3 Market Development of Composite Applications in the Years 2004 to 2010 (Source: Kinikin, Ramos 2004, Figure 4, Page 9)

In order to correctly estimate and exploit the possibilities and opportunities of composite applications, it is necessary to understand more precisely the change process that business applications have gone through since the introduction of business software.

1.2 The Evolution of Business Applications

A business world that is constantly changing in all aspects not only demands constant adaptation of organizational structures and business strategies but also subjects the information and related communications systems to continuous change. The evolution of business applications began with mainframe solutions and evolved through the client/server architectures to today's state-of-the-art service architectures.

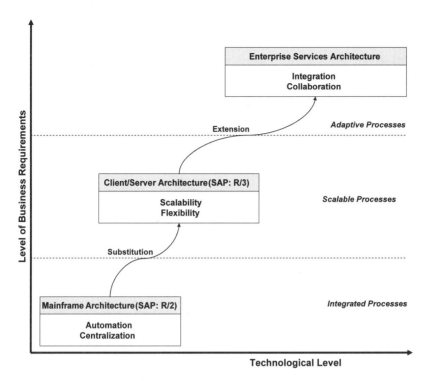

Figure 1.4 The Evolution of Architectures

1.2.1 Traditional Development and Architecture

Early business applications were developed for tasks or activities that were not business-critical and could be easily abstracted because they were mainly based on arithmetic operations. As a consequence, these applications were predominantly used in the financial area. As at that time there was hardly any standard software available for problematic areas, a specific application had to be implemented for every operation. With the introduction of mainframes, the usage rate of these applications increased to such an extent that a range of activities related to different business processes was automated as much as possible.

Central control of all processes and transactions and their collective processing through the stable operation and the installation of all applications on one system led to the main weaknesses of the mainframe approach: lack of scalability and flexibility.

After the data volumes to be dealt with and the business requirements had increased, central processing was replaced by a more flexible concept. The availability of personal computers (PCs) and the wide accep-

Mainframe

Client/server architectures

tance of network technologies led to decentralization in the form of client/server architectures which enabled several users to access the same data at the same time. A client places a request for a specific service, which is processed and then provided by a server. With the introduction of three levels—graphical user interface, application logic, and database—for independent control and administration, this model became the new standard. An increasing distribution of data processing on a variety of work stations (fat clients) led to a higher productivity for the end users and also increased the interoperability of applications. Although the scalability of system landscapes was improved with this approach, huge costs still had to be reckoned with in the operational and maintenance areas of heterogeneous landscapes.

The triumphal entry of the Internet through standardized communication protocols such as TCP/IP or HTTP led to many decisive improvements in this context. The hard-to-maintain installations on fat clients were replaced by Web browsers (thin clients) that communicated with the underlying layers via HTML. The growing possibilities of interacting with partners outside a company formed the foundation for new types of applications, such as Customer Relationship Management (CRM) and Supplier Relationship Management (SRM), which increased the scope of activities beyond the borders of an enterprise.

Enterprise Application Integration (EAI) As business processes increasingly reached across all available business applications, communication between the individual systems became a limiting factor in providing the required functionality. The creation of customer-specific interfaces between the systems involved was only a temporary solution. In the context of Enterprise Application Integration (EAI), an attempt was made to overcome this by abstracting the communication between applications with XML messages. Although this meant that different applications could interact by using a standardized format, the application processes still remained separate from each other so that integration only occurred locally and to a limited extent.

To map an individual business process, several applications had to be created which integrated a multitude of isolated systems along with their respective roles and decision makers. Along with the number of required connections between the systems, the complexity of the applications to be created rose significantly. EAI solutions thus led to a very dense network of applications and interfaces which could only be maintained with difficulty and at high costs.

1.2.2   Web Services, Service Oriented Architecture (SOA) and Enterprise Services Architecture (ESA)

Increasing integration complexity as well as the increasing focus on using existing investments in the most optimal way, led to a necessary rethinking towards new technologies in order to meet the dynamic business requirements. Instead of replacing heterogeneous system landscapes by a single new revolutionary solution to map all business processes, the focus was placed on an incremental growth and the use of existing system landscapes. Otherwise, as was commonly assumed, the competitiveness of companies was at a serious risk. Web services developed as the interface technology of the future, on which innovative and visionary architectures such as SOA or ESA from SAP are based.

Web Services

Web services emerged from the original efforts to achieve integration and interoperability between distributed software systems. They represent a new approach of meeting these demands.

Technically speaking, Web services are based on protocols that are widely accepted on the World Wide Web and are therefore defined by OVUM as follows:

> *A collection of industry-standard software packaging definitions, which specify mechanisms for software programs to send and receive data using an XML-based communication protocol (SOAP); and publish their capabilities using an XML-based interface definition language (WSDL).*[5]

The Web Services Description Language (WSDL) and the Simple Object Access Protocol (SOAP) define the structure of service descriptions as well as the call of provided methods.[6] In this context, the data exchange mechanisms such as message formats to be used, data types, or transport protocols between the Web service consumer and the Web service provider are defined in a Web service description (WSD) via WSDL. The exchange of data between the two entities then occurs via SOAP.

WSDL & SOAP

SOAP provides a way for applications to communicate with other applications independently of the operating systems used. The Hypertext Transfer Protocol (HTTP) and Extensible Markup language (XML) are used as mechanisms for information exchange in this context. SOAP specifies

SOAP details

---

5   OVUM (2002): *Web Services for the Enterprise: Opportunities and Challenges*, p. 41.
6   You will find further information on SOAP and WSDL at *http://www.w3.org*.

exactly the coding of the HTTP header and that of the XML file so that applications can communicate with each other bi-directionally.

UDDI Alternatively, the Universal Description, Discovery and Integration Specification (UDDI) can act as a mediator between these two basic technologies by defining formats, schemas and call types in order to generally provide a framework of available and callable Web services.[7] In this context UDDI is often compared to the yellow pages, as it enables companies to list themselves with names, products, locations and Web services provided. The UDDI project currently comprises 130 companies, some of which are among the largest global players. SAP AG is one of them.

This initiative is supported by WSDL. WSDL is a derivative of Microsoft's SOAP and IBM's Network Accessible Service Specification Language (NASSL) and replaces these two as a means to describe business processes in UDDI registers.

Figure 1.5 shows a simplified diagram of the ideal type of interaction flow between a Web-service consumer and a Web-service provider that are connected through a discovery service:

1. The Web-service provider publishes the Web service through a WSD on the discovery service, which in this example is produced by a UDDI-based Web service register.

2. A Web-service consumer searches through the discovery service for a suitable Web service.

3. The discovery service returns a specific number of Web services through the corresponding Web-service descriptions to the Web-service consumer. The consumer selects a relevant Web service.

4. Based on the selected WSD the interaction between the Web-service consumer and the Web-service provider occurs through SOAP.

This standardized and platform-independent communication formats enable the integration of existing applications, which, in turn, can be accessed by customers, suppliers, and other business partners even beyond a company firewall. Companies and organizations that maintain business relationships with each other can interact simply through Web services and selectively exchange data in ways that lead to the automation of business processes. Up to now, the lack of such automation has impeded such close cooperation.

---

7 You can find further details on the UDDI specification at *http://www.uddi.org*. The UDDI business directory of SAP AG can be found at *http://uddi.sap.com*.

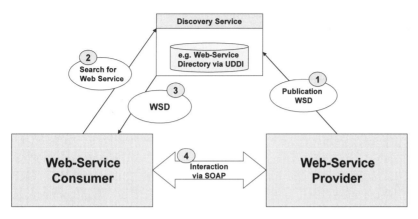

Figure 1.5 Simplified Description of the Functionality of Web Services

Web services are still at an early stage in their development and are mostly used for small tasks within individual applications. Logistic purchase-order monitoring or the provision of e-mail functionality are examples of these simple services. However, even Google, as the most widely used search engine on the Web, provides an API for a program-based search, that is leveraged by Web Services technology.[8]

Enterprise Services

The basic technology underlying Web services is not ground-breaking. The actual innovation and the enormous usage potential of Web services is based rather on the implementation of its concept in today's complex, multi-layered and heterogeneous IT system landscapes. This, however, will only become a reality if business-relevant business scenarios, which require services and extensive functionality from many different applications, are available as services that are easy to use. SAP has recognized and met these demands by expanding the concept of Web services to embrace enterprise services, and has placed the focus on the mapping of business functions. In contrast to Web services, enterprise services provide a variety of functions—independent of their respective providers—by combining the capabilities of Web services of different systems. By implementing this innovative approach, SAP can draw on its vast experience as a provider of standard business software.

Enterprise services are based on the same technological concept as Web services, but aim at usability for meeting the business requirements of a company. Web services thereby become reusable components of a business-relevant enterprise service.

Advantages of enterprise services

---

8 Please find more details on *www.google.com/apis*.

The resulting benefits are based on the following properties and advantages of the service-oriented approach:

▶ Enterprise services are *reusable*. Their underlying object-oriented design means code blocks or library classes for new (development) projects can be used or enhanced.

▶ Enterprise services are *easy to integrate and flexible*. As far as integration with other components is concerned, they are based on a generic interface. Enterprise services thus can reduce existing integration gaps, as components are enabled to communicate with each other. Each application that the enterprise service wants to use then connects to this interface, which means that the components can be easily changed or replaced.

▶ Enterprise services implement the principle of *encapsulation*. An application that wants to use a service doesn't need any knowledge of the actual implementation of this respective service. Enterprise services therefore abstract from the complexity of the underlying activities and systems.

▶ Enterprise services provide a *programmatic access*. Services carry out tasks for the end user; these tasks are visualized through a graphical user interface. The service itself, however, is only indirectly used by the end users, because it is initialized by applications that use their own user interfaces.

▶ Enterprise services are *distributable* across system boundaries. Their functionality can be provided in an existing internal infrastructure over the Internet.

Example   The business example of the cancellation of a customer order should clarify the enormous potential benefit of enterprise services. Several cross-functional activities across different systems must be carried out in this context:

▶ Sending a contract confirmation to customers

▶ Canceling the production order in the production plan

▶ Canceling the reserved materials requirement

▶ Canceling the customer order and sending the notification to the customer

You can consider each of these activities as a Web service or a service of an application from different systems (e.g. a CRM service and a production system). Combining these services into an enterprise service reduces the complex business process of reversing a customer order by encapsulating it. This results in considerable improvements regarding time savings and the logistical processing.

If you consider the investments in technology and in the development of applications that customers have carried out in times of the three-layer client-server architecture or even earlier architectures, it becomes clear that an approach is required to lower the total cost of ownership (TCO) and at the same time enable innovations.

<aside>Task: reducing the TCO</aside>

It is precisely at this point that SAP takes a crucial step further. It bases the potential of enterprise services on a consistent and structured foundation that takes into account the requirements of enterprise services in terms of scalability, performance, robustness, security, easy implementation, and maintenance. This guarantees a standard and efficient provision and use of enterprise services when implementing flexible applications for the future: the *Enterprise Services Architecture*.

Enterprise Services Architecture (ESA)

The strength of ESA lies in the combination of legacy applications and systems. The model is one of a standardized platform on which the applications work drawing on Web services of the middle layer. To the extent that communication between the components takes place via services, this concept corresponds to the SOA concept. Here, a large system is broken down into a variety of modular fragments, whereby the unmanageable complexity is reduced to smaller units. This results in several less complex parts, which are finally bundled by services to provide the envisaged functionality.

<aside>Modular fragments</aside>

The aim is to combine the heterogeneous set of existing applications and systems in order to provide a standardized abstraction to the applications of the top layer via Web services. With ESA, it will be possible to create the design for these applications. There are two main steps to be carried out in this context:

▶ Development of a graphical user interface

▶ Functional implementation of the enterprise services provided

In order to reduce the points of integration between applications and services the latter must be provided through a central instance which can communicate in a standardized way with the heterogeneous infrastructure. This level of standardization is represented by the ESA Platform, the main element of the framework. In combination with the underlying infrastructure, the ESA platform can then carry out the task of providing interacting applications with information and ensure that communication is possible.

Anatomy of the ESA The ESA platform consists of different logical layers, briefly described in the following section in order to clarify the structure of the ESA application stack:

- The *persistence layer* is responsible for the physical storage of application data in the areas provided for this.

- The *object layer* combines data from different sources and basic access methods to target-oriented business objects.

- The *services layer* contains all services which carry out the analysis and processing of these business objects.

- The *process layer* manages the sequence of steps that are carried out during the runtime of the application. They support the user in navigating through the entire process.

- The *user interface layer* (UI layer) represents the graphical user interface and enables the interaction with the user.

The platform functions as a central hub and provides the design, configuration and runtime environment for all service-based applications that are carried out on the uppermost layer of the architecture described. In addition, it serves other underlying systems as an integration point by using the system-specific applications that it supports with additional functionality.

Data and objects A combination of company data, the relevant services to work with this data, and processes which span the sequence of access makes up the ESA platform. Objects are created as new entities that collect data from underlying systems in the same way as the corresponding services in order to manipulate this data. Creating a comprehensive master model from data, services, and processes of the entire company represents a complex challenge. However, in creating a collection of master data, the platform spans the same functional scope as does a system landscape that implements all possible 1-to-1 interfaces. The model does not reserve its own copies of objects, in order to avoid redundant data. Collected objects are mapped to their original sources in order to ensure the consistency of the data and the reduction of the data volumes. In order to be able to model the relationship between objects, a mapping also takes place between the individual objects.

Even if standards for process descriptions exist these are only possible within the scope of the respective system boundaries. Extracting the application logic from the underlying systems and providing it in the form of a service wrapper makes it possible to describe and configure the implicit and envisaged processes in a central instance across different company applications. A clear separation between the process and the application logic makes the mapping of complete business processes possible. This concept is also decisively advantageous in addressing the changeability of business process, because its optimization or reorientation can be achieved without changing the actual implementation.

Comprehensive business processes

As the design process is carried out directly after the actual implementation, a continual, incremental improvement is necessary in order to meet new requirements. Because only a few dependencies continue to exist between individual components, the combinations of the components can be changed. This makes it easier to meet other requirements and achieve other goals.

In order to help customers to realize the benefits of ESA via SAP NetWeaver, SAP has initiated the ESA Adoption Program.[9] It helps companies to easily create and implement a tailored ESA environment that leverages the power of enterprise services. The program includes four key steps to support a customer's transition to ESA, which are illustrated in Figure 1.6.

ESA Adoption Program

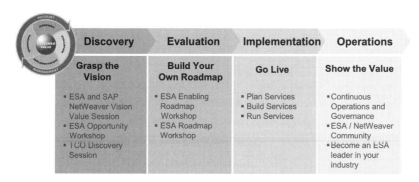

Figure 1.6 ESA Adoption Program

For each step SAP provides customers with a portfolio of field-tested support services, which encompass a variety of tools, templates, samples and workshops tailored to address separate needs of each organization. These services include an ESA and SAP NetWeaver vision value session, TCO

---

9   Details on the ESA Adoption Program can be found at *http://sdn.sap.com*.

discovery session, ESA enabling road-map workshop, and an ESA operations session on governance and security to support their enhanced IT environment.

All in all, the Enterprise Services Architecture is SAP's blueprint for service-based, enterprise-scale business solutions that offer the increased levels of adaptability, flexibility, and openness required to reduce total cost of ownership. It combines SAP's experience in enterprise applications with the flexibility of Web services and other open standards.

1.2.3 Composite Applications

Releasing functional potential

The ESA enables companies to finally respond appropriately to the dilemma of heterogeneity vs. flexibility by using applications that are themselves based on other applications: Composite Applications. Composite applications control the direct interaction with the end user, where the services layer provides its services to enable communication between traditional applications and composite applications. The main purpose of these applications is to make different functionalities available company-wide to all role players involved in parts of the business process mapped. In contrast to the implementation of isolated activities that are restricted to one system, additional benefit is thus generated from already existing investments, given that the functional potential of the entire IT infrastructure is made available. Entire business processes that stretch over a heterogeneous IT system landscape are homogenized through composite applications and thus integration gaps are reduced.

New functionality

The integration of isolated systems is complemented by the creation of new functionalities that are based on these systems but do not change them. As the composite applications are decoupled from the underlying levels by the standardized and intermediary layer, the system boundaries remain invisible for these types of application. It is possible to assign a business object of the composite application to several information bundles from separate data sources. This generates new relationships that in turn can be managed via services. In addition, composite applications promote collaboration in the context of each process step. This means all decision makers and role players can interact with each other at any time, are guided through the entire process, and are provided with the appropriate information.

The automatic referencing of data relevant to decisions from the respective source systems—in contrast to a manual collection of critical information—can enable an organization to reach decisions that are based on

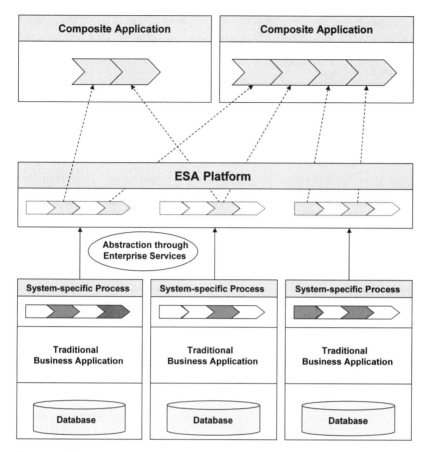

Figure 1.7 The Interaction of Composite Applications, the ESA Platform and the Underlying System Landscape

a precise judgement of established data. Therefore a composite application does not just represent data, but it can also call underlying systems and piece them together into a relationship, whereby high-quality results are attained. Through use of composite applications, persons responsible for processing as well as decision-makers can collaborate and interact in an efficient way, receiving guidance through the whole process and finally getting the right information at the right time and place.

The fact that these applications operate on a variety of components provides another basic potential advantage: The entire flow of the actual business process can completely undergo a continuous monitoring and direct analysis. You can view information on the process flow and the beginning and end dates of each process step at any time in order to identify bottlenecks and eliminate them.

Business process monitoring

Composite applications can reach a great level of flexibility as they exclusively interact with the well-defined services, objects, and processes of the ESA platform. As each layer that communicates with the application can be configured, expensive customer-specific developments can be avoided. This benefit is apparent in sinking operating costs and easier maintainability.

Composite applications have the potential to solve the familiar trade-off between tactical and strategic application development.

Tactical vs. strategic application development Traditional tactical developments aim for a quick solution to problems, based on reduced planning and evaluation activities, the use of speed-optimized tools and limited project scopes. In contrast, the focus in strategic application development is on engineering processes in systematic implementation of complex projects, which are frequently connected with high costs and are time-consuming. The following table clarifies this quite well.[10]

	Tactical development	Strategic development	Composite Applications
Reusability of the coding	low to medium	low to medium	high
Development approach	tool-controlled	model-controlled	parameter-controlled
Business driver	opportunistic	systematic	tactical
Requirements	simple	complex	simple
Scope	department-wide	company-wide	both
Qualifications	junior developer	senior developer	business analyst
Team size	1 to 6	6 to 60+	1 to 3
Validity of the coding	0.5 to 3 years	2 to 10+ years	undetermined
Budget	low to medium	large	low
Methodology	informal	formal, systematic	informal
Risk tolerance	high	low	medium

Table 1.1 Development of Composite Applications: A Comparison

---

10 Gartner (2003): *Service-Oriented Business Applications: Process Revolution or Next-Wave Hype.* Presentation at the Web Services & Application Integration Conference 2003, Baltimore.

	Tactical development	Strategic development	Composite Applications
Project duration	1 to 6 months	0.5 to 6 years	1 to 6 weeks
Integration	low	medium	high

Table 1.1 Development of Composite Applications: A Comparison (cont.)

1.3 Characteristics and Definition of SAP xApps

SAP reacted quickly and adequately to the new market and customer demands by introducing the extensive integration and technology platform, SAP NetWeaver. It implements the ESA step by step and creates the basis for mySAP Business Suite, mySAP ERP, and a new generation of service-based company applications: SAP xApps.

1.3.1 Composite Applications from SAP

SAP is pursuing the plan of developing all future SAP solutions according to the design of the ESA. This is the basis of Composite Applications from SAP. Based on mySAP Business Suite solutions that provide their functionality through enterprise services, composite applications will complete mySAP Business Suite and implement extensive functionalities and processes.

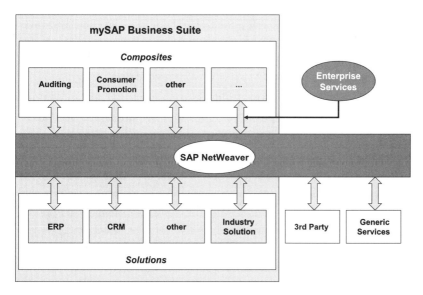

Figure 1.8 Composite Applications from SAP

mySAP Business Suite is a collection of tried-and-tested solutions that support customers in covering their most important business processes. Thanks to mySAP Business Suite, composite applications can draw on a wide range of existing functionalities from the following components:

▶ mySAP Customer Relationship Management (mySAP CRM)

▶ mySAP Enterprise Resource Planning (mySAP ERP), the successor to the R/3 system

▶ mySAP Product Lifecycle Management (mySAP PLM)

▶ mySAP Supplier Relationship Management (mySAP SRM)

▶ mySAP Supply Chain Management (mySAP SCM)

The composite applications from SAP that are integrated in the mySAP Business Suite thus provide great potential for enhancing the functionality of the suite by providing specialized or industry-specific functionalities through flexible linking, integration, or indirect adjustment of the different components or their sub-elements.

Composite applications provide SAP customers with decisive advantages to address the dynamics of the market and competition:

▶ **Lower implementation and upgrade costs**
Partners or customers can easily modify composite applications themselves, without affecting the underlying systems. This means that customers can adapt their solutions to the conditions of their infrastructure and can lower their deployment costs, because they no longer need to modify fixed programmed interfaces. When SAP supplies new business scenarios, the customer doesn't need to implement an upgrade to the components used. Customers can still implement new functions and in doing so pursue a more flexible and cost-effective upgrade strategy, resulting in fewer interruptions.

▶ **Scaling through a heterogeneous infrastructure**
Using mapping functions from SAP NetWeaver means that applications that work with XML-based protocols can be integrated at a fraction of the costs of traditional methods. SAP and its partners provide connectors for integrating established systems of other providers that are not XML-capable. Even legacy systems can be integrated in SAP solutions through Web services. Customers don't have to replace their existing solutions but rather continue to use them.

▶ **Faster market availability**
As composite applications are not affected by the release cycles of

their underlying components, they can be developed and implemented more quickly. Customers receive up-to-date solutions for critical problems which require their full attention, rather than having to wait six months or even a year.

▶ **Targeted industry solutions**
SAP uses composite applications in order to develop solutions even more efficiently. In particular, future industry solutions will be based on composite applications that map specific business scenarios. This means generic and industry-specific components will be used. For example, a solution to support the commercial use of copyrights in the media industry is being developed.

▶ **Investment protection**
Generic composite applications that provide business functions lead to a greater independence from the underlying components and their providers. This new development and provision approach is a win-win situation for both SAP and its customers. For the customers, this means lower TCO, and for SAP it means the possibility to deliver its vertical solutions more quickly.

1.3.2 SAP xApps

SAP had already begun in 2002 to implement the first solutions according to the design of the ESA—SAP xApps—to enable customers to respond in an appropriate manner to the dynamic changes in competition.

Based on the ESA principle, SAP xApps focuses on the continued use of existing functionalities in combination with the expansion of parts of the mySAP Business Suite or other solutions to new and innovative business processes. SAP xApps support companies in meeting the demand of continued innovation through a high degree of flexibility while at the same time lowering the TCO.

Innovation, flexibility, lower costs

SAP xApps are packaged composite applications through which SAP provides its customers with end-to-end business processes in order to implement these quickly and cost-effectively. Packaged, in this context, means that SAP xApps is an independently sold SAP product with its own release cycles and support and maintenance. This new product generation thus enhances the mySAP Business Suite and makes use of the already existing IT infrastructure of a customer. An SAP xApp therefore comprises the composite applications themselves and SAP NetWeaver, but not the functional applications to be integrated.

Packaged composite applications

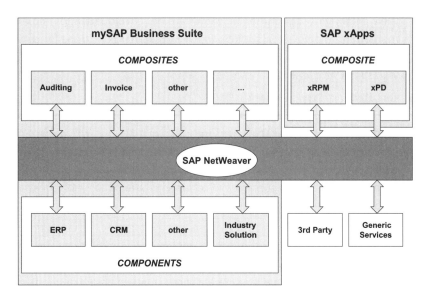

Figure 1.9 SAP xApps as Independent Enhancements of the SAP Solution Portfolio

Team work is especially promoted by SAP xApps in that the involved employees as role players and decision makers gain access to the relevant information and data in the various phases of the mapped business processes, based on their specific roles.

1.3.3 Properties and Requirements of SAP xApps

SAP xApps support both system and cross-functional business processes. This enables companies to implement business-critical strategic initiatives based on existing active investments at lower costs and reduced risks.

Properties This means SAP xApps can adopt the following properties:

▶ **Cross-functional**
SAP xApps can be used with many applications and information sources. This means critical and continuous processes can run in conjunction with the company strategy across heterogeneous systems. Thus they eliminate the functional silos of a company by providing flexible and innovative business processes.

▶ **Integrative**
SAP xApps use services to access the business logic and business objects of the underlying business applications. Through the use of Web and enterprise services, the implementation of the functionalities provided in the isolated applications is encapsulated within the SAP

xApp so that the end users and developers do not need to worry about this. In this way SAP xApps can execute flexible workflows or business processes independently of the underlying infrastructure.

Here the integration approach of SAP xApps is multi-layered, as employees, information and isolated processes are integrated in a strategic and innovative overall process.

▶ **Cross-team/company**
SAP xApps support the complex transfer of information by considering its context and relevance as well as the communication within companies. This faciliates and supports cooperation between work groups of different company areas (HR, R&D etc.), whereby a high-quality and thorough decision is achieved and the advantages of teamwork are realized. The term cross-company can mean that not only specific systems and employees are involved in the overall process to be mapped, but also that external business partners and customers or suppliers and their applications and systems can be involved.

▶ **Information-controlled**
SAP xApps enable intelligent processs that are controlled by decision-relevant business information. Based on continued monitoring and a real-time analysis of the overall processes or individual steps, the company is in the position to make informed strategic decisions whose effect can be continuously evaluated and which can be adjusted or revised as needed.

All these are properties of great importance for problem resolution in companies. The fact that SAP xApps provide them shows their great potential. In order to make use of the integrative strength of an end-to-end process, xApps must meet certain requirements:

Requirements of SAP xApps

▶ Services represent the foundation of SAP xApps. Therefore, you need Web-based, *modern and intuitive user interfaces* that provide the users with a consistent user experience and easy handling accross all *SAP xApps*.

▶ Within an SAP xApp, the services and user interfaces described are combined to business processes. In order to meet the requirements of the described concept, these processes must meet the criteria of *transparency, simplicity* and *flexible adapatability*.

▶ Content, i.e. process steps and UIs, must be provided to the relevant role bearers in a *Web-based and role-based* manner.

From these requirements of SAP xApps, extensive paradigms can in turn be derived in relation to the architecture model and the infrastructure needed for the creation of an SAP xApp:

▶ Model-controlled development and code generation

▶ Implementation of a service-oriented architecture

▶ Pattern-based user interfaces

▶ Decoupling of SAP xApps from the underlying transactional systems

▶ Standardized access to objects

These far-reaching requirements demand a variety of components that must exist in order to develop SAP xApps on a consistent foundation. As already mentioned, SAP xApps are based on a very suitable platform: SAP NetWeaver, SAP's integration and technology platform. It provides the exact components required:

▶ SAP Web Application Server

▶ SAP Enterprise Portal

▶ SAP Business Intelligence

▶ SAP Master Data Management

▶ SAP Mobile Infrastructure

▶ SAP Exchange Infrastructure

▶ SAP NetWeaver Development Infrastructure

▶ SAP NetWeaver Developer Studio

▶ SAP Comosite Application Framework

A detailed description of the components in SAP NetWeaver can be found in Chapter 2, *The Architecture of SAP xApps.*

1.3.4 SAP Composite Application Framework

In order to achieve the required consistent user experience across various SAP xApps the developers of SAP xApps must have a homogenous programming model and an agreed-upon scope. Different SAP xApps often use the same or similar elements, such as an overview view of relevant objects of an application. In order to achieve the envisaged homogeneity, such elements should be identified and provided through patterns. This is why SAP developed the SAP Composite Application Framework (CAF), which carries out the described tasks and acts as an intermediary between the relevant components of SAP NetWeaver and the SAP xApps.

Integrated in SAP NetWeaver, the SAP CAF provides a development platform with a variety of tools, methods, rules, user interface patterns and services that make a fast and easy development of SAP xApps possible.

In the future, through the provision of SAP CAF, it will also be possible for customers to implement innovative business processes in a standardized, flexible and simple way by using their own developments of composite applications. Composite applications developed by customers are referred to as custom composite applications.

Custom Composite Applications

The principles of the CAF will be described in Chapter 2, while Chapter 3 provides an example of an xApp development on the basis of SAP NetWeaver CAF.

1.3.5 Advantages of a Close Integration with SAP NetWeaver

In addition to the advantages of composite applications already discussed SAP xApps provide further benefits:

▶ **Lower innovation costs**
SAP xApps enable customers to achieve innovations with lower costs. Due to SAP xApps customers no longer have to resort to niche products or complex changes to existing applications when implementing innovative business processes. Their approach ensures that the costs of the initial development and maintenance are considerably reduced throughout the entire lifecycle.

▶ **Decreasing innovation risks**
SAP xApps enable customers to base their development on the same platform that SAP uses: the SAP CAF. Customers receive the support of SAP and its partners. Development costs are kept lower and simple integration with SAP applications or third-party applications is ensured, which means that IT costs are kept at a manageable level. The use of SAP xApps developed by SAP and its certified partners means customers can lower their risks, not only because they are integrated in the service network of SAP but also because they can be sure that they are investing in highly sophisticated solutions.

▶ **Flexibility and speed**
SAP xApps use the SAP CAF as a basis. This means the development of innovative SAP xApps by SAP Industry Business Units, solution groups and partners can be accelerated. Customers recognize the advantages of speedily developed business-critical solutions which they require for their central business requirements.

1.4 The Developers of SAP xApps

From the above descriptions it has become clear that the concept of SAP xApps is characterized by openness. SAP does not insist on being the only inventor and developer of SAP xApps. Rather, an SAP partner program was especially created for this effort, enabling SAP to develop new SAP xApps solutions itself or in cooperation with its partners and, in doing so, expand the range of innovative and adaptable business processes.

1.4.1 SAP as a Developer of SAP xApps

SAP has many years of experience in the development of standard software. Based on a broad customer base, SAP taps into the pulse of the era and hits on exactly what customer demands are in terms of further development. Due to intensive cooperation and its frequent position as a trusted advisor, SAP can absorb the many requirements and desires of customers and provide suitable solutions. It is precisely due to SAP xApps that new opportunities are available to implement innovative business processes and strategies.

However, SAP does not act alone in the creation and implementation of these solutions; instead it can rely on a close-knit network of partners. As a result, SAP and its partners already possess a remarkable assortment of SAP xApps. Section 1.6 contains a list of SAP xApps currently available and gives short descriptions of selected examples. Chapter 4, *Implementation Examples*, contains a detailed introduction of the two SAP xApps, SAP xCQM and SAP xPD, which are both based on the SAP CAF.

1.4.2 The SAP xApp Partner Program

SAP global partner program
The SAP Global Partner Program is a unique system with 1,500 partners worldwide and 120,000 certified SAP partner consultants. The focus here is not on gaining the largest possible number of partners but rather on establishing a global SAP partner network based on quality and continuity, which should keep customers satisfied over the long term.

Partner categories
In order to provide SAP customers with a broad and valuable offering of innovative SAP xApps through a cost-effective and scalable partner network, the SAP xApps Partner designation was born. This means that an adequate pool of qualified resources can be guaranteed in the areas of technology, sales and marketing for the development and sale of the solution as well as for the implementation and operation on the customer side. The close linking of SAP xApps to SAP NetWeaver also becomes

clear in the integration of the SAP xApps partner program into the SAP NetWeaver partner initiative.

A long-term environment of cooperation behind a common goal and activities can achieve great benefits and added value for all participants.

Win-Win situation for partners and SAP

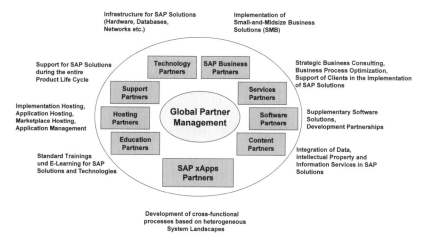

Figure 1.10 SAP Partner Categories

Advantages for the Partners

A main advantage for SAP xApps partners lies in the free use of SAP NetWeaver as an integration and technology platform that facilitates the integration of the partner applications. In addition, the participants in the SAP xApps partner program can benefit from the wealth of experience and far-reaching support by SAP in development.

SAP NetWeaver as a platform

Through access to the broad SAP customer base, partners generate an essential advantage in the sales area. Involvement in the SAP marketing initiatives, "Powered by SAP NetWeaver" and "SAP xApps Partner," participation in SAP events, the right to use product-specific titles and logos, and the common appearance in multiple SAP communication channels all give SAP xApps partners large competitive advantages in marketing.

Sales and marketing

In addition, SAP xApps partners are kept up to date via Internet-based communication tools and have the chance to questions and exchange information. Information channels include:

Information

▶ Access to the SAP Partner Portal (*http://service.sap.com/partnerportal*)

▶ Integration into the SAP Developer Network (*http://sdn.sap.com*)

▶ Subscription to the SAP Global Partner Newsletter

Advantages for SAP

SAP established a strategic initiative through the SAP xApps partner program in order to meet growing and dynamic market requirements. It is exactly this tight partner network which bundles the process, industry and implementation knowledge that strengthens SAP NetWeaver by networking standard technologies and openly integrating leading non-SAP products. This results in a further positive outcome for SAP, as partners increase the level of know-how and provide new products, expanding the SAP product portfolio and securing new markets and customer segments while maintaining consistent quality standards.

1.5 Ideal Procedure for the Creation of an SAP xApp

Due to the availability of the SAP CAF, partners and future customers are in the position to implement applications that correspond to the technical concept of composite applications. For this reason we will now skim through an ideal procedure when creating an SAP xApp.

The implementation process of an SAP xApp, from the idea to the final delivery and maintenance, occurs in six sequential phases which are tested and completed with several milestones.

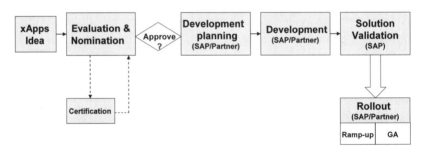

Figure 1.11 Procedure for Developing an SAP xApp

The idea of xApps Typically, at the beginning of the development of an SAP xApp there is an innovative idea which is either created by an SAP partner or internally at SAP based on specific customer requirements. In order to enter into the subsequent phase of evaluation and nomination, the idea contributor needs a detailed business case that describes the xApps idea to be developed in its technological and business functionality as well as a business scenario that should contain the following items:

► **Process and solution description**
The essential principle for judging a potential SAP xApp is a description of the currently exisiting technological and process-oriented problems and a detailed description of the envisaged solution (business process, role bearers involved etc.).

Business scenario description

► **Market opportunities**
The person responsible for the concept names the market opportunities of the envisioned SAP xApp on the basis of a detailed market analysis and documents the potential by naming customers interested in purchasing the solution, referred to as customer prospects.

► **Economic benefit**
It must be made clear that customers, partners and SAP will profit from the possible SAP xApp. Parameters often used are e.g. TCO, return on investment (ROI) or planned sales.

► **Industry knowledge and position**
In the case of an envisioned SAP xApp, which is to be created with the intensive participation of an SAP xApps partner, the partner's actions must make it clear that they know the relevant market and target industry very well and that the partner assumes a leading and prominent position in it.

► **Synergy with the SAP solution portfolio**
From a business and process-oriented perspective, it must be made clear that the future SAP xApp has synergies with the current solution portfolio of SAP.

The submission of this business case into the SAP-internal decision process launches the nomination and evaluation phase in which the chances of success and the compatibility of the possible SAP xApp are evaluated on the basis of the global SAP product portfolio.

Evaluation and nomination

The end of this phase is represented by the decisive milestone of the SAP xApps process: the decision as to whether or not the nominated xApp will be developed and hence integrated into the official solution portfolio.

If the SAP xApp is to be developed in cooperation with a partner, a partner certification process can be initiated, which if successful results in the procedure described above.

After the decision milestone has been completed with a positive decision, the next phase begins: development planning.

Development planning

In this phase all the relevant steps for developing the approved SAP xApp by the involved parties, i.e. the participating departments of SAP and the partner, are planned.

The focus here is on the following topics:

▶ Designing the entire architecture of the SAP xApp

▶ Expert planning and scheduling of the required resources

▶ Organization and execution of the knowledge transfer to the SAP xApp partner (xApp methodology, SAP NetWeaver know-how, SAP Solution Production and quality standards)

▶ Determining and allocating the budget

The phase is finally concluded on the basis of the worked out documents, in particular the ARC sheet which comprises the architecture and the resource planning.

Development After detailed planning and acceptance of the business case, the development phase begins. This also can be initiated while the development planning is being carried out. The main person responsible for the development phase is the respective solution owner of SAP, i.e. the corresponding global business unit, industry business unit or business solution group. If the SAP xApp is produced by a partner from the SAP xApps partner program, large parts of the development phase can be carried out by the respective SAP xApps partner.

The development phase essentially contains the following work steps:

▶ Creating the software requirement specification (SRS)

▶ Composing the development specifications and their transformation into source code

▶ Quality assurance

▶ Executing test activities (testing product units, performance, test cases etc.)

▶ Documentation

After developing the solution, the major focus shifts to the implementation of pilot implementations for the customer prospects named in the evaluation and nomination phase. This is supposed to guarantee a solution which matches the customers' requirements.

Each SAP solution that is supposed to appear on the SAP price list must successfully go through the solution validation phase. In this context, a corresponding customer project is simulated internally at SAP. The installation and configuration of the SAP xApps solution is carried out and evaluated solely on the basis of the documentation and tools provided. This "first customer project" is implemented by a team that corresponds to the team structure recommended in the documentation in terms of size and the required qualification profiles.

After the newly developed SAP xApp has proved and documented the completeness of the solution, the intended functionality and the fulfilment of the quality requirements, the customer rollout begins. This is divided into two phases. First, during the ramp-up phase of the new SAP xApp there will be a controlled market introduction where a limited number of select customers will be provided with the product. These customers can avail themselves of the relevant software in order to implement the solution with development support by the partner or SAP. The ramp-up phase of an SAP product generally lasts for between six and 12 months. Before it begins, criteria are established, for instance the number of reference or live customers. These criteria must be fulfilled in order to officially end the ramp-up phase and to switch to the general availability phase (GA) of the solution.

1.6 First Implementation Examples

The process described moving from the idea to the development and rollout of an SAP xApp has already been described several times.

Figure 1.12 provides an overview of the first available packaged composite applications which were implemented by SAP and its SAP xApp partners.

In order to emphasize the innovative potential, the following section will provide a few short examples of SAP xApps that were developed by SAP or in cooperation with an SAP xApp partner.

Detailed descriptions for SAP xApp Product Definition and SAP xApp Cost and Quotation Management, which are solutions based on the CAF are contained in Chapter 4, *Implementation Examples*.

→ SAP xApp Product Definition
→ SAP xApp Resource and Portfolio Management
→ SAP xApp Cost and Quotation Management
→ SAP Global Trade Services

→ SAP xApp Emissions Management by TechniData
→ SAP xApp Integrated Exploration and Production by Accenture
→ Visual Information for Plants by NRX
→ Manufacturing Performance Intelligence by Lighthammer
→ Workspace Solution B2B Retail Mgmt by Accenture
→ Pricing Analytics by Vendavo
→ plannerDA by BristleCone
→ Service low by Digital Fuel
→ PharmaConnect by EZCommerce

Figure 1.12 SAP xApps Portfolio

1.6.1 SAP xApp Resource and Portfolio Management (SAP xRPM)

Business pain points

Managing extensive portfolios is today seen as a very complex, almost impossible task. This is especially true if the required information on different departments, employees and IT applications is distributed throughout an enterprise. In these circumstances it is difficult to gain an overview of the current projects, let alone control them.

This means project portfolios often do not match the strategic company goals, budgets and timelines are not adhered to, and resources cannot be optimally and effectively used. Transparent, valid and prepared project, resource and portfolio information for all role players are often missing.

Research studies confirming this point to the fact that only a quarter of all IT projects are completed successfully, i.e. by adhering to the content-related, time, financial and technical guidelines.

SAP xRPM as a solution

SAP xApp Resource and Portfolio Management (SAP xRPM) takes on these challenges and provides companies in the IT, R&D, and services sectors with an integrated solution. SAP xRPM integrates data from existing company applications such as HR or finance systems and provides executives, project managers, and team members with relevant, valid and current project data in a timely role-based manner. This leads to consolidated and harmonized decisions regarding financial and personnel resources from the strategic to the operational levels of projects and portfolios which match the business goals.

The main functional areas of SAP xRPM can be divided into portfolio and program management and expertise and resource management, all of which will be discussed briefly in the following section.

The project dashboard is the central point of entry. It gives you an overview of the relevant project data and states the status of a project regarding different key performance indicators (KPIs) such as the budget, time planning or resource assignment by using clear metrics. This central view of the performance and risk-specific information is essential for a successful management of company-wide portfolios and projects. SAP xRPM provides the option of classifying projects as master and sub-projects in order to support an effective portfolio management. A variety of reports are available in order to evaluate the entire portfolio or individual projects on the basis of selected KPIs. Through definition and use of critical success factors, the projects and the portfolio can work in unison with the strategic orientation of a company. Based on this, the project prioritization enables the identification of projects with the greatest potential to reach the desired goals. In addition, different portfolio scenarios within a what-if-analysis, based on a selection of projects and project suggestions, can be simulated in terms of resource requirements and assignments, budget allocation, time frames, and additional factors, before measures specific to the project or the portfolio are taken.

Portfolio management

Through program management, SAP xRPM integrates data such as project tasks, phases, or milestones from different project management systems through a standardized data exchange format. This means project management functions and data from cProject, the SAP module Project system, Microsoft Project in the client and in the server version, and from Primavera can be consolidated through SAP xRPM and made transparent. In this context, SAP xRPM provides a wide range of functionalities regarding project control, management and reporting, for instance in the form of role-based, operational workflows.

Program management

Resource management in terms of SAP xRPM covers capacity management as well as the project-specific resource assignment.

Resource management

Here capacity management focuses on the macroscopic inspection of resources within the given organization. SAP xRPM provides a complete and consolidated view of the resource offering and of the corresponding resource requirement for the projects so that resource managers have a detailed insight into the capacity situation across organizational and functional limits. This company-wide transparency opens up the opportunity for companies to use their resource capacities in the most optimal manner. In addition, SAP xRPM provides the option of identifying key functions and requirements of projects, of forecasting their future requirements and finally of being able to decide on adequate resources, for example in the form of new hiring or employee training.

The project-specific resource assignment focuses on a microscopic view of the use of resources. Essentially it centers on the issue of assigning the correct people at the right time to a suitable project. SAP xRPM establishes a transparent relationship between the timely and qualitative requirements of projects and the availability and qualifications of employees in order to meet this requirement.

Expertise management
In order to be able to optimally assign resources, you need easily understandable and complete employee profiles that contain information on qualifications and availability. SAP xRPM can use existing data, for example from mySAP HR or provide team members or their managers with multiple options for the easy entry and collection of the relevant data.

Structure of SAP xRPM
SAP xRPM is one of the first xApps developed by SAP. Figure 1.13 provides an overview of the architecture of SAP xRPM.

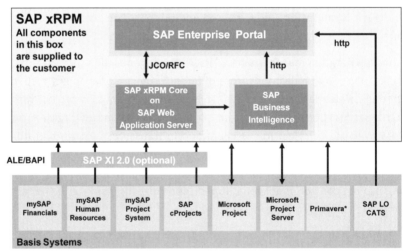

Figure 1.13 Simplified Architecture of SAP xRPM

1.6.2 SAP xApp Emissions Management (SAP xEM) as an Example of a Partner xApp

From the broad spectrum of packaged composite applications developed by SAP xApps partners registered as system integrators or independent software vendors (and in cooperation with them), we will introduce SAP xEM in this section.

Legal regulations and guidelines regarding energy consumption and the emission of greenhouse gases based on the Kyoto protocol e.g. or the US Clean Air Act or the IPPC guidelines by the EU set new challenges for companies. Companies are obliged to provide detailed emission reports and to present them to environmental authorities. If specific emission guidelines are not adhered to, the company may not only be perceived negatively by the outside world but face sanctions that affect the regular business operation or even lead to the closure of entire plants.

Business pain points

Companies in which an efficient emission management is in place can receive emission credit notes by exceeding emission guidelines, which they can offer to the newly established emissions-trading market.

Due to the distribution of the required emission data and functions of a production plant in different departments, areas and systems of a company it appears almost impossible for experts and is very time-consuming to establish a functioning and effective emission management:

> *The current solutions for emission management have a large problem: They do not provide the possibility of accessing manufacturing applications and data. SAP xAPP Emissions Management is based on SAP NetWeaver and does not have this problem. It is an integrated solution with a comprehensive functional package.[11]*

SAP xAPP Emissions Management as an integrative solution provides a central and role-based access to this emission-specific data and also to tools for control, calculation and documentation of the emissions. Communication and information processes, the improvement of the environmental portfolio, and a sustainable increase in environmentally friendly trading are supported as well.

SAP xEM as a solution

SAP xEM comprises the following functions, which enable an efficient emissions management:

---

11 Jim Bausano (2004), Vice President and Director, Air Quality Services Energy, Environment & Systems CH2Mill.

► Evaluating and analyzing emissions with the help of scenarios to calculate and display emission data

► Legal security and the monitoring of regulations through task monitoring, schedules, processes and rules as well as fixed information flows by role-based workflows

► Compliance reporting by automatical creation and dispatch of documentation and reports

► Trading with emissions rights and cross-company scenarios, including forecast creation and transaction processing

► Supporting company management in the areas of controlling, planning, risk management, stock management and management processes

► Additional functions such as failure management, discharge due to accidents, the emission of volatile substances, modelling and forecasting

SAP xEM is based on the SAP NetWeaver technology and integration platform and combines processes, information and people across technological and organizational boundaries. The rough structure of SAP xEM is illustrated in Figure 1.14.

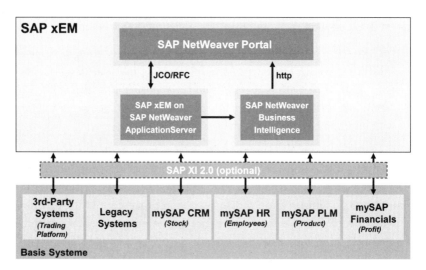

Figure 1.14 Simplified Architecture of SAP xEM

SAP xEM was developed in cooperation with the independent software vendor and SAP xApp partner, Technidata AG, which was awarded the SAP Pinnacle Award for this.

1.7 Possible Decision Criteria for Developing an SAP xApp or a Custom Composite Application

In this chapter the particular characteristics and the ideal procedure for developing an SAP xApp are described. The possible decision criteria with regard to the development and implementation of an SAP xApp will be listed and elaborated on in a summary, before an architectural model of an SAP xApp is introduced in Chapter 2.

The starting point is the goal of creating an IT solution for a business process. Alternative solutions will be contrasted against SAP xApps as a possible solution.

1.7.1 Business Criteria

Creating an SAP xApp as standard software demands certain investments for development, marketing, and maintenance. The business process must therefore be sufficiently universal in order to ensure there is a corresponding market potential for the new solution. In general, this potential only exists in newly conceived or newly established processes, which represent a growing market.

Market potential

Criterion	Character	Solution
Market potential	Sufficient market potential for the solution, i.e. the business process is universal and will become more important for companies in the future. Competitive solutions are not or only insufficiently available.	SAP xApp
	The process is specific and has a limited market potential.	Custom Composite Application Enhancement of existing standard software

Table 1.2 Business Decision Criteria

1.7.2 Criteria Determined by the Characteristics of the Business Process

The advantages of an SAP xApp come to the fore when flexibility and cross-functional cooperation are required in the process.

Flexibility is one of the main criteria. SAP xApps enable changes to be made to the IT solution in harmony with business requirements in a sim-

Flexibility

ple manner. The flexibility potential of SAP xApps exists in three areas which could serve as decision criteria:

▶ **Process configuration**
Modified user interactions or application services can be reconfigured easily in a new sequence by the process engine. This means a process selection can also take place dynamically during runtime depending on the existing information.

▶ **User interface changes**
Independence from the user interface business logic enables modified user interfaces to be adapted and added as required.

▶ **Changes to the application logic**
By using components which are separated from each other modified or even new services can replace existing ones without changing the entire application. In part, the changes to the object model of the user interface are available without additional programming effort. Via Web services, external services can be used in the SAP xApp.

Cross-functional process
A cross-functional process is supported by SAP xApps primarily by using SAP Enterprise Portal. Participants work in the process with role-specific views and services. These can be provided to the user through the portal according to their role. Furthermore, integration of collaborative services including groupware applications is possible.

Criterion	Character	Solution
Process flexibility	Is the business process subject to forseeable adaptations and modifications which affect the general process flow, participating roles and specific activities?	SAP xApp or Custom Composite Application
	Process is relatively stable	Customer-specific development Enhancement of standard software
Cross-functional character of the process	Are different roles involved in the process that carry out different views and activities on the same objects? Is communication between the participants important in this context?	SAP xApp or Custom Composite Application
	Restriction to specific functions in the company.	Enhancement of standard software Best-of-breed solution

Table 1.3 Decision Criteria Determined by the Characteristics of the Business Process

1.7.3 Criteria Determined by the Type and Source of the Information

Implementation of an SAP xApp is particularly useful if the information to be integrated and the data already in the company exist within a heterogeneous system landscape. Based on the type and source of the information, three decision criteria can be considered:

▶ **The type of information distribution across different applications**
If the information required in the process is already existing in other systems or if it is required there, the SAP NetWeaver platform provides convenient modules to integrate the information in a flexible manner.

▶ **Novel information emerges**
An SAP xApp possesses its own persistence. New objects and connections can be stored there which are not available in other systems.

▶ **Structuring of the information**
An SAP xApp can combine both structured data and documents. The CAF Repository Manager provides both types in SAP Knowledge Management. The KM component enables a powerful search regarding both types of information.

Criterion	Character	Solution
Distributing information across different applications	The necessary information for the process is available in different systems or is required there.	SAP xApp or Custom Composite Application
	Information remains limited to one application.	Enhancement of standard software
Novel information emerges	In the process new information emerges. This can be enhancements and changes to existing objects.	SAP xApp or Custom Composite Application
	Information and object structure generally exist in existing applications.	Enhancement of standard software
		Using a portal solution
Character of the information	For cooperation in the process a combination of structured data and less structured information such as documents is important.	SAP xApp or Custom Composite Application
	In the process structured data or documents are required.	Using knowledge management systems
		Self-programming of a database application

Table 1.4 Decision Criteria Determined by the Type and Source of the Information

2   The Architecture of SAP xApps

Based on the principles already discussed, an ideal type of architectural model of SAP xApps will be developed in this chapter. The main emphasis will be put on the basis for SAP xApps: SAP NetWeaver with its components. In this context, you will focus on the SAP Composite Application Framework.

The description of the architectural model of SAP xApps is divided into three parts. After a short overview of SAP NetWeaver, we will describe NetWeaver components that provide comprehensive functionality and tools for SAP xApps. The second part deals with the structure and functionality of the most important component in the context of SAP xApps, the SAP Composite Application Framework (CAF). The third part of the chapter merges all the previous information into one general architectural model of SAP xApps.

If you are already familiar with SAP NetWeaver and its components, you can skip the first part and continue with Section 2.3.

2.1   SAP NetWeaver Overview

In order to make the conceptual leap from a service-oriented architecture to the development of composite applications, you must first understand the relationship between the Enterprise Services Architecture (ESA), SAP NetWeaver, and the SAP CAF.

As described in Chapter 1, *SAP xApps—Basic Principles*, SAP NetWeaver represents the third generation of application platforms for SAP. Analogous to the R/3 platform, which enabled the three-level client/server architecture, SAP NetWeaver introduced the actual implementation and realization of the ESA.

SAP NetWeaver to enable ESA

As previously discussed, there are usually productive heterogeneous system landscapes on the client side. These consist of applications from different vendors and various technologies. In order to meet the customers' requirement for integration, SAP provides the most comprehensive integration and application platform currently available on the market: SAP NetWeaver. Based on existing systems, SAP NetWeaver supports the integration and development of applications in heterogeneous system landscapes and thus reduces the TCO of the IT landscape.

Interoperability ensures a low TCO Given the variety of different applications in productive system landscapes, a basic factor for achieving a low TCO is the interoperability of the technology platform. IT departments face the challenge of supporting the growth of the enterprise and at the same time protecting previous investments. In order to accomplish this two-sided task, SAP NetWeaver provides complete interoperability with IBM WebSphere and Microsoft .NET.

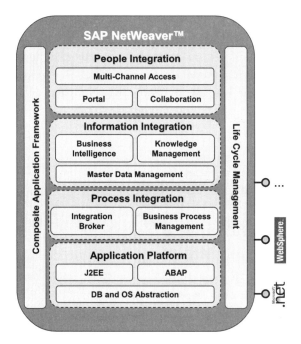

Figure 2.1 An Overview of SAP NetWeaver

Before describing the functionality and structure of the SAP CAF in Section 2.3, we will first address the components available with SAP NetWeaver, which play an important part during the development and implementation of SAP xApps.

2.2 SAP NetWeaver Components

SAP NetWeaver connects people, information and business processes beyond enterprise, organizational, and technological boundaries. With SAP NetWeaver, SAP provides an integration and technology platform based on open standards, which consists of four layers:

- ▶ People integration
- ▶ Information integration
- ▶ Process integration
- ▶ Application platform

Next, we will address these layers and their corresponding applications and components. Because the application platform is crucially important for all other SAP NetWeaver components, it will be discussed at the beginning of this section.

2.2.1 Application Platform

The SAP Web Application Server provides a complete development infra-structure for developing, distributing, and running platform-independent, robust, and scalable Web services and business applications. The SAP Web Application Server supports both ABAP and Java as well as Web services.

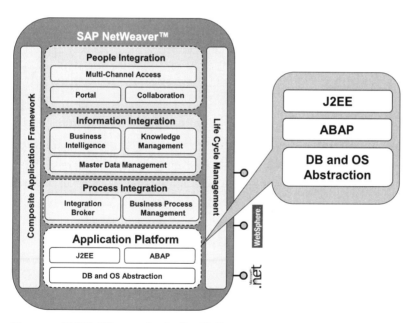

Figure 2.2 SAP NetWeaver—Application Platform

The ABAP development and runtime environment and the corresponding Java component enable development of complex business applications while not having to explicitly observe technical details like process and storage management, multi-user functionality, database connections, and

Abstraction levels

the like. Application development is also carried out irrespective of the underlying platform. The SAP Web Application Server completely detaches the application source code from the used operating system and database.

Apart from the pure ABAP or Java editor for creating ABAP or Java source code, respectively, the development environments of ABAP Workbench and SAP NetWeaver Developer Studio are completely integrated in the server. In combination with the Java Development Infrastructure (JDI), they offer support for developing comprehensive projects. This is ensured by the following functionalities:

Development environment

- ▶ Versioning control
- ▶ Structuring of development objects
- ▶ Development tools and editors for interfaces
- ▶ Support of multilingual text elements and messages
- ▶ Connection to corresponding transport systems (Transport Organizer in ABAP and Change Management Service—CMS—in the JDI)
- ▶ Direct access to all data definitions via the ABAP and Java dictionaries, respectively
- ▶ Debugging functionality
- ▶ Various test and analysis tools
- ▶ Modification support

With its SAP Web Application Server, SAP provides a homogeneous infra-structure for both ABAP- and J2EE-based applications. Therefore, all business objects and interfaces can be used in the same way both in the Java and in the ABAP environment.

ABAP development projects are managed directly in the system, meta-data and source code are stored in the database.

ABAP component

The ABAP programming language combines the benefits of an object-ori-ented language with those of an integrated 4GL language. It provides the typical OO language constructs like classes, interfaces, inheritance, etc. In addition, many server services, which are embedded in other languages as libraries and have to be addressed via APIs, are integrated directly in the language. These include the direct usage of all data types managed in the central ABAP dictionary and the integration of the database access in particular.

The runtime environment ensures that every ABAP program automatically receives an open connection to the central database of the system so that an application programmer does not need to worry about the opening and closing of database connections. ABAP objects include Open SQL, an SQL dialect independent of the database vendor, as a direct part of the language. Using this dialect, databases can be accessed directly without having to go via an API or a class library. Buffer mechanisms on the application server ensure a highly scalable, complex database access.

Integration of database access

The runtime system provides its own locking mechanism for synchronizing accesses to data in the database. This prevents two transactions from changing the same database data simultaneously. Updating enables the mapping of business operations in completed transactions, ensuring data integrity.

In the past, the interfaces of classic SAP applications were based on the SAP GUI. Apart from output of data in lists, Dynpro technology gives you the option to program dialogs to be displayed in the SAP GUI at runtime via a proprietary protocol. This type of UI programming is still possible. Additionally, new UI programming techniques can be applied.

SAP GUI

The server-side scripting approach is used by the Business Server Pages model (BSP). Much like JSPs, this model enables the creation of HTML-based web applications with integrated ABAP code. The BSP model is based on the Internet Communication Framework, which is located at a lower level and allows the implementation of ABAP-based services which answer HTTP and HTTPS requests.

BSP

In order to create documentation and multilingual applications, you can use the integrated documentation and translation tools. New applications can be documented directly, managing the documentation texts in a similar way as development objects. Using the translation tools, multilingual texts can be created separately from the actual program development. The connection to the transport enables the building and management of even the most complex documentation and translation landscapes.

The J2EE Engine is an integral component of the SAP Web Application Server that implements the J2EE standard (Java 2 Enterprise Edition). This standard was defined by the Java Community according to the rules of the Java Community Process and is protected by the copyright of Sun Microsystems. Since November 2002, SAP is a member of the Executive Committee of the Java Community.

Java area

The SAP J2EE Engine supports component-based enterprise technologies and enables quick development and installation of secure, scalable, and easy-to-organize applications. The portability of these applications is guaranteed by the support of many operating systems and database platforms. The SAP J2EE Engine complies with the current JMX and J2EE standards and implements JavaBeans, servlets, JSPs, JNDI, JMS, and Java mail according to the standards specified. It provides scalability, availability, reliability, support for current security standards, caching, dynamic load balancing, options for data replication and clustering of web pages and components, as well as a wide range of functionalities for administration, configuration, and monitoring.

Enhancements of the standard   The SAP Web Application Server not only complies with the J2EE standards as a J2EE-certified application server but also extends these standards with comprehensive functionality which meets the high quality requirements of large-scale enterprise development projects of Java applications. For this reason, the Java component of the SAP Web Application Server features the following enhancements:

▶ SAP Java Connector (for connecting the Java and ABAP components)

▶ Java Persistence (implementing a layer which is independent of the database)

▶ Web Dynpro (framework providing a development and runtime environment for creating professional, high-quality, cross-platform Web UIs)

▶ SAP NetWeaver Developer Studio and SAP Java Development Infrastructure

SAP NetWeaver Developer Studio   *SAP NetWeaver Developer Studio* is the SAP environment for developing Java-based business applications structured in layers. It provides consistent access to all Java development tools, and serves as a central point of entry for all SAP infrastructure components. All Java developers greatly benefit from not having to switch between different development environments for the UI or the business logic. In fact, the SAP NetWeaver Developer Studio provides the option of centrally developing, assembling, installing, and running applications. Therefore, it is not relevant whether SAP technologies like the Web Dynpro Java Dictionary or standard technologies like J2SE, J2EE, or XML are being used.

SAP NetWeaver Java Development Infrastructure   The SAP NetWeaver Developer Studio provides access to the *SAP NetWeaver Java Development Infrastructure* (JDI). It extends the concept of an Integrated Development Environment (IDE) with server-side services that centrally provide development teams with a consistent development environment and support them during software development throughout the entire life cycle of a product. The JDI consists of tightly connected central services for design, implementation, building and testing purposes which can be used in a local as well as in a central environment. All units are composed of well defined components. They improve the reusability of software and the management of extremely different dependencies of application modules.

The SAP NetWeaver JDI includes the following components:

▶ *Design Time Repository* (DTR) for central storage, versioning, and management of Java source code and other resources. It provides an automatic mechanism for conflict detection and conflict resolution.

▶ The *Component Build Service* (CBS) creates the corresponding runtime objects like Java archives which can be installed on the central J2EE server. The CBS creates incremental builds and updates them automatically with the dependent components taking the dependent resources directly from the DTR.

▶ The *Change Management Service* (CMS) takes the results of the build process from the CBS and initializes the distribution and installation in the J2EE server environment.

▶ During this process, the *Software Deployment Manager* (SDM) is responsible for installing and updating the software components on the J2EE server. On demand, it offers modification support. Every time a new component version needs to be installed, the CBS calls the SDM on the relevant target system.

▶ The *Java Dictionary* supports the global definition of tables and data types, as does the ABAP Dictionary.

▶ With the *SAP Java Test Tools*, components can be easily tested, started, stopped, and debugged. In doing so, it is not relevant whether the components reside on a local or a remote instance of the SAP Web Application Server.

2.2.2 Process Integration

Process integration supports smooth business processes in a heterogeneous IT landscape. Cross-system business processes can thus be defined, controlled and monitored.

The following key functional areas are included in the process integration:

▶ Integration broker

▶ Business-process management

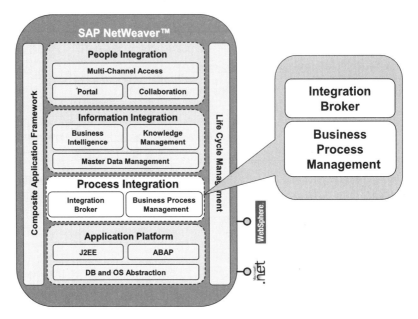

Figure 2.3 SAP NetWeaver—Process Integration

Integration Broker: SAP Exchange Infrastructure

With the SAP Exchange Infrastructure (SAP XI), cross-system business processes can be put into practice. This provides the option of combining systems from SAP and other vendors in different versions and implementing them in different programming languages (Java, ABAP, etc.). SAP XI is based on an open architecture and primarily uses open standards (especially from the XML and Java world). It offers services that are indispensable in a heterogeneous and complex system landscape: runtime infrastructure for exchanging messages, configuration options for controlling collaborative processes and message flow, design and execution of cross-system business processes, and B2B support, as well as options for transforming message contents between sender and recipient.

SAP XI is adapted to generally accepted standards in order to be open to the integration of non-SAP systems. Therefore, the central concept is an XML-based communication via HTTP: Application-specific content is transferred via messages in a customizable XML schema from the sender to the recipient through the so-called Integration Server.

Sender and recipient exchanging messages via the Integration Server are decoupled from each other. This decoupling makes it easy to combine systems which are technologically different. Every system that can exchange messages with the Integration Server is thus able to exchange messages with all other systems connected to the Integration Server. SAP XI supports the following approaches for communicating with the Integration Server: **Integration Server**

► Direct communication via proxies which are generated into the application systems based on a description in WSDL

► Communication via adapters. This is enabled by creating message exchange interfaces in the application system.

Simple message processing on the Integration Server is stateless, which means that the Integration Server is not aware of any semantic correlations between different messages. Using cross-system business processes running on the Integration Server, you can describe logical dependencies between messages and define additional conditions for the message flow. These processes of cross-system business process management can be centrally modeled and maintained with SAP XI. **Stateless messages**

Like cross-system business processes, the entire integration knowledge of a collaborative process is stored centrally in SAP XI: objects during the design phase reside in the Integration Repository; objects during the configuration phase are stored in the Integration Directory. The exchange infrastructure thus obeys the principle of *Shared collaboration knowledge*: Information about a collaborative process no longer has to be collected from the systems involved but can be retrieved centrally. This procedure significantly reduces the costs of developing and maintaining distributed applications.

SAP Business Process Management

The SAP Business Process Management extends the SAP Exchange Infrastructure by a stateful processing of messages. The state of a business process is made persistent on the Integration Server. Thus, a business process can wait infinitely or according to a schedule for incoming messages. In addition, messages within a business process can be further processed; they can be collected and then be sent in a specific order. **Stateful messages**

Cross-system business process management is integrated in the SAP XI in that Business processes are objects in the Integration Repository or Integration Directory and are integrated with the other objects such as message interfaces etc. For defining a business process during the design phase, the Integration Builder in the Integration Repository provides a graphical process editor.

During the configuration phase, the recipient determination is set for the business process in the Integration Directory of the Integration Builder.

At runtime, the business process engine runs the business processes. The business process engine is part of the Integration Server. The execution of business processes can also be monitored via the monitoring feature of the integration engine.

2.2.3   Information Integration

Information integration provides both structured and unstructured information in a consistent and easily accessible way: Users are granted continuous access to consistent information, irrespective of its location.

Components involved

Information integration is achieved using three components:

▶ Business intelligence

▶ Knowledge management

▶ Master data management

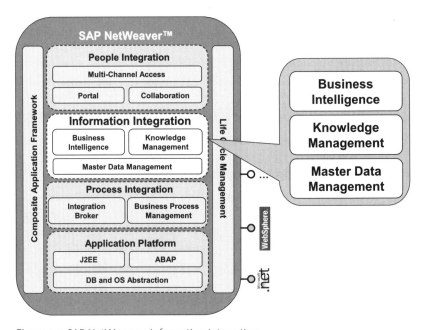

Figure 2.4 SAP NetWeaver—Information Integration

SAP Business Intelligence

Enterprises urgently need to report, analyze and interpret enterprise data in order to stay competitive, optimize processes and react quickly and appropriately to market changes. The SAP Business Intelligence component provides a data warehousing functionality, a business-intelligence platform as well as a suite of business-intelligence tools for enterprises to achieve this goal. With the toolset provided, relevant business information from productive SAP applications and all external data sources can be integrated, transformed and consolidated in SAP Business Intelligence. It offers flexible reporting and analysis tools to support data evaluation and interpretation and enables the distribution of information. Well-analyzed data leads to well-informed and effective decision-making and actions that are in line with business goals.

Figure 2.5 Overview of the Architecture of SAP Business Intelligence

Data warehousing with SAP Business Intelligence is the basis for a comprehensive solution for converting data into valuable information. Integrated and enterprise-specific data warehousing provides information and knowledge to the decision makers of an enterprise who can then take goal-oriented actions. Data warehousing with SAP Business Intelligence enables the following actions for data from any source (SAP and non-SAP) and relevance (historical and up-to-date):

Data warehousing

- ▶ Integration (data retrieval from source systems)
- ▶ Transformation
- ▶ Consolidation
- ▶ Cleanup
- ▶ Storage
- ▶ Retrieval for analysis and interpretation

The central tool for data warehousing tasks in SAP BI is the Administrator Workbench.

Business Intelligence Platform

Another functional area is represented by the Business Intelligence Platform. It provides a technological infrastructure and various analytical technologies and functions:

- ▶ *Online Analytical Processing* (OLAP) is used for preparing vast amounts of operational and historical data. The OLAP processor enables multi-dimensional analyses according to different individual perspectives.
- ▶ The *Meta Data Repository* enables you to display information about the metadata objects of the BI system on the running system or to use this information irrespective of the operation of the BI system.
- ▶ Planning applications are created with *Business Planning and Simulation* (BI-BPS). Fields of application range from simple manual data entry up to complex planning scenarios.
- ▶ Special analysis procedures like data mining can be carried out with the *Analysis Process Designer* (APD). Using an analysis process, information can be merged in the BI system in order to create new information.

Business Intelligence Suite

The *Business Explorer* is the component of the SAP Business Intelligence which provides flexible reporting and analysis tools for strategic, tactical, and operational analysis and decision support for enterprises. These tools include query, reporting, and analysis functions. Employees with the appropriate access authorization can evaluate both historical and current data in different levels of detail and from different perspectives (e.g. via the web or in MS Excel).

Using *BEx Information Broadcasting*, pre-calculated documents with historical data or links with live data can be distributed via e-mail or published in the enterprise portal from the SAP Business Intelligence.

The Business Explorer enables a broad range of users to access the information in SAP Business Intelligence. Information can be distributed via the SAP Enterprise Portal, an intranet (Web Application Design), or

mobile presentation devices including WAP- or iMode-enabled mobile phones, or Personal Digital Assistants (PDAs).

The Business Intelligence Suite provides a very broad functionality, which we will now describe.

The data basis of SAP Business Intelligence is divided into complete data areas (InfoProviders). The SAP Business Intelligence dataset is analyzed by defining queries about InfoProviders in BEx Query Designer. By selecting and combining InfoObjects (attributes and key performance indicators) or reusable structures in a query, you determine the way in which the data of the chosen InfoProvider can be analyzed.

Query, reporting, and analysis

The data analysis based on OLAP reporting enables a simultaneous analysis of multiple dimensions (e.g. time, place, product, etc.). You have the option of carrying out any variance analyses (e.g. plan/actual comparison, fiscal year comparison). The data is shown in a table and is used as a starting point for a detailed analysis to answer a variety of questions. Numerous possibilities of interaction, such as sorting, filtering, exchanging attributes, or local calculations allow for a flexible data navigation at runtime. The data can also be visualized in graphics (bar chart, pie chart, etc.). In addition, you have the option of analyzing data with a geographical reference (e.g. attributes like customer, sales region, country) on a map. Using exception reporting, deviating and critical objects can be determined. Messages about deviating values can be sent automatically (through background processing in the reporting agent) via e-mail or SMS, or can be spotted at a glance in an alert monitor.

Data analysis is eventually carried out in the BEx Web.

BEx Web

Web Application Design provides the option of implementing the generic OLAP navigation in both web applications and business intelligence cockpits for simple or even highly individual scenarios. Highly individual scenarios with custom interface elements can be achieved with standard markup languages and web design APIs. Thus, the Web Application Design comprises a broad range of interactive web-based business intelligence scenarios that can be adapted to specific needs using standard web technologies.

With the BEx Web Application Designer, the desktop application for web application creation, HTML pages can be created containing BI-specific contents such as tables, charts, or maps. These can be saved via URLs and shared by means of the intranet or mobile presentation devices. In addition, you have the option to integrate web applications as iView in an SAP Enterprise Portal.

BEx Web Analyzer provides an independent, comfortable web application for data analysis which can be called via a URL or as an iView in the SAP Enterprise Portal. In BEx Web Analyzer, you can open a query or a view, respectively, or define a new query. Using tabs, you have the possibility to change from the tabular into the graphical view, query information about the selected data provider and call the BEx broadcaster.

Developer technologies SAP Business Intelligence provides further developer technologies: the BI Java SDK, Open Analysis Interfaces, and a Web Design API.

▶ Using the *BI Java SDK*, analytic applications can be created which enable access to multidimensional (OLAP) and to tabular (relational) data. The BI Java Connectors, a group of four JCA-enabled (J2EE Connector Architecture) resource adapters, implement the APIs of the BI Java SDK and thus make it possible to combine the applications created via the SDK with different data sources.

▶ The *Open Analysis Interfaces* provide various interfaces for connecting front-end tools from third-party vendors.

▶ The *Web Design API* and the table interface enable the realization of highly individual scenarios and sophisticated applications with customized interface items.

Business Content A key advantage of SAP Business Intelligence is the provision of business content. This includes preconfigured role- and task-oriented information models based on consistent metadata. Business content supplies selected roles in an enterprise with the range of information needed to fulfill their tasks.

These information models primarily include roles, workbooks, queries, InfoSources, InfoCubes, ODS objects, key performance indicators, attributes, update rules, and extractors for SAP R/3, mySAP.com Business Applications and other selected applications.

Business content can be used without adjustments or can be adjusted, i.e. refined or made more general, or used as a template or example of self-created business content and thus enables a quick and cost-saving start-up of SAP Business Intelligence.

SAP Knowledge Management

Within the SAP Enterprise Portal, the SAP Knowledge Management provides a central, role-specific point of entry for unstructured information from different data sources. It makes its entire functionality and all configuration options available via iViews of the SAP Enterprise Portal. Unstructured information can exist in different formats, e.g. as text documents, presentations, or HTML files. The employees of an organization retrieve such information from various sources like file servers, an intranet or the World Wide Web. Through a generic framework, SAP Knowledge Management integrates these data sources and provides access to the information contained therein via the SAP Enterprise Portal.

Access to unstructured information

The SAP Knowledge Management functions assist in structuring information and making it available to the target groups. These features include for example the search, classification or subscription of information. These options can be applied to all contents of the integrated data sources, depending on the technical conditions.

Features like discussions, feedback, or sending any objects from KM folders via E-mail are tightly integrated in SAP Knowledge Management and enable joint work on documents irrespective of roles and departments. In addition, parts of SAP Knowledge Management are reused in the collaboration component of SAP NetWeaver, e.g. for storing documents in collaboration rooms.

SAP Knowledge Management supports the SAP NetWeaver scenario of Information Broadcasting. Using the BEx Broadcaster and the comprehensive knowledge management functionality, business information from the SAP Business Intelligence can be made available to a broad range of users via the SAP Enterprise Portal. The following objects from SAP Business Intelligence are appropriate for storing in KM folders:

Information broadcasting

▶ Documents with pre-calculated reports;

▶ Links to BEx Web Applications and queries with live data.

The features of the SAP Knowledge Management, e.g. the subscription of documents, can be applied to these objects. For representing BI objects in KM folders, there is a customized user interface which can be adapted according to specific requirements.

SAP Knowledge Management comprises the subcomponents SAP Content Management (CM), and search, retrieval, and classification (TREX), and provides the following functionality.

Integration of repositories	Typically, information is stored in various repositories, e.g. on file servers, in groupware systems, or document management systems. Using several pre-configured repository managers, SAP Knowledge Management integrates these repositories and provides a central point of entry for their contents in the SAP Enterprise Portal. Through open programming interfaces (APIs), customers and partners can develop repository managers for additional storage systems.
	In addition, it provides the option to store documents in a KM-specific repository.
Navigating folders	In an iView, portal users can navigate through the folders of all integrated repositories as they would on a file server and access the documents contained therein. Access to folders and documents is controlled using authorization. The user interface for navigation in folders can be configured flexibly and adjusted to different roles. End users can customize the display of the user interface. Open interfaces enable the extension of the user interface to integrate proprietary features in the standard system.
Search	The search function finds documents in all repositories that are integrated in SAP Knowledge Management. In the search results list, the system shows only those documents for which the user has read authorization. Using a web crawler, the contents of websites can also be added to indexes in order to make them available for the search function in the SAP Enterprise Portal.
Taxonomy and classification	A taxonomy is a hierarchical structure of categories in which documents are classified according to content, organization or other criteria. Documents physically stored in different repositories can still be assigned to one category. A taxonomy enables portal users to navigate a hierarchical structure that is consistent throughout the organization even though the data storage environment is heterogeneous. After the initial configuration, the system runs an automatic classification for new and changed documents.
Content Management Services	Content Management Services enable the use of functions that can be applied to contents of all connected repositories according to the technical conditions. These include subscriptions, ratings, public valuations, feedbacks, or personal notes. In addition, the Content Exchange Service provides the possibility of importing documents from external sources into KM repositories.
Creating and publishing	Every portal user can create information in the SAP Enterprise Portal, provided he or she has the appropriate authorization for a KM folder. Docu-

ments created with PC applications can be uploaded to KM folders. Alternatively, this information can be created directly in the web browser using forms. The corresponding publication process is supported by various functions like e.g. an approval workflow.

Documents and other objects have properties that can be assigned values. Thus, objects are enhanced by metadata which the system can evaluate in different ways. Therefore, the knowledge existing in the organization can be used more effectively because a higher hit rate can be achieved during the search process. In this context, you can specify the properties certain types of objects can or must have. New properties can be defined if needed, based on the given requirements.

SAP Master Data Management

SAP Master Data Management (MDM) provides a central and consistent framework for the maintenance, management, and installation of master data. It is based on an open and web-based architecture designed for collaboration within organizations and enterprises. The design solution guarantees data integration across different systems, physical locations, and different providers or business partners. Based on the data harmonized using SAP MDM, collaborative E-business scenarios in heterogeneous IT system landscapes will be supported.

SAP MDM enables storage, change, and consolidation of master data while ensuring its consistent distribution to all applications and systems of the IT landscape. Thus, every employee of an enterprise receives current and valid information about products, product catalogs, business partners or documentation. That information can flow from all areas, including engineering, procurement, manufacturing, marketing, sales, or service.

Storage, change, consolidation of master data

Apart from system integration, SAP MDM supports the management of master data in their general cross-system context throughout all business processes. The main factors are:

▶ Accessible master data

▶ Coordinated knowledge of master data

▶ Merged processes

By integrating heterogeneous systems spread across various locations, SAP MDM enables an extended use of IT investments already made for business-critical data. In addition, an effective management of master data results in a significant reduction of data maintenance costs. In this context, consider the accelerating effect on business processes as well as the positive impact on decision-making.

Master data for comprehensive processes Application systems included in the MDM process use master data objects independently of each other. One reason for this is the often quite heterogeneous data models of the individual applications. In order to be able to establish business processes across different systems or to ensure consistent access for analytical applications in heterogeneous IT environments, it is essential to integrate and consolidate master data that is shared but stored in different places.

Business scenarios SAP MDM supports three different business scenarios:

▶ Consolidation

▶ Harmonization

▶ Central Master Data Management

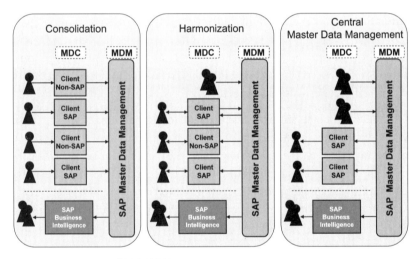

Figure 2.6 Scenarios of SAP MDM

If SAP MDM is implemented, the different application systems are defined as Master Data Clients (MDC). With SAP MDM, adapters for different systems like SAP R/3 Enterprise, SAP CRM or SAP SRM are supplied.

SAP Master Data Management Consolidation SAP MDM Consolidation entails the process of consolidating master data used in different application systems. This scenario can be applied to different master data like business partner, product or technical assets.

The SAP MDM allows for searching, tracking and consolidating master data and provides the information required for deletion in the connected application systems. In short, the MDM consolidation enables you to identify identical or similar master data objects in each system, so that a cleanup can be carried out in the respective application, if necessary. The main purpose of these scenarios, however, is to transfer information about identical master data entries to the SAP Business Intelligence so that a unified and collaborative evaluation can be effected.

SAP MDM Harmonization not only enables the consolidation of master data but also persistent data synchronization throughout the entire system landscape in order to avoid future inconsistencies. Nevertheless, the local creation and change of master data is still permitted.

SAP Master Data Management Harmonization

The harmonization scenario therefore includes the consolidation described previously, extending it so as to enable a consistent maintenance and distribution of master data entries. This consistency is ensured mainly by the use of global attributes that contain master data information and are relevant throughout the entire enterprise and their IT environments.

The use of SAP MDM Harmonization guarantees that all client systems are provided with master data after the distribution and makes sure that business processes are carried out consistently and securely. Client applications provide the option of extending the distributed master data entries with additional attributes of only local relevance. This scenario can be applied to master data objects like business partners, products or product structures.

Another scenario would be the central master data management that allows for the central maintenance and management of complete data records for master data. Since maintaining small parts of available master data attributes is often inefficient, SAP MDM additionally supports the central maintenance of complete object definitions including dependencies on other objects on the master data server.

Central Master Data Management

Although the central management is based on the harmonization of master data, it still does not permit the direct maintenance of data or related attributes in the local systems. Neither the local creation and change of data nor their extension with local attributes is allowed in this context.

In central master data management, every single distribution step is updated by an active state management so that the distribution process can be carried out and logged in a controlled and transparent way.

2.2.4 People Integration

People integration provides the relevant functions and data to the right people.

Despite the steadily growing system variety, end users expect to find consistently designed, user-friendly interfaces with central access and unlimited collaboration features.

Central features | People integration includes the following central features whose implementation is described in the following sections:

▶ Multi-channel access

▶ Portal

▶ Collaboration

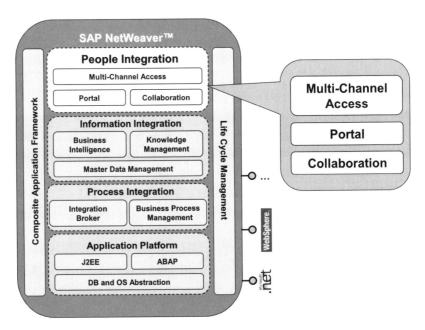

Figure 2.7 SAP NetWeaver—People Integration

Multi-Channel Access: SAP Mobile Infrastructure

SAP Mobile Infrastructure is a technological solution based on the SAP solutions for mobile business, giving mobility to both SAP and non-SAP applications.

SAP Mobile Infrastructure is installed locally on a mobile presentation device and features a web server, a database layer and native business logic. Thus, employees working remotely are independent of networks and can edit and finish time-critical business processes offline. For synchronizing data between mobile presentation device and backend, the SAP Mobile Infrastructure provides synchronization and data replication tools.

SAP Mobile Infrastructure uses the following open industry standards: **Open standards**

▶ Java

▶ Extensible Markup Language (XML)

In addition, the SAP Mobile Infrastructure features Java Virtual Machine and provides an open programming model which developers can use to create mobile applications.

This system architecture allows both mobile presentation devices and networks to be platform independent. Most different mobile presentation devices are supported, e.g. Personal Digital Assistants (PDAs), laptops, and smart phones.

SAP Mobile Infrastructure can be operated via a standard browser and a non-browser user interface. It uses a client/server architecture (see Figure 2.8). **Structure of SAP Mobile Infrastructure**

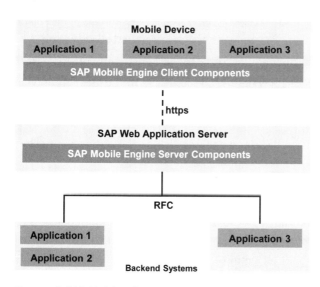

Figure 2.8 SAP Mobile Infrastructure—Simplified System Landscape

The SAP Mobile Client is used as a runtime environment for mobile applications. Via a defined API, it supplies mobile applications with generic services. These services include: **SAP Mobile Client component**

- Data persistence (local storage of data)

- Data synchronization (data exchange between the client and the server component of SAP Mobile Infrastructure)

- Application management

- Tracing (log and trace files which can be sent to the server for monitoring purposes)

- Configuration (administration of system and user attributes)

- Programming models for user interfaces (local UIs based on JSP/AWT)

- User management

SAP Mobile Server component The SAP Mobile Server does not belong to the mobile part of the solution. It is divided into a J2EE server component and an ABAP server component.

The J2EE server component of SAP Mobile Server runs on the J2EE stack of the SAP Web Application Server. It receives compressed data from the mobile device via HTTPS and forwards it to the ABAP component via SAP Java Connector (JCo). In addition, it includes a web console that enables system administrators to prepare applications to be installed on devices, to manage the deployment of the application at user and role level, and to access installation-specific log and trace information of mobile presentation devices.

The ABAP server component of SAP Mobile Server runs on the ABAP stack of the SAP Web Application Server. It carries out such tasks as managing data containers and detecting and calling relevant back-end applications, and is responsible for large parts of the synchronization process.

The applications on the back-end systems include the business logic and process the data transferred from the devices.

SAP Enterprise Portal

The SAP Enterprise Portal allows for a consistent and role-based access to SAP and non-SAP information sources, enterprise applications, repositories, databases, and services within and outside of organizations—all integrated in a homogeneous user experience. It includes tools which enable you to manage, analyze and relate this knowledge to each other, to exchange it and thus work effectively as a team.

With role-based content and multiple personalization options, the portal enables its users—from employees and customers to partners and suppliers—to focus exclusively on data and information relevant for the daily decision-making process.

Seen from the architecture point of view, the portal platform's central component is the *portal framework*. It contains the portal runtime in which all processes and operations of the portal are run. The portal runtime includes the connector framework for integrating enterprise information systems (EIS), along with portal components like the Page Builder that are executable HTML-generating Java programs. In addition, it contains portal services including e.g. caching and the user-management service. These make functionality available to portal components and other services.

Components of the portal platform

The portal framework is a logical environment made up of a collection of software components. Some of these facilitate the implementation of iViews. Others are interfaces of the portal infrastructure taking over, for example, the following processes:

Portal framework

▶ Creation of portal pages and assigning the corresponding layouts

▶ Managing layouts (styles and themes)

▶ Accessing required resources during runtime

In this framework, three components are of major significance:

▶ The *Portal Runtime* (PRT) running iViews

▶ The *Portal Content Directory* (PCD), a service-oriented implementation of the portal infrastructure which presents an interface with the database to be shared by the SAP Web Application Server and the portal

▶ The *database*, which acts as a central place for managing a collection of data specific to the portal and which provides this data selectively to corresponding processes at runtime

In addition, the portal framework supports common standard technologies and protocols:

▶ Hypertext Transfer Protocol and Secure Sockets Layer (HTTP and HTTPS)

▶ Protocols and services for authentication, e.g. the Lightweight Directory Access Protocol (LDAP), Active Directory Services, digital certificates, and logon tickets

▶ Java Database Connectivity (JDBC), a vendor-independent database protocol for connecting Java software with a database system

- ▶ Simple Object Access Protocol (SOAP)
- ▶ SAP Java Connector (JCO), a proprietary SAP interface which enables SAP systems to communicate with Java applications
- ▶ P4, another proprietary SAP protocol of the J2EE Engine which is based on RMI (Remote Method Invocation) and allows both synchronous and asynchronous communication of components across networks
- ▶ Hyper-relational Navigation Protocol (HRNP), a proprietary SAP protocol which is used for providing Drag & Relate functionality within iViews

Processing a portal request Figure 2.9 shows a summary of the SAP Enterprise Portal components described and illustrates the process of a portal request.

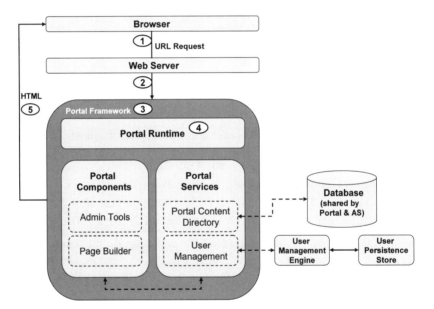

Figure 2.9 Process of a Portal Request

1. If a user calls an iView, the client sends an HTTP or HTTPS request to the web server.
2. Based on the URL, the web server detects the existence of a portal runtime (PRT) request and starts the PRT.
3. The PRT analyzes the request and asks for the following elements:
   - ▶ Object from the PCD, either a page or an iView to which the request refers

- User-specific data like personalization information regarding page or iView, logon language and the like

- Additional attribute information

4. If the user who submitted the request has the corresponding authorization for the object requested, the following information is provided:

- Portal component to be run, e.g. the Page Builder

- Profile—a number of properties that have to be passed on to the portal component. This can be a set of properties of an iView or of a page.

The PRT eventually receives an instance of the portal component to be executed and provides it along with additional information from the PCD.

If the request refers to a page, the Page Builder is the portal component to be activated. It searches the information received, composes the page accordingly, and creates the corresponding HTML output.

If the content of an iView is requested, however, the PRT activates the appropriate components to produce HTML, which are supported by portal services, if necessary.

The initial portal page and all its content, for example, is composed and created by the Page Builder.

5. The HTML page created is transferred to the browser.

Via interfaces, the portal platform uses the security mechanisms provided by the J2EE Engine of the SAP Web Application Server. In particular, this includes user authentication, Single Sign-on (SSO), authorization management, and secure communication. The portal requires an authentication service to establish an SSO mechanism which uses encrypted cookies to safely select and use user-specific authorization and authentication data across extremely different sources.

Security

Collaboration for SAP NetWeaver

The collaboration component of SAP NetWeaver includes services which support communication and collaboration in enterprise-specific business processes. It gathers team and project group members across time zones and geographical distances. To this end, virtual rooms are made available to users in which they can organize their tasks and share documents, applications and ideas.

The services of the collaboration component are tightly linked with the portal and the Knowledge Management platform, which will be discussed in Chapter 3, *The SAP Composite Application Framework*. The integration of applications, e.g. of evaluations from the SAP Business Intelligence, is of significant relevance in collaboration scenarios.

The retrieval of collaboration services can be easily configured. They can be provided in several places within the portal, e.g. in the collaboration launch pad or the user detail iView.

Predefined templates are available when creating virtual rooms for the collaboration of teams and project groups. A room enables the members to access common data and services, irrespective of their usage site.

For collaboration in the SAP Enterprise Portal, the e-mail and scheduling services implemented in your enterprise (e.g. Microsoft Exchange or Lotus Domino) can be integrated.

Deferred collaboration A deferred collaboration is supported in the portal through the following functions:

▶ Online discussions

▶ Online management of tasks, sessions, documents

▶ Online gathering of feedback, evaluations, comments

Real time collaboration Likewise, there are many options for real-time collaboration in the portal:

▶ Interactive online access to applications

▶ Interactive online exchange of information

▶ Integration of third-party services, e.g. from WebEx

2.2.5   SAP Solution Lifecycle Management

Before discussing the SAP Composite Application Framework, this section will give you a short overview of the SAP Solution Lifecycle Management (SLCM). Within SAP NetWeaver, the SLCM has a key function in providing the tools required for the entire lifecycle of the solution, from the implementation to the productive operation up to continuous changes and upgrades.

Tools and functions The SLCM supplies a wide range of tools and functionalities such as installation and upgrade documentations, tools for managing SAP licenses, tools for solution monitoring and system management, comprehensive statistics regarding system performance and load, high availability concepts, the application log, and tools for customizing, testing and data archiving. In addition, the Solution Manager provides central access to tools, methods and pre-configured contents which can be used during evaluation and implementation of the solutions wanted. In operational mode, it also presents options for managing and monitoring systems and business processes of the solution landscape and for handling the solution support.

After this comprehensive overview of SAP NetWeaver and its components, we can now turn to another element of the technology and integration platform described here, one which plays a decisive part in developing and implementing SAP xApps: the SAP Composite Application Framework (CAF).

2.3 SAP Composite Application Framework

The SAP CAF is a standardized platform for developing applications. It contains the tools, methodologies, rules, UI patterns and services required to create composite applications quickly and cost-effectively. The basis of it is SAP NetWeaver, which makes its wide range of components available via the CAF as a central point for application development.[1]

With CAF, developers can build innovative SAP xApps using enterprise services made available by the complex and heterogeneous components of the underlying systems.

While SAP and its partners use CAF for creating packaged composite applications, customers will be able to use this framework to develop composite applications and create specific solutions. Thus, enterprises have the possibility to either develop innovative solutions themselves or choose from the broad solutions pool provided by SAP and their partners.

2.3.1 Vision

The following sentence expresses the vision which is the motivation for the efforts of the development team:

> *With the CAF, business applications can be built onto other applications without programming a single line of code.*

Daring? Provocative? Impossible?

---

1 Since Composite Applications and SAP xApps are identical as far as their technical requirements and implementations are concerned, both terms will be used in parallel from now on.

These were the reactions when SAP produced this vision for the first time. Still, we want to show that it is possible to a surprisingly great extent to create applications in a purely model-based way and (almost) without any programming effort.

Growing complexity in development

Today's business applications are no longer expected to function as monolithic blocks in a machine but to reuse functionality from existing systems, integrate data from other systems, and structure all these in a new process. It is precisely this expectation, however, which places ever higher demands on the developers. Developers have to stay up to date on more and more technologies and systems that are changing more and more quickly. In addition, the requirements concerning functionality, flexibility, and adaptability of business applications by the user departments are constantly rising.

Taking the burden off the developers

With SAP NetWeaver and especially with the included SAP CAF, SAP provides a platform with systems, technologies, and tools which meets these modified conditions. These technologies enable you to generate model-oriented source code and tables while hiding complexities that are not relevant in the current context. In this way, this platform allows for a stronger integration of non-developers into the application development process and results in reduced pressure on the developers. They are relieved of the creation of important but repetitive and unchallenging source code, e.g. reading and writing methods or calls for authorization checks. This enables them to concentrate more on the demanding parts of the application, such as business rules.

2.3.2 Comparison

Many questions concerning the CAF refer to the Unified Modeling Language (UML) and SAP Business Intelligence (SAP BI). While developers immediately look for modeling in the CAF with UML, others have to struggle more with understanding the differences from other technologies. Therefore, here is a short comparison of UML and SAP BI.

UML

According to the remarks on *www.uml.org,*

> "*...the OMG's Unified Modeling Language (UML) helps you specify, visualize, and document models of software systems, including their structure and design, in a way that meets all of these requirements. (You can use UML for business modeling and modeling of other non-software systems*

too.) [...] You can model just about any type of application, running on any type and combination of hardware, operating system, programming language, and network, in UML."

UML is a powerful tool for modeling business applications and also other applications irrespective of underlying technologies. This is advantageous in that developers can use the same modeling language in the most different application areas. It is a tool for universal system modeling.

A downside is that because of its wide usability it is extremely generic so that it offers less support for a more limited focus.

In other words: the exclusive aim of the CAF is the creation of business applications. Therefore, the objects involved do not have to meet any more general requirements, and certain assumptions can be taken for granted.

Reduction of complexity

One of these assumptions in the CAF is that there is always a persistence, either local or remote.[2] For this reason, a service created with `create`, `read`, `update` and `delete` methods is always created as a rule. As a result, these can be generated additionally with complete source code. Language and time dependencies are characteristics specified under these assumptions already. In this case, too, the corresponding source code and the table structures can be generated automatically.

Thus, this more restricted focus allows for a collection of tools which is more abstract than the source code level and permits purpose-oriented, code-free application development. So to a certain extent, the CAF also addresses non-programmers.

The common UML tools, however, were mostly designed for developers and also express this in their nomenclature. They contain classes, class relations, etc.

SAP Business Intelligence

What is SAP Business Intelligence?

SAP Business Intelligence (SAP BI) is a system and a technology which enables you to create *analytical* applications based on models and metadata. It unifies the view of data from extremely different back-end systems. The SAP BI technology provides the tools, the business content, the

Definition of SAP BI

---

2 Although no transient attributes, i.e. attributes which do not have persistence as such, can be defined in the entity service, the application services can map this functionality quite well.

business scenarios, and the analytical applications. Structured data is pre-aggregated, transformed and extended with other structured and unstructured data. All of this can take place either in real time or after a time lapse. The data used for analysis can be stored in SAP BI as well as in back-end systems. The majority of the source code for data loading, transformation, storage, and navigation is generated, just like the underlying data structures in table format.

Now let's compare this to the CAF.

Definition of CAF The CAF is a technology which enables you to create *transactional*[3] business applications based on models and metadata. It unifies the view of data from extremely different back-end systems. The CAF technology provides the tools, the xApps, the business scenarios, and the transactional applications. Data is transformed and extended with other structured and unstructured data. All this takes place in real time. The data can be stored in the CAF as well as in the back-end systems. The majority of the source code for transformation, storage, and navigation is generated, just like the underlying data structures in table format.

Historical affinity Although these are rather exact definitions of both technologies, they are very similar to each other. This can be explained easily through their history: The foundation members of the CAF team all formed the Business Content team, and play a significant role in today's development of the Business Content in SAP BI. The team developed content themselves and managed and coordinated all SAP-internal content development groups.

After the increased integration of Business Content with transactional parts, the team was split in the year 2002, and one part was the development team which generated the idea and design of the CAF.

An advantage in this regard was the wealth of experience in developing and maintaining Business Content projects, the familiarity with the technology and the network of contacts in the individual applications within SAP which developed from this and was not to be underestimated.

In fact, someone who has experience with BI generally comes to grips with the background to CAF philosophy very quickly. And this begs the question as to why CAF did not already exist. But we do not want to get into these discussions at this point ...

---

3 The CAF is not exclusively defined for transactional applications, even though especially source code and persistence are generated for transactional applications at the moment.

2.3.3   SAP Composite Application Framework—Principles

The aim of the SAP CAF lies in the support of developers in quick, effi-   Modeling
cient and cost-effective implementation of composite applications. It
increases the productivity of the development and change process of
applications by a development process based on modeling and code generation. The CAF supports this approach through multiple tools for the
three layers of a composite application:[4]

▶ Processes

▶ User interfaces

▶ Services

In the traditional application development, a group of developers formu-
lates requirements from the business side in source code on the basis of
a previously processed specification. By contrast, the development of
composite applications using CAF focuses on modeling the planned
application, on whose basis the CAF then creates the application code.
CAF is therefore a type of modeling tool for applications. Numerous tools
of the CAF connect the relevant elements of the application (processes,
services, entities and UIs) with one another. The functionality providing
these elements is controlled and described by metadata.

Patterns and templates on all levels of the CAF enable the implementa-   Patterns
tion of the required homogeneity of the application and the efficiency of
its development.

The CAF provides a standard view of the entire development project,   Abstraction
although a variety of components like SAP NetWeaver or functional units
of the heterogeneous IT landscape of the customer are to be integrated.
This complete view of developing and installing the application is enabled
without having to know these components. In a traditional case, specialized development tools would be required for each individual application. The concept behind the CAF development approach spans the
abstraction of these components to a model. They are not directly called
but rather addressed through an interface which is provided to the corresponding abstraction layer. Each level of CAF contains tools which are
based on metadata. A "developer" who models his or her application only
maintains the attributes of this metadata. The actual implementation is
performed by the system as it interprets the provided metadata and auto-

---

4 The tools provided per layer by the Composite Application Framework are
   described in detail in Chapter 3, *The SAP NetWeaver Composite Application Framework*, and are used for implementation of a concrete deployment.

matically generates the corresponding source code. Through the CAF, business experts are able to create an application without having to write program code. Developers can refine and enhance the machine coding at a later stage as required. The focus of the development therefore does not lie in the programming but rather on the business logic being implemented.

The different abstraction layers of the CAF increase the reusability of development components and reduce the complexity of the application. Each level communicates exclusively with its adjacent levels so that elements of an implementation can be changed and exchanged without affecting other parts of an application. This facilitates the maintenance, support and changeability of the application and can be achieved at reduced costs. However, we should not neglect the fact that the enhancement or change of an application created through CAF is not attached to its coding but rather to its model.

Reusability of components

2.3.4 General Structure of the CAF

The CAF spans the relevant runtime environments and the development tools for each of the abstraction layers referred to. This capability makes it possible to design effective and highly functional applications. It closes the gap between the components that provide isolated services, and the composite application which uses these services. This occurs by combining the functionalities and their provision for the users through a central instance. Based on SAP NetWeaver, the SAP Composite Application Framework makes the entire range of functions of the components contained for developing composite applications available through a central toolset.

Figure 2.10 displays a clear distinction between the design time and runtime and the three abstraction layers of the SAP CAF. We will deal with these more closely in the following sections.

Process Level

The process level defines the route which a composite application takes during its runtime from the viewpoint of the business process. The business process mapped generally consists of different steps which either require interaction with a user or with a workflow-based system.

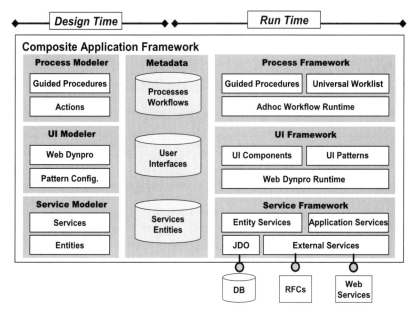

Figure 2.10 The SAP Composite Application Framework

Guided Procedures is a tool with which collaborative business processes can be modeled during design time and runtime while meeting the requirements of the interactive and dynamic processes of composite applications. Planning a business trip, requesting a holiday, or bringing on a new employee are all examples of such processes. The progression of each individual process step is maintained in order to determine which tasks have been completed and which operations must still be performed. The development of the process can be followed by process administrators through a monitor called the *dashboard.* The individual work packages for each user are displayed in the guided procedures inbox. In this way the collaborative aspect of an application is implemented, and the user is given a point of entry to the respective instance of a Guided Procedures process.

Guided Procedures

Guided Procedure processes consist of sequential phases which must be carried out in order to complete a business process. Phases are also divided into steps which are carried out sequentially as well as in parallel and can all be processed by the same person or different people as required. A (work) step is linked to precisely one activity, an *action,* which is automatically carried out by the system or one actual person. An action is an executable unit which describes precisely what must be done in a specific process step.

Structure of a Guided Procedure

Actions   Actions can take on different forms:

- Simple workflow actions (e.g. transmitting, authorizing, denying)
- Generic actions (e.g. sending an e-mail)
- Data entry actions through a specific user interface
- Automated actions (e.g. calling a web service which is running in the background)
- Actions to promote collaboration (e.g. starting an online discussion or survey)
- Specific actions (e.g. starting an additional guided procedure)

The main advantage of actions lies in the fact that as independent units they can be reused in any number of process templates. By defining actions, services, and also the following application types can be called:

- Web Dynpro components
- Interactive forms
- URLs

Design time   The process flow with all relevant phases, steps and actions is defined in a *Guided Procedures Template*. The design time of the guided procedure provides the developer with two of the tools implemented in the Web Dynpro that can support and accompany him or her in the creation of a guided procedures template and in defining actions.

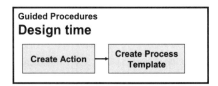

Figure 2.11 Guided Procedures—Design Time

Action design time   The first tool is the Action Design Time. It enables the definition of actions which must contain the following elements:

- Information on the required parameters to call an application or a service
- List of required resources (input parameter)
- List of deliverables (output parameter)
- Language-dependent texts on resources and deliverables
- Mapping between the resources of the action and the parameters of the application

As a sample screen for the action design time, Figure 2.12 shows the definition and configuration of the "Shuttle Booking" action which calls the Web Dynpro application "com.sap.CshuttleBooking."

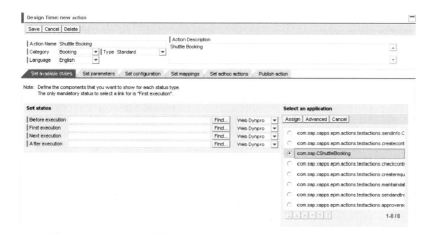

Figure 2.12 Action Design Time — Sample Screen

The second tool, process template design time, gives the developer the ability to define guided procedures templates. This is done by naming and determining the sequence of phases. The phases are divided into operations that will eventually be assigned actions and process roles which carry out these activities. In addition to controlling the process flow, other tasks are also supported by the process template, e.g., the determining of read authorizations on individual instance steps, the determining of authorizations on the template itself, or context mapping.

Process template design time

In Figure 2.13 the process template design time is shown for the template "LoanRequest." Here, the process flow is configured in three phases to process the loan request.

Such a guided procedures template can be started during runtime and processed as an actual process instance. During instantiation, the process roles assigned to predefined operations in the process template are assigned to the actual processors. During the runtime of the application, extracted information from the user profile and the user entries is evaluated. This occurs together with the evaluation of the context, which is managed by every instance of a guided procedure. Based on this data, the results of an operation can be transferred to the next action. The context determines the recipient and parameterizes the subsequent action. At the same time the activities carried out undergo monitoring and analysis in order to receive information on the entire process.

Runtime

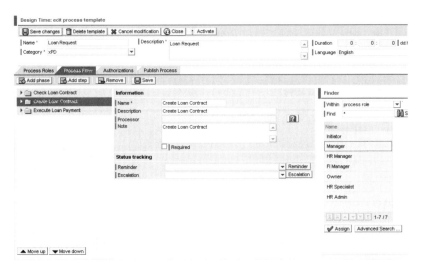

Figure 2.13 Process Template Design Time—Sample Screen

Guided procedures provide an extensive user-interface framework for the runtime. For example, it supports operations which must be executed by a user through providing additional information on the work progress and on the next activities. As soon as an operation is completed by a service or a user, the user responsible for the next operation is required to complete this operation. All those involved can monitor the entire process according to their assigned roles.

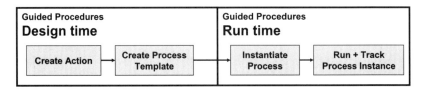

Figure 2.14 Guided Procedures—Lifecycle

Interactive forms   A great advantage of guided procedures is the integration of interactive forms. Processes which are frequently manually processed in companies can be handled in electronic form with all the advantages resulting from this. As they are static, do not contain any complex user-interface elements and are self-explanatory, they can be used by employees without great change-management difficulty. The use of these interactive forms within the scope of guided procedures can occur in different ways. As an example you can imagine an application process which is started by an interactive form. A company provides an application form on its website. Applicants fill this out and click on the send button. This starts an internal process which reads the applicant data from the form and stores it in the relevant back-end systems. In additional operations, this data is checked; the applicant is invited, and after further steps may be hired.

User Interface Level

The interaction with the user is controlled by the user interface (UI) level. The SAP Composite Application Framework uses the Java Web Dynpro modeling tools provided by SAP NetWeaver and supplements these with UI patterns and pattern components with which a homogeneous, flexible and easily configurable and reusable user interface can be created. This results from the principle of separating the presentation and application logic. Similar to the Model View Controller concept (MVC), a Web Dynpro application consists of three main components:

Model View Controller principle

▶ **Model**
The model encapsulates operations on the underlying levels and is responsible for data exchange of the components in both directions, i.e. toward and away from the components.

▶ **Controller**
Events, actions and logging tasks are managed by the controller of the components. In addition to the management and organization of the complete business logic and interaction, the controller is also responsible for the context of the component. The context is a temporary memory for the data flow to the model and away from it. A component can also interact with other components. Its Interface Controllers are used for this. In order to enable data exchange between different components, a mapping of the contexts involved is implemented.

▶ **View**
Views contain the presentation logic and finally represent the screen which will be displayed to the end user. A view is either individually assigned to a window or grouped to viewsets. These consist of different views and can present dynamic content based on the user entry and context.

Web Dynpro supplies a declarative metadata model for the development of a user interface in order to reduce the programming time and effort. This abstraction automatically generates the implementation of the components. Projects are directly created in SAP NetWeaver Developer Studio in order to make all tools of CAF available through a central point of entry. The SAP CAF makes use of it and extends it with useful Web Dynpro patterns such as the **ObjectEditor** pattern for editing business

Declarative metadata model

objects, the **ObjectSelector** pattern to search for business objects or the **Dashboard** pattern to display them.

To illustrate this, Figure 2.15 shows the use of the **Dashboard** pattern as an overview of concepts, where different concept properties such as title, author or status are displayed. Besides a filter function and the structuring of the concept through a tab, the **Dashboard** pattern provides different navigation options. By clicking on a title, for example, the corresponding details of a concept can be called.

Figure 2.15 Dashboard Pattern Runtime

The configuration of patterns is implemented by the application developers who are supported with practical CAF tools. Usually, the manual writing of code lines is obsolete. If the functionality provided by patterns is not sufficient, you can access the multiple Wed Dynpro options, and UIs can be developed through Web Dynpro Foundation.

Figure 2.16 shows the screen for simple configuration of the **Dashboard** pattern in order to receive the concept overview already displayed at runtime. For instance the **AUTHOR** and **STATUS** fields displayed and the second tab with the title **Accepted** are defined.

Repetitive labor-intensive and time-consuming coding to create UIs and to establish the connections with respective data sources is avoided by using Web Dynpro and SAP Composite Application Framework, as these operations are provided to the developers through the UI patterns and data models encapsulated for reuse.

User interfaces structured in this way can be used in two ways: Either by integrating them in the processes of a composite application, or directly as iViews in the SAP Enterprise Portal.

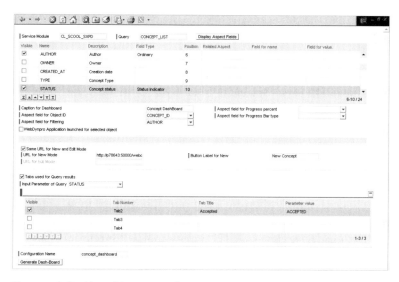

Figure 2.16 Dashboard Pattern Configuration (Design Time)

Service Level

As was clear in the description of the process level, guided procedures can be used to create a simple composite application, which is enabled by the Web services provided by the underlying systems. It is accessed by the required processes and the corresponding UIs of the application to be created.

In the typical case, however, not all required services are provided by the underlying functional components. These components are needed to implement the desired functionality. The problem is that different applications and systems offer different object models, and resolving these differences requires complex mapping. Further, a continuous and consistent user interface within the entire composite application raises the possibility of semantic breaks. If you call to mind the requirement of SAP xApps in accessing data of any heterogeneous system landscapes, it is quickly clear that the CAF requires a level which supports the processes and UIs with consistent, semantic, continuous and system-independent services. The service layer of the SAP Composite Application Framework fulfills this task by doing the following:

Consistent services

▶ Building a complete and consistent data model by defining entities and data types. Work with the entities created is done through assigned entity services, which generate corresponding tables, table relations, dictionary elements and lifecycle methods for reading, writing and deleting data.

▶ Creating external services which in the scope of the CAF act as wrappers for Remote Function Calls (RFCs) and Web services. This ensures that the functionalities already existing from the underlying applications and systems can be reused. In addition, there is also an option to import descriptions of RFCs and Web services into the CAF in order to read and manipulate data from the connected systems. In this context, the external elements of a mapping are used in order to meet the semantics of the composite application. External services can be used by the entity and application services.

▶ Defining and creating application services to contain the business logic of a composite application by using operations of external, entity or other application services. There is also the option to enhance the business logic by adding specific source code sections. In the end, the application services transfer the relevant data to the user interface.

Service modeler

The functionality described is provided through a modeling tool, the *Service Modeler*, which stores the relevant data in the corresponding metadata repository. In this way, the process and the user interface levels can access a consistent and continuous data model and service network, which protects against semantic breaks and delivers the desired flexibility within the scope of the entire composite application.

In Chapter 3, *The SAP Composite Application Framework*, the application and the functionality of all tools of the CAF are illustrated by implementing an example xApp.

2.4 Architectural Model of SAP xApps

The previous descriptions of SAP xApps, the structure of SAP NetWeaver and the SAP CAF are merged in an architectural model of SAP xApps in the following section.

In this context, the focus is on SAP NetWeaver with its components that have already been described and which are used within the scope of SAP xApps to accomplish multiple tasks in integrating people, processes and information and providing an application platform.[5]

Similar to the implementation of the Enterprise Services Architecture, SAP NetWeaver provides a growing pool of enterprise services through which the functionality of different components of the mySAP Business

---

5 The use of SAP NetWeaver and its components in the context of SAP xApps is illustrated in Chapter 4, *Implementation Examples*, using the example of SAP xApps SAP xCQM and SAP xPD.

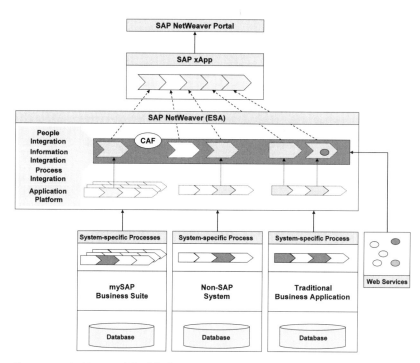

Figure 2.17 Architectural Model of SAP xApps

Suite are mapped and can be made available. Supported by the SAP Exchange Infrastructure, data can be transferred from heterogeneous back-end systems to SAP NetWeaver. There is also the option of implementing standard web services to access their functionality provided. The SAP Composite Application Framework is the link between components of SAP NetWeaver and an SAP xApp. It combines the options of guided procedures, processes and UI frameworks and patterns to an extensive and homogeneous collection of tools which simplify and accelerate the development of SAP xApps through a model-driven approach. In this way, SAP xApps can be created quickly, consistently and in a homogeneous manner and can be mapped and implemented as "applications to applications."

Content and functionality of the SAP xApp is finally provided through the SAP Enterprise Portal for end users based on their role.

3 The SAP Composite Application Framework

This chapter explains step by step all concepts, components and tools of the CAF. Through development of a sample xApp, you will get to know its functions and advantages in the fast and flexible implementation of composite applications.

3.1 Introduction

The SAP Composite Application Framework (CAF) consists of two parts: a designer and a runtime component. While the designer is most often installed locally on the developer's computer, the runtime component can be installed locally or on a specific server.

In order to make it easier for those converting from the ABAP or SAP BW world to the world of SAP NetWeaver and the SAP Composite Application Framework or those new to the concept, the corresponding tools, functionalities or concepts from ABAP and BW will be summarized in brief again at many stages in this chapter. This can be easily seen by a corresponding note in the margin similar to the one next to this paragraph. It must be mentioned upfront that not all CAF parts have counterparts in ABAP and BW and if they do they don't necessarily have the same functions. The references are merely meant to support you in your considerations. Occasionally, throughout the text, tips and tricks to handle the framework will be inserted as marginal text.

Comparison to ABAP/BW

The CAF designer is the central tool for working with the SAP CAF to create and customize composite applications and SAP xApps. The CAF Designer is supplied as a plug-in with SAP NetWeaver Developer Studio, which is in turn based on the open source initiative Eclipse by IBM (*www.eclipse.org*). Eclipse, the integrated development environment, basically consists of a runtime kernel with precisely specified interfaces. The functionality of the runtime kernel can be enhanced by additional plug-ins. As a matter of fact, Eclipse already possesses many plug-ins in the standard version. Each of these has been developed for a specific task area and can be integrated with other plug-ins or in turn use their parts. Plug-ins for various applications are created and offered by many software companies and programmers. There are "perspectives" for the plug-ins that enable the developer to use the functionality of the plug-ins in a specific context. A plug-in can be used in several perspectives, and one perspective can in turn use several plug-ins at the same time.

The SAP NetWeaver Developer Studio sets itself apart from the Eclipse standard version by the fact that it contains additional plug-ins developed by SAP. Among these are perspectives for the Design time Repository (DTR), for Web Dynpro, for the Java dictionary, or for EJB development. Most of the modeling tools of the CAF Designer were developed as plug-ins for Eclipse in the Java programming language, and they use both standard Eclipse plug-ins and SAP plug-ins.

Comparison to ABAP The ABAP workbench is the integrated development environment for the ABAP world. The plug-ins developed by SAP in Eclipse are very similar to the functionality in the SAP NetWeaver Developer Studio of the workbench.

Runtime components In addition to the CAF Designer, runtime components are available on the J2EE servers. These comprise authorization checks, metadata model, UI patterns, generic services, and services used internally by the CAF. An application developed with the CAF Designer is installed on the J2EE server, where it uses the runtime components.

This chapter describes and uses the functionalities which are available with the first version of CAF within a sample scenario.

3.2 Scenario xFlights

By using a simple and easily understandable scenario, we can show the different aspects of developing an SAP xApp and the way development tools are used. This scenario is available as a demo application for the CAF and can be used for demonstration purposes. Reference will constantly be made to this demo application in the following chapters.

3.2.1 Scenario

Roles The task is to create an application to book flights for business trips. In the scenario there are three groups of people which will be referred to as "roles" in each case:

▶ Traveler (employee)

▶ Travel agent

▶ Manager of the traveler

The employee is supposed to go on a business trip by airplane. For this, we need the necessary data concerning departure location, departure time, and destination. The travel agent then looks for the flight connections and sends the employee a list with several flight connections. The employee in turn decides on one of the offers. The travel agent then books the flight and transfers this information to the manager of the employee for approval. Figure 3.1 illustrates this example.

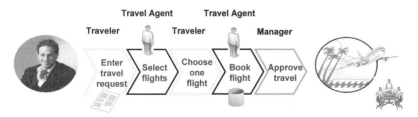

Figure 3.1 Scenario—Booking a Flight

This little example already contains the entire complexity that application developers would encounter in practice. We now want to translate the example into the CAF terminology.

ABAP developers might be familiar with this example, as the *flights* example is always referred to in the R/3 system and the documentation available there as well as in the training documentation. This is one reason we decided to use it.

Comparison to ABAP

3.2.2 Modeling

The scenario elements can first be translated into *entities*. Entities are clearly identifiable units. In our case the "employee" is an entity that is assigned certain "attributes," i.e. properties. As the traveling person, the employee will remain the same entity even though in a different form, for which other attributes now also become important. The "travel agent" and the "manager" are also entities. All the entities mentioned refer to a general entity which we will call **person**. This person has a "last name," a "first name," a "title," "address," "telephone number(s)," and many other attributes (see Figure 3.2). A person can have several characteristics and can appear in the role of manager, employee, or travel agent.

Entities

Let us now look at the other entities, **Flight**, **Departure location**, and **Destination**. **Flight** is an entity that can have attributes such as "flight number," "flight duration," "departure time," "arrival time," and "price." **Departure location** and **Destination** are characteristics of the general entity **Location**.

Figure 3.2 Entity "Person" in the CAF Designer

All entities, their attributes, and the relationships between the entities of applications can be defined in such a manner. This is generally the case independently of CAF, and follows a model known in classical application development as an *Entity Relationship Diagram*.

In this simple example—"a person must go on a flight; another person books the flight, and a third person in turn authorizes the flight"—there already exist quite a few entities and relationships between entities.

The entities must in turn be converted as logical structures into the technical objects for implementing an application. Tables, relationships between tables, and program routines to read, write, delete, change and search in these tables represent the underlying basis of each entity. In CAF language, an entity is referred to as an *Entity Service*. In the next chapters these two terms will be used interchangeably.

Entity Services are related to each other either as attributes of one another or through the business logic. For example, the entities **Person** and **Address** are linked together as attributes, while the entity **Flight** is only related with the entity **Person** through the business-process logic. A person books a flight. Before a flight is booked it must first be checked to learn, among other things, if the desired class is available, if a vegetarian menu can be offered on board, and if the flight displayed is the cheapest or the shortest in a selection of flights. All these rules and conditions should be taken into consideration by the system.

In the CAF, *Application services* map these rules and conditions, which are a part of the business-process logic. Application Services are either directly related to Entity Services or can perform operations independently from them. The services required for our scenario comprise the reading and writing of data to the Entity Services from a remote back-end system or a local database such as a currency conversion or from the display of the menu plan during the flight. We will discuss in detail later exact definitions of and differences between entity and application services and local and remote data storage, among other things.

Business process logic

The entry and display of data for the user occurs through user interfaces (UI). For each sub-area of the xFlights application, different UIs are necessary depending on the task, the user, the role and the data.

User interface

For example, a travel request can be entered through an electronic and interactive form. In our case, however, we'll use a Web dynpro (see Figure 3.3). This can be similar in appearance to the paper version previously used in the company, thus avoiding complex employee training. The travel agent then sees a list of all traveler requests, selects one to be processed and begins the search for flight variants.

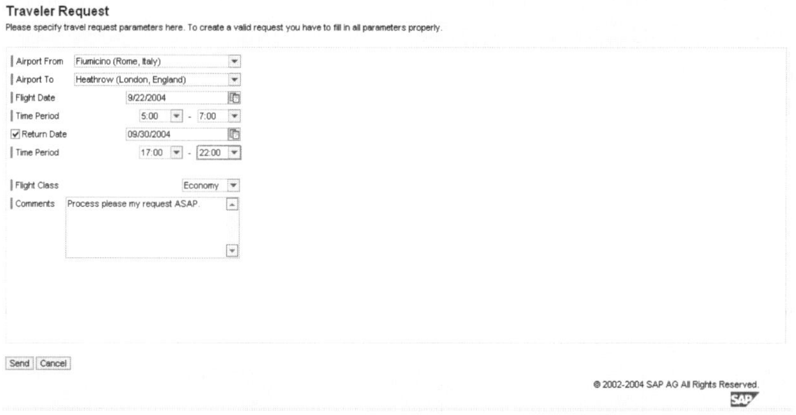

Traveler Request
Please specify travel request parameters here. To create a valid request you have to fill in all parameters properly.

Airport From	Fiumicino (Rome, Italy)	▼
Airport To	Heathrow (London, England)	▼
Flight Date	9/22/2004	🗐
Time Period	5:00 ▼ - 7:00 ▼	
✔ Return Date	09/30/2004	🗐
Time Period	17:00 ▼ - 22:00 ▼	
Flight Class	Economy ▼	
Comments	Process please my request ASAP.	

Send Cancel

Figure 3.3 User Interface "Traveler Request"

Depending on the travel profile that the traveler has maintained previously (desired flight class, non-smoker or smoker, membership number for bonus mile program, preferred hotel chain, car rental company etc.), the flight variants are already filtered to match this profile. After the flight has been chosen and booked in cooperation with the traveler, a message is sent to the manager with a request for approval.

Business process This cooperation represents the collaborative aspect of an application. The employees work together to organize the trip. The application must be intelligent enough to map this business process and all variants of this cooperation. The process is structured into process steps and phases, some of which are dependent on each other and some can run in parallel. The technology used for this in CAF is called *Guided Procedures*.

3.2.3 Building an Application in the Classical Way

How would you build the application described above in a modern company with the tools and technologies available today without CAF? Let's take a look at this.

Dream ... The project generally begins with a cup of coffee or tea. The employees from the business department sit together with those from IT and discuss the problem of how to book business trips in companies. In an objective discussion on the issue, it quickly becomes clear that the single solution in order to move away from the paper office and prevent flights from being booked too late or incorrectly, is to build a new application.

In order to create an application, the process must be defined. What is the normal way to do this today? What would be the ideal case for it? To this end the people from the business departments describe "their" business process, the systems they work with, who the users are etc. For example, the data for the person is stored in an R/3 system; however, there is no travel profile available for this person. The flight data can be received from an external application that is accessed via a Web browser. The CRM system provides information on the travel agency, and so on.

The IT people try to analyze this information and separate it into individual steps in order to derive the necessary technical information from it. The project team with members from all the departments affected, begins with specifying the application, creating a schedule and assigning work packages.

After several iterations and inquiries, the project is started with an initial official kick-off. Project plans are worked out; technological decisions are made, and tasks are defined and assigned to the team members. The process is defined with a modeling tool. Then an entity relationship diagram is derived for the table structure. With a UML (Unified Modeling Language) tool, structures and relationships of the program classes for reading and writing and the mapping of business rules are created; the different systems are connected, and the user interfaces and the buttons, fields and other elements to be positioned within them are created. Now the programming and implementation of the individual parts of the application begins.

All parts of the applications are all compiled within one process, and after a test phase the application can be handed over to the people in the business department for productive usage.

If all went as smoothly as just described, this would be great! As we all know there are frictional losses that are caused by the different use of concepts ("Vegan has a different meaning than vegetarian?"), incorrect assumptions ("A traveler usually only takes part in one bonus mile program."), generally accepted norms which have not been specified ("If you fly with Delta it is always Business Class, but the boss must always authorize this."), and qualifications of the developer ("We program everything as long as it is in Perl!"), not to mention the different views and goals of the participating employees and departments.

These views and goals cannot be avoided even with the best technical tools, whereas the formerly named misunderstandings and the like can. Today, modeling and programming are carried out with tools and technologies that require employees with good technical knowledge that includes such techniques as UML modeling, entity relationship, programming, and integration.

If different technologies and systems are implemented in such an application, the problems really begin. A lot of time is spent finding out which interfaces are to be used, requesting data from an existing system and integrating it into the new application.

If data is to be entered for which no files existed previously, the creation of tables and programming the relevant code is necessary in order to create data, delete it, read, change, or search for it. Displaying data in a "thin client" (e.g. a UI in a Web browser) or "fat client" (where frontends must be installed on users' computers) has effects on the functionality, the architecture, the use, maintenance, and future enhancement of the application. Even if everything was exactly specified, the complex testing and error search in the coding still remains to be done. This has absolutely nothing to do with the business-process logic but rather with the relatively simple and less intelligent read and write methods. All application components must more or less be created "manually."

... and reality

Nightmare ...

The smallest misunderstandings ("A traveler can participate in several bonus mile programs at the same time.") can therefore have great effects on the development. For example, for the bonus-mile program a cardinality of 1..1 must be converted to one of 1..n in the entity which results in another table. The coding to add this data correspondingly to a request and to enable multiple entries of this value in the UI must also be taken into account in the programming.

If such misunderstandings occur frequently, the schedule for the development project can be affected and the entire project can be at risk. There are numerous possible causes for necessary changes. It often happens that important requirements only emerge after the specification has been completed and the development has already begun.

If a "fire and forget" mentality prevails in the project work ("Here is my specification, now go and do it, and come back when you are finished."), and the project result is not regarded as a commonly achieved goal ("I only wrote the specification, but it describes something completely different to what THEY have done."), this is a good time to stop and consider what could be accomplished with new tools.

What is better about the SAP Composite Application Framework? First of all: You don't have to "walk" anymore but you can "drive." Coding and table structures, UI and processes are generated. They do not have to be programmed manually any more.

To complete the allegory: "Walking" meant that a developer had to wear heavy mountain boots and had to carry a large rucksack filled with provisions in order to climb the craggy and cliffy valleys and peaks of the technology and system landscape. Now the person from the involved department who is familiar with the well-paved sidewalks and streets, wearing his sneakers and with cameras dangling from his neck, can take a cable car and hover over the valleys and peaks. Of course, he will not get to know all the idyllic, secret and hidden corners of the mountainous IT landscape, but at the end of the day he will be able to say: "I was there, and would like to recommend it to everyone!"

In the same way, the CAF enables non-programmers to model many parts that in the past were reserved for the programmers. This not only lightens the programmer's load, but brings about a faster redesign due to direct experience with the tool and a better adaptation of the application to the actual requirements through timely feedback. In addition, employees from the user department identify personally with the solution; the application becomes their "baby." The enthusiasm grows and the result much more closely satisfies the requirements and wishes of the requesting business department and enterprise.

This is not only important for the successful development of an application from a psychological point of view, but it corresponds much better to the Enterprise Services Architecture (ESA) approach, because the CAF can be decomposed into consumable services. It also affects maintenance, an issue we will consider in more detail.

3.3 Architecture and Tools of the SAP Composite Application Framework

3.3.1 General Remarks

What components does the SAP Composite Application Framework (CAF) comprise? Figure 3.4 shows both the development and the run-time components. Both sides are closely related to each other due to the metadata repository.

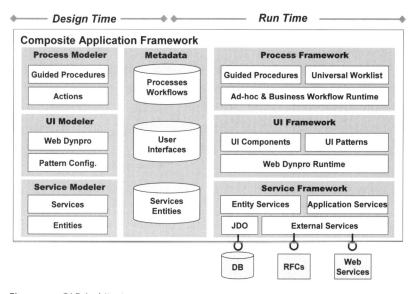

Figure 3.4 CAF Architecture

First we will take a look at the design and modeling tools.

Design Time

By installing SAP NetWeaver Developer Studio, the perspective can be called using the **Composite Application Service** name in Developer Studio. This perspective is required in order to create the different components of an application with the CAF. It contains the following tools for the creation of business applications:

Tools

▶ **External Service Modeler**

In order to access the function modules of an ABAP-based system such as the R/3-system or to access other systems through Web services CAF offers an import dialog for Remote Function Calls (RFCs) and Web services. This dialog publishes the RFCs as a Web services in the CAF so that they can be called and used by other CAF services.

▶ **Entity Service Modeler**

This tool is used to model Entity Services, their properties, attributes, and relationships to each other. As a result you finally receive tables and access to external storages, and the generated coding of the read and write methods required for this.

▶ **Application Service Modeler**

The business logic is created with this modeler. Parts of the coding are also generated here. In contrast to the External and Entity Service Modelers, however, you can use this modeler to manually insert additional coding.

▶ **UI Modeler**

This modeler enables the display of data and the reuse of form templates. It is generally known as SAP Web Dynpro.

▶ **Guided Procedures**

Individual sub-applications can be "bundled" with guided procedures. Guided procedures describe collaborative process flows and trigger actions.

This chapter describes the individual modeling tools in detail.

Runtime

In addition to the CAF designer, *CAF runtime* consists of the components required for the runtime environment. It runs on the J2EE server. Parts of the CAF runtime include the Business Intelligence Meta Model Repository (BI MMR) and a CAF-specific library.

BI MMR

BI MMR represents the basis for all metadata. The CAF metadata model is created in the BI MMR. Objects which describe a CAF-based application, their properties and relations can be stored here.

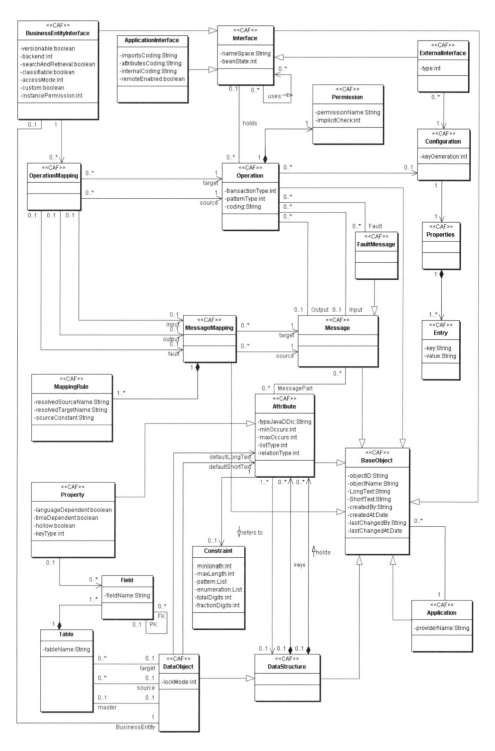

Figure 3.5 CAF Meta Model

Figure 3.5 illustrates how the metadata for the different types of services, operations, mappings, interface definitions, properties and their relationships to one another are mapped in the metadata model. For the runtime the metadata is stored in the SAP NetWeaver database, for the design time it is stored locally as XML files and in a cache[1].

> The BI Meta Model Repository was developed by developers from the SAP Business Intelligence area. In BI, metadata is used in business content. This experience led to the idea of a metadata model which, in turn, led to the BI MMR functional library referred to above, which is based on the standards of the Object Management Group (OMG, *http://www.omg.org/*).

The tables and coding can be generated on the basis of this model, as we will describe later in more detail.

Libraries Both the CAF and CAF MP libraries provide all the required supporting program codes during runtime. This contains authorization checks, logging and tracing, calls to systems and technologies such as SAP Knowledge Management, the integration of collaboration functionality, and so on.

Other important tools, even if they are not CAF-specific, are the Software Deployment Manager (SDM) and the Visual Administrator.

Software Deployment Manager The Software Deployment Manager is used for the installation, i.e. deployment of the above-mentioned libraries. The path to this application is quite concealed and usually has the following structure on a Windows operating system:

..\usr\sap\<SAP-System-ID>\JC<instance no>\SDM\program\ RemoteGui.bat

For an SAP system ID *J2E* and an instance number 00 it could look as follows:

C:\usr\sap\J2E\JC00\SDM\program\RemoteGui.bat.

Visual Administrator The Visual Administrator is a tool to manage the J2EE server. You can use it to set parameters or to switch on monitoring and tracing, among other functions. In a Windows operating system, the path structure to this application usually is

---

1 In a Windows NT system the MMR cache is located at *C:\WINNT\Temp*.

..\usr\sap\<SAP-System-ID>\JC<instance no>\j2ee\admin\go.bat

For an SAP system ID *J2E* and an instance number 00 it could look as follows:

C:\usr\sap\J2E\JC00\j2ee\admin\go.bat

3.3.2 Installation

The CAF Designer is already integrated in the installation of SAP NetWeaver Developer Studio. Only the runtime libraries require a subsequent installation on the J2EE server.

In contrast to the ABAP world, where both the development tools and the runtime are called from the server, SAP NetWeaver Developer Studio is installed locally on the developer's computer. The runtime environment, that is to say the J2EE server, can either be installed on the developer's computer or on a remote server. A completed project is then either remotely or locally installed or—in Java terms—deployed on the J2EE server.

Comparison to ABAP

In order to use the development tools and runtime environment with a reasonable level of performance, both a smart CAF application developer and a correspondingly high-performance hardware are prerequisites.

3.3.3 Life Cycle of a Composite Application

In a complete life-cycle of an application, which begins with the description of the business case and the specification, the following are necessary when development begins: integration into a Java Development Infrastructure (JDI), the definition of naming and coding conventions, an assignment of work packages and responsibilities, the creation of documentation and translation, and testing.

After its successful development, the application must be "packed", installed and/or delivered, depending on whether the application was developed by SAP, an SAP partner or a customer. Then the maintenance period begins, and if necessary a further development of the application for which a maintenance and support landscape is required. By using the JDI and the corresponding NetWeaver components, these prerequisites are fulfilled.

3.3.4 Composite Application Project

After successfully installing SAP NetWeaver Developer Studio and the J2EE server and meeting all the requirements, the development phase can begin. To do this, a project of the type "Composite Application" must be created in the Composite Application Service perspective. A project in SAP NetWeaver Developer Studio is basically a structuring element that, as a logical unit, contains all the relevant objects of a part of the application.

The created project, which is represented as the first project in this perspective, actually contains six other projects in the background. These additional projects are a dictionary, an Enterprise Java Beans (EJB) module, a metadata, an Enterprise Application Archive (EAR) file, a User Management Engine (UME) permission, and a Web dynpro project. All of these project types were created with the SAP-specific plug-ins supplied with SAP NetWeaver Developer Studio.

A composite application project is assigned to a Java package, which is named in the form PROVIDER + PROJECT. PROVIDER is the company name, although a special syntax is used: You take the URL of the website of this company and assign the elements in a reverse sequence to it, `sap.com` thus becoming the PROVIDER `com.sap`. PROJECT is the name of the project, in our case `xflights`. The name of the package would then be `com.sap.xflights`.

Comparison to ABAP The corresponding part of an ABAP development project is the package which in the past was also referred to as development class.

The SAP Composite Application Framework thus simplifies the view and handling of the different layers and components of an application. If we create such a project for our flight booking example, five projects exist in the background. As a CAF developer, this detail is only of minor interest. In spite of this, however, for a better understanding we should cast a glance at the individual projects.

Dictionary Project

All the table, view, data element, and domain information is saved in the form of XML files in the dictionary project. All changes to the services that were carried out with tools from CAF Designer and which affect the dictionary objects are stored in the source directory of the project.

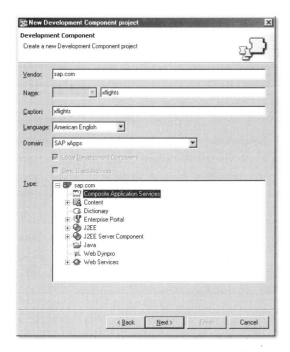

Figure 3.6 Creating a CAF Project

When creating a build of the Composite Application Project an SDA file is generated and stored in the deploy directory. In this context, SDA stands for *Software Deployment Archive* and is the format for supplying SAP applications that had been developed in other programming languages than ABAP.

SDA

When deploying the archive on the J2EE server, the tables, views, data elements and domains are created or, if necessary, changed in the underlying database and the relevant metadata is stored. This generates the local part of the persistence for the application.

The pendant to the Java dictionary in the ABAP world is called the ABAP dictionary, also abbreviated to DDIC (pronunciation: [de:dik]).

Comparison to ABAP

EJB Module Project

In the EJB Module Project, all coding of the entity and application services is contained in a compiled status in an Software Component Archive (SCA) file. This file is integrated into the enterprise project during the build creation and then stored in the relevant deploy directory. An SCA file represents a version of a software component. It contains a number of SDA files in the corresponding version.

SCA

This project can be compared to Transactions SE37 and SE38 for creating, calling and activating reports or function modules.

The SCA file comprises all services and interfaces as well as JDO (Java Data Objects) and mapping files of the composite application project.

Metadata Project

An EAR file is created in the metadata project and is also stored in the deploy directory. This file contains the metadata of the CAF project so that this information can be provided during runtime. This metadata describes all Entity Services, application services, relationships, operations and so forth.

Enterprise Project

The enterprise project in an EAR file contains the compiled code and references to the dictionary and metadata projects.

Web Dynpro Project

In the Web Dynpro project, a Web Dynpro model that is based on the definitions of the entity and application services is automatically generated and stored. This model is necessary so that the fields of the entry templates can be mapped to the operations and fields of the underlying services and thus the data can finally be displayed.

In order to use the Web Dynpro models and to create Web Dynpro foundation UIs, separate Web Dynpro projects should be created which reference to these CAF-specific Web Dynpro projects with such a model.

UME Permissions Project

When building a UME Permissions project an SDA file is generated and created in the deploy directory. This process is similar to the dictionary project.

3.3.5 CORE

CORE is a specific CAF project with objects that can be used by any xApp.[2] In some cases the architecture of the SAP Composite Application Framework prohibits the use of objects from other CAF projects.[3] This

---

2 In the classical ERP view CORE has a different meaning and refers to core applications such as FI, CO, HR etc.

ensures that unwanted and hard-to-resolve dependencies between individual projects are avoided. In addition it can be avoided that in order to use one application you have to install all other applications as well.

For example, the application xPD Product Definition is not allowed to use objects from the project xIEP Integrated Exploration & Production (an xApp from the oil and gas industry). Otherwise, every customer who wants to use xPD would be forced to install the xApp xIEP. The same condition applies in reverse.

You will need to re-use existing services on the one hand and on the other hand to access the same entities for the integration of different applications. **Document** and **Category** are among the many such entities.

For this reason, there is an exception to the restrictions and therefore the concept of the CORE project was introduced. The CORE project was delivered by SAP together with CAF and contains all data types, services, UI patterns and guided procedure templates that were identified as generally reusable during the development of other SAP xApps. This is the only project that can be referenced and used by all other projects. Changes to its objects can only be implemented by SAP. This ensures that no changes are made to services and patterns that could affect other SAP xApps.

The CORE project itself does not appear as an independent project in the Service Explorer. The CORE objects are shown in the models at the corresponding points.

You can find a complete overview of all the data types, Entity Services, application services, and UI patterns supplied with the CAF in the CORE project in the corresponding sections of this chapter and in the appendix.

In the following section the components of a CAF-based application, and the CAF terminology use will be introduced.

---

3 This is only partly true. Objects from other CAF projects can be integrated as Web services. But we'll come to that later.

3.4 External Services

The CAF can call functionality from back-end systems in two different ways: by remote function calls (RFCs) and by Web services. Both are referred to as "external services" in the CAF.

External services can be re-used by both Entity Services and application services. External services cannot be changed during design time and runtime in the CAF. Only the selection of the underlying backend system mapping to the operations and fields of the entity and application services is possible at both run- and design-time. (You can find more information on the other two service types in Sections 3.5 and 3.6.)

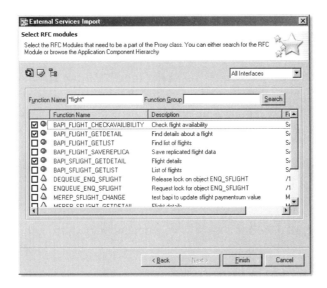

Figure 3.7 External Service — Import Dialog

Each system and application that enables communication through RFCs and Web services can be integrated in a CAF-based application irrespective of its location. For instance, all SAP Knowledge Management Services supplied as standard in the CORE project with the CAF (**Document**, **Discussion** etc.) are real Web services.

The CAF-specific application services, in turn, can be provided as Web services to other applications.

External services are always stateless due to the design of RFCs and Web services. Calling an external service opens and closes the session within this call.

Remote Function Calls

RFCs represent the most frequently used method to communicate with an ABAP-based SAP system. RFCs are interfaces that enable a communication with programs (so-called function modules) of an SAP system from outside.

The metadata of RFCs can be imported with the CAF and are then made available to the entity and application services. During import, all methods and their input and output parameters are notified to the CAF and are made available for the CAF services.

Metadata import

ABAP systems also use *transactional RFCs*. These run asynchronously. That means that although data which this RFC receives are written in a database table the transaction can only be completed by an explicit COMMIT WORK.

tRFC

Web Services

Web services have become widely accepted in recent times as the interface standard for communication on the World Wide Web across application and system boundaries. Independent of platform, program language, and technology, Web services enable systems and applications to exchange data and to start actions of any type. For the Web services, WSDL (Web Service Description Language) files are imported that can be retrieved from a directory or a UDDI[4] server.

External services (and entity and application services that we will describe in further details later on) are the cornerstone of an Enterprise Service Architecture and are used to flexibly create business applications.

3.5   Entity Service

3.5.1   Introduction

The Entity Service Modeler is a tool that can be used to model Entity Services, their attributes, methods, relationships with other Entity Services as well as their general properties and behavior. The task of an Entity Service is to save and access application data. The data can be made accessible in a local storage in a backend such as an R/3 system or a Web service. You will find more information on the different persistences in Section 3.5.3.

---

4 You can find information on Universal Description, Discovery and Integration (UDDI) at *http://www.uddi.org/*.

You can call the Entity Service Modeler in SAP NetWeaver Developer Studio by creating a new or changing an existing Entity Service. Both actions open an editor that provides all properties that can be modeled, as well as attributes and relationships of the Entity Service, in several tabs as well as in the Properties window. In addition, this editor enables you to make changes depending on your selections. The (technical) name of an Entity Service can also be changed at a later stage and it will be registered on the name server during the check-in phase into the Design Time Repository (DTR, see also description of DTR in later chapters) provided the development takes place in the Java Development Infrastructure (JDI).[5]

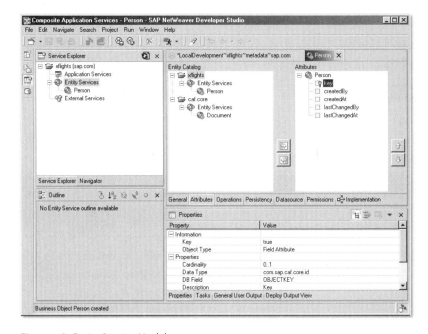

Figure 3.8 Entity Service Modeler

In the ABAP world, the name server corresponds to the catalog of repository objects (incl. Table TADIR) and the global TADIR (for cross-system and cross-release developments in ABAP systems).

3.5.2 Modeling

The first general properties of a new Entity Service are the name, the package, and a short descriptive text. The Entity Service is automatically assigned a unique number ("GUID") and creation and change dates as

---

5 If the name already exists, the check-in is canceled and an error message occurs.

well as creation and change users are logged simultaneously. Thus the Entity Service is uniquely described.

The attributes and properties affect both the number of tables generated and the scope of the coding which is generated as an Enterprise JavaBean (EJB).

Several entities have already been identified for our xFlights scenario, and Table 3.1 shows a list of selected entities.

Entity	Selected attributes of the entity
Person	LastName, FirstName, Address
Flight	CarrierID, FlightNumber
Airport	Name, Altitude, Latitude
Plane	PlaneType, MaxSeats, FuelUsage
Address	Streetname, ZIPCode, City, Country
FlightSchedule	DepartureTime, ArrivalTime, FlightNumber
Booking	Person, Flight, Date
Business Partner	lastName

Table 3.1 Selected Entities for xFlights

As already mentioned the entity **Person** is described by last name, first name, title, address, telephone numbers(s) and other attributes. On closer consideration it becomes apparent that these attributes have different characteristics. The person has only one last name but can have several first names. The person can also have several addresses and telephone numbers.

Characteristics of attributes

Addresses and telephone numbers can also be divided into several different attributes. Thus the address consists of country, region, city, zip code, street, and street number. The telephone number can be broken down into country code, area code and extension.

This requires different types of modeling for which it is important to know which options are available to map this data. The CAF provides three additional types of attributes here in addition to the standard attributes which cannot be changed: simple, complex and entity-service attributes.

Standard attributes

When creating an Entity Service five attributes are automatically created. These attributes are: "key," "createdAt," "createdBy," "lastChangedAt" and "lastChangedBy." The attributes cannot be changed or deleted and possess the cardinality 1..1 for "key" and 0..1 for the remaining four. Every Entity Service thus contains a main table with at least five of these attributes, regardless of whether it is locally or remotely persisted.

Meaning The meaning of these fields becomes clear when you consider the names. "Key" which is defined as GUID, is the unique primary key for this Entity Service, "createdAt" and "lastChangedAt" provide the change history of the data records in date fields, and "createdBy" and "lastChangedBy" are used to store the change user as a 255-digit key of the UME.

The "lastChangedAt" attribute is also important because it is used for the delta extraction of data into the BW. You will find a more precise description of the BW extraction in Section 3.9.

Rules for attribute properties The appendix of this book contains a tabular overview of all rules which itemize the property changes to all attribute types and describe the dependencies.

Simple Attributes

Simple attributes are generally simple data fields. In a table they would correspond to a column. In the **Person** example the attribute "last name" would be a simple attribute.

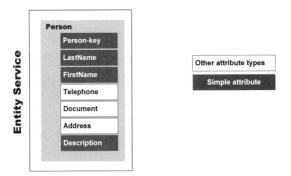

Figure 3.9 Simple Attributes and their Mapping in the Database

Language and time dependency In the CAF world, a simple attribute can also be identified as language or time dependent which entails the creation of an additional language or time-dependency table. However, such an attribute can only be identified as language dependent if it is of the basic type "string" and has the cardinality 0..1.

Only one language table is created per Entity Service. In the language table, an additional field is used for every language-dependent attribute. This field is no longer available in the main table. In Figure 3.10 this aspect is illustrated using the field "Description."

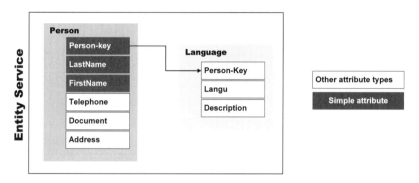

Figure 3.10 Language-Dependent Simple Attributes and their Mapping in the Database

Simple attributes can possess the cardinality 0..1 and 0..n or 1..1 and 1..n respectively if they were entered as mandatory attributes at the same time (the "mandatory" property is set to "true"). Regarding the database, the cardinality 0..n and 1..n means that an additional table is created with a primary key and an attribute. For this and all additional tables which are created for an Entity Service for the persistence, the name can be changed in the **Persistency** tab. In the main table itself a foreign key is then created which is a GUID for the CAF. In Figure 3.11 this is illustrated using the field "FirstName."

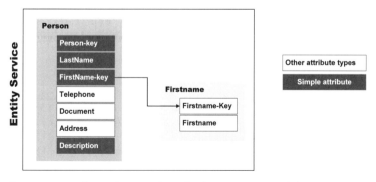

Figure 3.11 Simple Attributes with Cardinality 0..n or 1..n and their Mapping in the Database

Simple attributes can also be defined as keys by selecting the "key" property. This makes them automatically mandatory input fields and the cardinality is set to 1..1. This cannot be changed subsequently. However, in the database these attributes are not key fields but rather receive a unique index. The standard attribute "key" is created as the only key field in the database itself.

Attributes which were defined as mandatory input fields or as keys are automatically transferred as arguments into the CREATE method of the Entity Service.

Modeling tip   As a rule of thumb, simple attributes are used if the attribute should not be divided into additional sub-attributes and cannot exist independently from the referenced master data record. It should only be identified as language dependent if the values entered have a commentary or description field character. Reusable language-dependent texts such as "color" should be modeled as separate Entity Services.

Specific data types for attributes as are required for using currencies and units will be described in Section 3.13.1.

This attribute type and all other types can be sorted in any way in the **Attributes** tab of the Entity Service Modeler.

Complex Attributes

Complex attributes have several data fields. The data is stored in an additional table in the database. In the **Person** example, the "Telephone" attribute is a complex attribute which consists of the fields "Country code," "Region code," and "Extension."

A complex attribute can also be created with the cardinality 0..n (one person has several telephone numbers). The sub-attributes themselves can only be simple attributes and can have a cardinality of 0..1. A sub-attribute cannot be a mandatory attribute (i.e. the "Mandatory" property cannot be set to "true"). Complex attributes can neither be language-dependent nor defined as mandatory input fields.

Regarding the database, this means that an additional table with several attributes is created. In the attribute of the main table, a foreign key is then stored which is a GUID for the CAF.

Modeling tip   As a rule of thumb, complex attributes are used if the attribute is to be divided into additional sub-attributes and cannot exist independently from the referenced master data record. This means that, for instance, a telephone number makes no sense in most cases without the corresponding person.

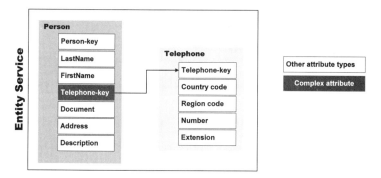

Figure 3.12 Complex Attributes and their Mapping in the Database

Entity Service Attributes

Entity Services can have other Entity Services as attributes. To create such an attribute a user can simply drag an Entity Service from the "Entity catalog" to the attributes in the "Attributes" tab. Technically speaking, this results in a foreign-key relationship. In the **Person** example the "Address" attribute would be defined as a separate Entity Service that can in turn have simple ("Street"), complex ("Geographical coordinates"), and Entity Service ("City," "Country") attributes. This means that one and the same address can therefore be used both separately and in other Entity Services, for instance as a company address and as an address for several employees.

Entity-service attributes have a cardinality of 0..1 or 0..n. They cannot be set as language dependent at this point. This must be defined in an Entity Service, which is used as an attribute. Entity-service attributes cannot also be defined as keys in this Entity Service. | Cardinality

In the database, an additional join table is created as a result. Thus another table is implemented between the main table of the Entity Service and the Entity Services used as attributes. This join table contains three fields: a separate primary key, the foreign key for the Entity Service, and the foreign key for the Entity Service attribute. Although both of the foreign keys alone would be sufficient for uniqueness, it was decided to create an additional key.

As a rule of thumb, entity-service attributes are used if the attribute is to be divided into additional sub-attributes and can exist independently from the referencing master data record. | Modeling tip

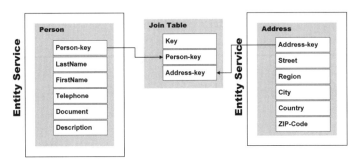

Figure 3.13 Entity Service Attributes and their Mapping in the Database

Cascading deletion   Although an instance of an Entity Service attribute can exist independently of the referencing master data record, a cascading deletion is sometimes necessary. Therefore it is possible to define the Entity Service attribute as an association or composition in the properties section. If you select Composition, referenced data records in the Entity Service attribute are also deleted when carrying out deletions in the referencing Entity Service.

Figure 3.13 shows that when modeling with the CAF, extensive database structures are created very quickly.

Custom Appends

Enhancement project   In the current version of CAF SAP, xApps are supplied as Java archives but not as Java projects with the metadata. In order to be able to perform changes to the application that go beyond the configuration, an enhancement project can be created. In such an enhancement, project, custom appends can be created that enable customers to model additional attributes for the Entity Services supplied.

3.5.3   CORE Services

As already mentioned, with CAF some CORE Entity Services are supplied in the CORE project by default. These services are frequently used and they are cross-application entities that can in general only be changed to a limited extent by application developers. SAP is planning to add an entire range of Entity Services to this project in future versions of CAF.

As a matter of fact, there are already more Entity Services supplied with CAF than those described in this chapter. These mainly involve persistence for business rules, permissions, object metadata etc. required during runtime. These Entity Services are available to the CAF only internally and during runtime. They are installed with the CAF library.

Along with CAF the following additional CORE Entity Services are provided:

CORE services supplied

- ▶ Category
- ▶ CategoryValueSet
- ▶ Document
- ▶ Discussion
- ▶ DiscussionRoom
- ▶ Principal
- ▶ Topic

Category

Instances of entities can be categorized using the Entity Service **Category**. For example, the passengers can be divided into different categories according to "menu requirements," "smokers/non-smokers," "frequent flyers," etc. Several values can exist for each category, and these can be selected via the Entity Service attribute "CategoryValueSet." The category itself is modeled as language dependent.

The assignment of categories to data records is carried out via the UI pattern **Classification Assignment**. Maintaining the value list is carried out either through the *KMIndex UI* or the values are uploaded from SAP Knowledge Management. In either case, the values are stored in the local persistence. You can find the link for this UI in the appendix.

Assignment to data records

CategoryValueSet

This Entity Service is an attribute of **Category** and contains the value list for different categories. If, for example, a category is called "Menu requirements," the lists of values can contain "Vegetarian," "Kosher," "Meat," and "Pasta." The list of values is also modeled as language dependent.

Maintaining the list of values is also carried out through the *KMIndex-UI*. The values are stored in the local persistence. By using this UI, existing taxonomies can also be loaded from SAP Knowledge Management into the local persistence for further use.

Category and **CategoryValueSet** together form a two-level hierarchy that can be used to categorize data records.

Modeling tip In contrast to the **CustomEnumType** (see also Section 3.7.5), which is displayed as a dropdown field in the UI, a UI pattern must be used to categorize a data record. To do this, a more flexible two-level hierarchy is provided.

CategoryService

As one of the last changes, the hierarchy functionality has been added to the CAF support packages. This functionality enables you to create hierarchies with as many levels as you wish. In addition, several hierarchies can also be created for the same values. The assignment to the object instances is carried out in the UI pattern **Classification**.

Document

By using the **Document,** any file types can be checked in to SAP Knowledge Management, where they can be requested from and edited. Typically, these file types are Word documents, text files, PowerPoint files, PDFs, and so forth. If this CORE Entity Service is used as an attribute for another Entity Service, a field of the data type rid is created in the main table for the Entity Service. This data type then has a foreign key relationship with the document.

The Entity Service **Document** has the following attributes:

▶ Key (String)
▶ parentFolder (String; 0..1; key attribute)
▶ parentFolder (String; 0..1; key attribute)
▶ title (String; 0..1)
▶ description (String; 0..1)
▶ link (String; 0..1)
▶ contentLength (long; 0..1)
▶ contentType (String; 0..1; contains the MIME type information)
▶ relatedObjectRids (String; 0..n)

In the application the UI pattern **Attachment** is used as the user interface.

124 The SAP Composite Application Framework

Discussion

If **Discussion** is used as an attribute of an Entity Service discussions, users will be able to discuss individual instances. These postings are stored in KM.

DiscussionRoom

In contrast to the Entity Service **Discussion**, **DiscussionRoom** enables you to restrict the access to a discussion. You can grant authorizations to those who are permitted to take part in the discussion. This Entity Service also provides the functionality to send invitations to users to participate in a discussion.

Principal

Principals are used in the Entity Service **DiscussionRoom** and represent the individuals invited, i.e. the users authorized for this **DiscussionRoom.**

Topic

This service is used by the Entity Service **Discussion.** Each discussion can have one or several topics.

Currency

This service is used internally in order to attach currencies to numerical attributes.

ExchangeRate

This service is used internally in order to execute conversions into other currencies on attributes with attached currencies.

UnitOfMeasurement

This service is used internally in order to attach units of measurement to numeric attributes.

UnitConversionSimple

This service is used internally in order to be able to perform simple conversions on attributes with units of measurement.

3.5.4 Persistence

As already seen the modeling of an Entity Service has major effects on the
persistence. Deciding on a specific attribute type can be critical for additional tables in the local database. The created tables follow a naming
convention, which has the prefix XAP_ and has a generated key as its
actual name. Due to length restrictions for databases supported by SAP,
the table names cannot be longer than 18 characters. For this and other
reasons, a decision was made to assign the name of tables in this form
instead of generating any "meaningful" names. Other reasons were the
potential conflicts between attribute tables with the same names in different Entity Services, conflicts when installing several xApps with the
Entity Services bearing the same names, and also the ever-present temptation among application developers to directly access the tables. Instead
of this direct access, the corresponding APIs of the Entity Services should
be used.

The tables with the rather cryptic names of XAP_<14-digit ID> can be
renamed in the modeler by the developer. The names are registered on
the name server during check-in to the DTR. If the name already exists,
the check-in procedure cancels with an error.

Other factors affect the table structure. In addition to the attribute type,
its data type and the key property, these factors are the language dependency, time dependency, the cardinality, and the decision concerning the
use of a local or a remote persistence. A precise explanation of these factors follows.

Language Dependency

Language table If an attribute is referred to as language dependent, a language table is
created that contains the foreign key of the data record, the language,
and the corresponding text as fields. For each language-dependent
attribute, an additional field is created in this language table. Depending
on the user log-on language, the text is selected and displayed in the corresponding language during the application runtime.

An attribute which was identified as language dependent cannot have a
cardinality of 0..n or 1..n.

Time Dependency

Information as to when a value was valid can be mapped through the
time dependency of attributes. The "last name" or the "address" of a per-

son can be time dependent. This property is stored in an additional table that contains the fields "Key," "Value," "Valid from," and "Valid until." Depending on the period of validity of the request, the corresponding value is selected from the time-dependency table and then displayed.

Cardinality

If there is a 0..n or 1..n relationship between the Entity Service and the attribute, additional tables will only be created in cases where this modeling cannot be mapped by the existing table structures. An attribute that was identified as mandatory ("Mandatory" property is set to "true") can only have cardinalities of 1..1 or 1..n.

Remote and Local Persistence

In an Entity Service with local persistence, at least one table is always created. As already mentioned, the number of tables can vary according to the type of modeling. If the Entity Service was already deployed once on the J2EE server (which means that tables were created in the database) and if subsequent changes are then made to the attributes affecting the persistence (i.e. the tables), the following cases can be differentiated:

Subsequent changes

▶ Positive changes
Attributes are added. In a new deployment these attributes are generated as additions to the existing tables. The data remains in the tables.

▶ Negative changes
Attributes are removed. This is not permitted. During deployment at the latest, the J2EE server sends error messages and the deployment cancels.

Subsequent changes that have an impact on the language and time dependencies and the cardinality are only possible to a limited extent. The installation must previously be "undeployed,"or deleted on the J2EE server.

So far only the local persistence was taken into consideration. In addition to saving data in the local database on the J2EE server, the CAF also provides the option to "remotely" read the data, to change it, save it, and to delete it. In this context "remote" means that data is stored in a back-end system, i.e. a downstream system. Back-end systems in CAF are all those systems whose data, is separated from the local CAF database, no matter how it is stored.

Remote persistence

In an Entity Service, a "mixed" persistence, i.e. a local one as well as a remote one can be set as an attribute by using other Entity Services. For example, a **Person** Entity Service can be made completely locally persistent with its simple and complex attributes. On the other hand, the "address" attribute, which is an Entity Service itself, can be made persistent in a remote form in a back-end system. The same applies in reverse: Both the data of the Entity Service and all its attributes can either be stored completely locally or remotely.

In fact, an Entity Service which is identified as remote always has just one local table in which the standard attributes and the information on relationships with other Entity Services are stored. This means no changes have to be performed on the backend systems.

The use of a remote persistence from an Entity Service requires mapping to an external service. For each method (`create`, `read`, `update`, `delete` and the arbitrarily definable `findBy`-methods), an individual external service can be referred to. The methods of the external service are then mapped to the methods and fields of the Entity Service. In the current version of the CAF, there are still some functional limitations. For example, the developer has to ensure that the data types match.

In general, it doesn't make sense to use transactional RFCs in the Entity Service. It is better to use these in the application service, as otherwise another `COMMIT` command (in our specific case the ABAP command is `COMMIT WORK`) must be released.

If you take a closer look at "mixed" persistences, the problem of a "distributed commit" emerges. By this we mean that the data to be written into distributed systems actually arrives there without any interruption. Nothing is worse for data consistency than having the write access to a system canceled due to concurrent accesses, locks set, unavailable systems, or inconsistencies while the relevant data was updated in the other system. If persistence exists in one single system only, you have more or less complete control and therefore always have the option of a rollback. However, to ensure a clean update in distributed systems, all participating systems have to permit a two-phase commit. An example would be to first check in the course of a test update if the data can be written so that it can be actually written in a subsequent update. Unfortunately, most systems do not offer any two-phase commit, and some of the external services used do not even provide rollback functionality.

The CAF, or to be more precise SAP NetWeaver, for these reasons currently provides no options for using generic functionality during a distributed commit. This should not be a reason for ruling out the creation of composite applications with SAP xApps, as in many cases either no distributed commit is required or it can be bypassed by taking other actions.

Access to the Local Persistence

But how do the operations access the local database? This occurs "indirectly" using Java Data Objects (JDO). JDO is an API developed by Sun in order to be able to access data from any data sources through Java. JDO makes access to the data sources transparent for the developers and requires no SQL knowledge.

JDO

JDO is not used directly in the Entity Services but via the CAF-specific **DataAccessService**. During creation, two additional files with the endings .jdo and .map are created. The .jdo file contains the relationships between the Java class and the database table and is required when the CAF project is being built. During the build, the **PersistenceCapable** interface is implemented in the Entity Services on the basis of the .jdo file in order to enable the JDO use.[6] The .map file can then read out these relationships during runtime.

Access to the Remote Persistence

In order to receive data from a back-end system or to save it there, external services are used and mapped to the operations. By mapping we mean the assignment of methods and parameters of the Entity Service to methods and parameters of the external services.

External Services

Not all operations of an Entity Service must be mapped to the same one, to a different one, or to any external services. It is conceivable that the read method READ is mapped to an external service A, the FINDBY-method XY to an external service B, and the write method CREATE to no external service at all, but that it stores the data locally. A practical example illustrates the mapping of the FINDBY methods to the BI-SDK[7] Web service in order to search purchase order data and line items from SAP Business Intelligence. If this required data is found, it is once again read from the R/3 system and the changes are saved there. The reason for

---

6 If the class is decompiled, you can see this extension in the code. In the original project code the extension is not available at this point in time.
7 Business Intelligence Software Development Kit. This SDK enables you to access data from SAP NetWeaver Business Intelligence via Web services.

using this solution can be an already heavy load on the R/3 system. Due to the previous filtering performed by BW this load does not increase excessively.

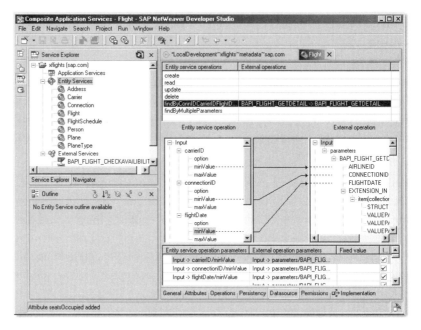

Figure 3.14 Mapping an External Service to an Entity Service

Changes Similar to the local persistence, in a remote persistence the operations can only be changed in so far as the mappings are adaptable to the methods and parameters. If more transformations or adaptations are to be executed, then either the external service itself must be changed correspondingly, or it must be carried out in the application service that is located at the next higher level.

Operations

Operation types The query and storage of data from the persistence in the Entity Services is enabled by five operation types:

1. CREATE
2. READ
3. UPDATE
4. DELETE
5. FINDBY

If the Entity Service is defined with local persistence, the first four operation types (the *CRUD operations*) cannot be changed. In the generated coding, these four methods[8] are created. For local persistence, adjustments and transformations in the coding can only be executed in the application service.

The arguments of the CREATE method can be set in the **Attribute** tabstrip of the Entity Service Modeler. When creating attributes that were defined either as keys or mandatory input fields, the CREATE method is also enhanced by the corresponding arguments. When calling the CREATE method in order to create a data record, these arguments must be transferred also and cannot be empty.

Attributes

The FINDBY operations represent a special case. Depending on the number and type of the attributes, several of these can be created. The search parameters are selected using a dialog wizard. Possible input parameters are standard attributes, simple attributes, the sub-attributes of complex attributes, and attributes of Entity Service attributes. With the exception of the Entity Service attributes, all other attributes referred to here can also be used as output parameters for the search. For the Entity Service attributes, only the respective keys are returned. If attributes of the Entity Service attributes themselves are required as return values, they must be queried separately in the application service.

By default, you can carry out a restricted search with a placeholder in the FINDBY operations in the case of local persistence. The character * (asterisk) acts as a placeholder. The restriction given by using JDO means you can only run queries of type "aa*" or "*zz", i.e. the placeholder symbol can only be the first or the last character of the search term. In the case of a remote persistence, the FINDBY operation supports every type of placeholder and position which is supported by the remote operation used.

Search with placeholder

FINDBY operations require an object of the type com.sap.caf.rt.bol.util.QueryFilter as a transfer value. It is clear from the nine constructors of this class that several types of query filters are possible, and these can adopt both individual values and intervals and conditions.

Transfer value

A query filter can look as follows:

```
QueryFilter filter1 = new QueryFilter("HelloWorld");
QueryFilter filter2 = new QueryFilter("Hello*");
```

---

8   The terms "method" and "operation" are used as synonyms.

In addition, based on the settings in the Entity Service, operations are created such as

```
searchidxForBOInRelatedDoc
```

This operation belongs to the Entity Service **Document** and runs a search for all data records which contain a reference to a document. The operation then returns a list of results.

During generation, in the complete coding authorization checks, logging and tracing and other calls are automatically created as well.

3.5.5 Generation, Build and Deployment

While the services are being created and changed, the metadata also is being created, links are being created, and coding and interfaces are being generated. For an executable application, Java dictionary objects (DDIC) such as tables, data elements, domains, views and metadata, and program and interface classes are required. During generation, these files and configuration files are once again regenerated and during the final build three archives are stored per CAF project. The archives contain the information on the DDIC objects, the metadata, and the compiled coding.

Consistency check During the build itself, in addition to compilation, all references are also checked once again and the consistency of the archive is ensured. If the consistency and links to references cannot be produced, the build cancels with an error message.

Subsequent action If the build was successful, the archives can be "deployed" on the J2EE server. By "deploying," we mean the process of copying this archive to the server and the execution of subsequent activities. A subsequent action is, for instance, the creation of tables and database structures by calling the information contained in the dictionary archive to execute corresponding SQL statements.

During the deployment, a check is run to see if the specified references are valid. If this is not the case, the deployment is usually canceled with an error message. However, if the deployment took place without error, the services are available to the application. The tables are created in the local database and are waiting to be populated.

The entire process of generation, build, and deployment is executed in one step and transparently for the user.

The comparable functionality in the ABAP Workbench would involve generating or activating objects.

Comparison to ABAP

Java Dictionary

Tables and their relationships to each other can now be created in the database by using the information in the Java dictionary project.

Metadata

The metadata is stored in the metadata project. In the more than a dozen sub-directories of the Meta Model, the definitions of interfaces, attributes, data objects, fields, mappings, operations, authorizations, properties and tables are stored in XML files. At least two XML files are created for each of the definitions referred to, even small application projects can contain several hundred XML files.

Since these files are regenerated each time you use the CAF Designer to perform changes to the services, modifications executed on XML files with non-CAF tools are lost.

Apart from this, changes to the services, depending on the extent of these changes generally also affect more than half a dozen XML files.

Coding

The generation of the services is based on coding templates and metadata definitions. The coding templates for external, entity and application services and their interfaces can be found in the plug-in directory of the CAF Designer under `com.sap.caf.designer` in the sub-directory `templates`. More than two dozen templates are available there and can be used according to the relevant definition.

Templates

The coding that is generated in such a way is then stored uncompiled in the source directory of the EJB module project, the built archive that is ready for deployment is stored together with the compiled Java classes in the Deploy directory. Coding for Entity Services (and also application services) is generated in the form of sessions beans.

As the Java classes are regenerated each time you use the CAF Designer to perform changes to the services, modifications executed on Java classes with other tools are lost. We would therefore strongly advise you against making changes directly in the generated coding even if the temptation is great.

Note

We would also advise you against making arbitrary changes to the coding templates in the `templates` directory. SAP will not provide any support if these templates are changed by application developers (i.e. developers who are not part of the CAF team). In addition, a future upgrade to a new CAF release can be made more difficult or even impossible, as SAP reserves the right to change these coding templates to make them incompatible, if necessary.

> **Excursus: Why Are Session Beans Generated?**
>
> The purpose is to provide a standardized service interface. Therefore, all services are session beans (entity and application services). By using JDO, the beans are also made persistent and the generation of entity beans would be too much generated coding. However, the generation of other types of coding, depending on the task at hand, is not ruled out for the future.

Four methods are created by default for an Entity Service, namely the `create`, `read`, `update` and `delete` methods. In addition, `findBy` methods are generated, provided that these were generated by the developer on the **Operations** tabstrip. There are also some attributes and set methods that are not available for general use. For example, the `setKey` method cannot be used in order to set a separate key. This method is only used internally.

3.5.6 Testing

ServiceBrowser

After successful deployment services can be tested on the J2EE server with the *ServiceBrowser* by calling them from the context menu of the service explorer in the CAF design time. In the subsequent screen you can then see all the services registered on the server.

You can find the link for this and all other tools in the appendix.

Comparison to ABAP

In the ABAP world the ServiceBrowser corresponds to Transactions SE37 and SE38 for changing and executing reports and function modules.

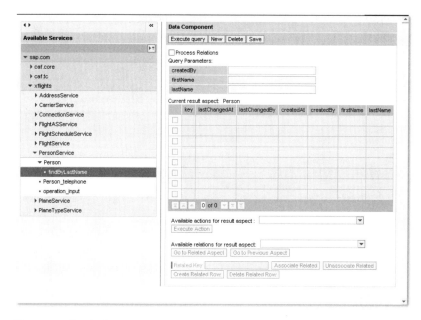

Figure 3.15 ServiceBrowser

3.5.7 Authorizations

The CAF employs the UME supplied with SAP Enterprise Portal to check user authorizations. In the Entity Service Modeler in the **Permissions** tab-strip the authorizations check generally takes place at the object level ("Should an authorization check be carried out for this Entity Service?") and switched on or off at the instance level. The term "instances" refers to the individual data records in this case.

If the authorization check was switched on at the instance level, an access-control list (ACL) is created for each instance. This list contains information on each data record for which authorizations are permitted for which users or roles. The corresponding code sequence can then be executed in the application service. There is an administration interface to maintain the ACLs (see Figure 3.16). ACL

In addition to maintaining ACLs, you can also create rules (business rules) and conditions there. The authorizations created can be imported and exported as well as propagated to referenced Entity Services.

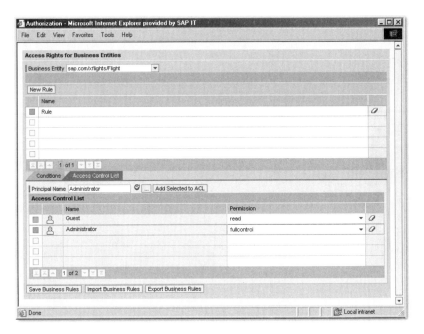

Figure 3.16 Authorization Maintenance for Users, User Groups and Roles

UME actions UME actions must be available so that the UME can work with the authorizations for operations of the application services. You can create these in the CAF Designer using the Application Service Modeler.

The administration tool **Principal Authorization Report** is used in order to be able to view the rule-based authorizations of a user for an Entity Service for all instances (see Figure 3.17).

You can use this tool to display the authorizations but not to change them. The authorization data can also be downloaded locally.

The reverse view of data, namely the display of authorizations for all roles and users on one instance of an Entity Service occurs with the UI illustrated in Figure 3.18.

Calling this UI, does not return any data at first because both the configuration (and hence the Entity Service) and the instance are required. The configuration takes place in the screen displayed in Figure 3.19.

The data cannot be changed here either. In order to transfer the instance, this UI can—for example—be called from the **ObjectSelector** (of the **ObjectList**).

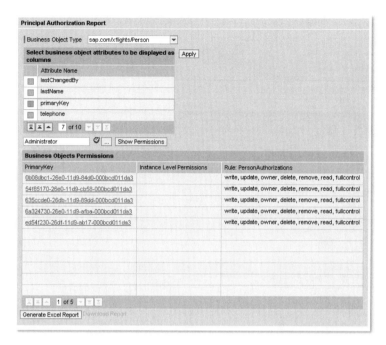

Figure 3.17 Principal Authorization Report

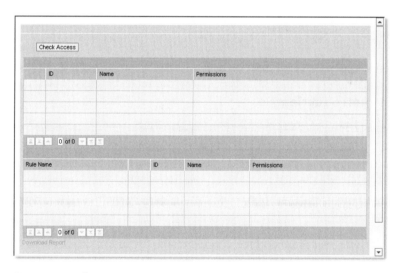

Figure 3.18 Authorization Report

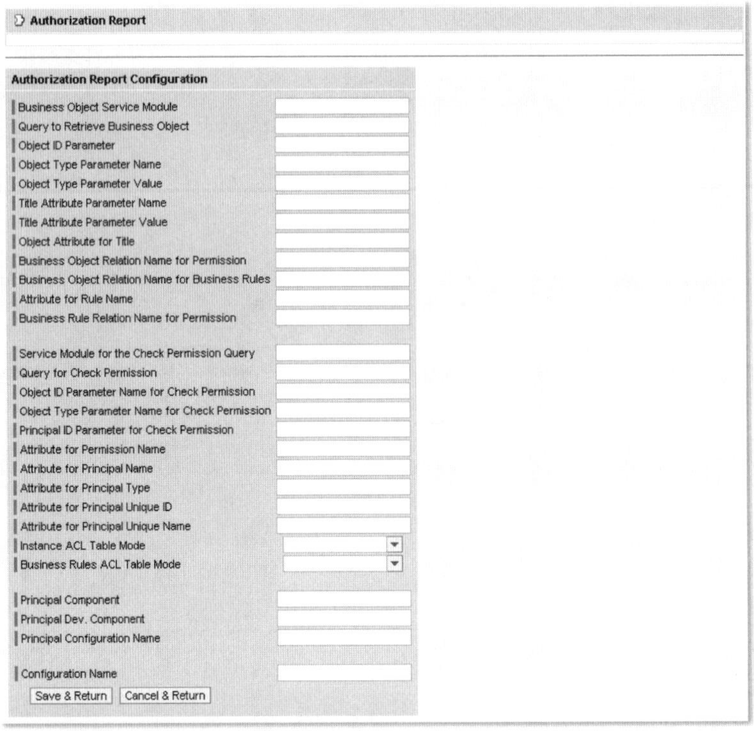

Figure 3.19 Authorization Report Configuration

3.6 Application Services

3.6.1 Introduction

Business process
logic The Entity Services described up to now primarily deal with generation of
code for the relatively simple and redundant, but—provided they are to
be programmed manually—coding-intensive tasks of data reading and
writing, which are prone to errors. Application services, by contrast, contain the "intelligent" part of the application, namely the business process
logic.

Application services are also the only way for entity or external services to
get in contact with the UI in the CAF architecture, according to the Model
View Controller principle (MVC).

In the xFlights example, the most important application services would
mainly be those for booking flights and all others which execute searches
for data records in the Entity Services. Figure 3.20 provides an overview
of the application services in the sample scenario.

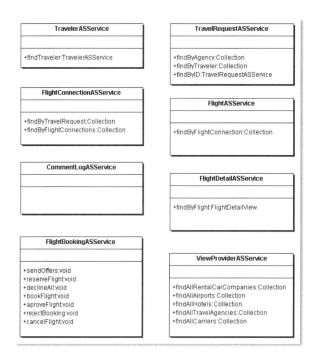

Figure 3.20 Application Services for xFlights in UML Form

3.6.2 Modeling

Application Service Modeler

The *Application Service Modeler* used for modeling appears quite simple at first glance but contains a high degree of flexibility. Among other things, it can be used to define the transactional behavior of an application service, its usability for other applications, and the use of external, entity and other application services, as well as their operation, input and output parameters, and the exceptions.

These properties of the application services enable the CAF to generate the general scope for coding, which then provides the application developer in specifically marked locations with the option to specify the business process logic through specific Java coding. These marks can look as follows:

```
//@@custom code start - checkBirthDate()
...
//@@custom code end - checkBirthDate()
```

Operation types

In order to ensure the operations for the User Interface are readable they must be typed. Readable in this context means easier to interpret, so that the screen can be customized accordingly, for instance. There are seven operation types available for selection in the Application Service Modeler:

1. Custom

2. Create

3. Read

4. Update

5. Delete

6. FindBy

You already know the last five operation types from the discussion of Entity Services. They are used in the application services, for example if the operation is only to forward data from the UI to the Entity Service or vice versa, and thus a large part of the coding entails mapping parameters of the entity and external services and those of the UI. Nevertheless there is the option of adding your own coding in order to execute different transformations or checks, a choice which is not possible in the Entity Services. The operation wizard of the Application Service Modeler and the **Operations** tabstrip in the modeler (see Figure 3.21) reduce some of the workload for the developer once the operation type is selected by automatically creating the number of arguments, the operation of the return type, and so on.

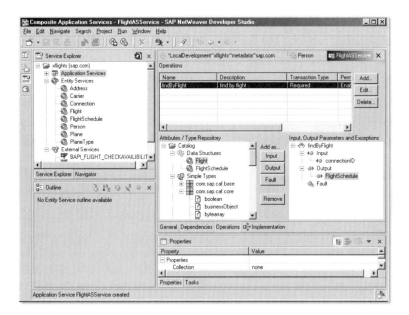

Figure 3.21 Creating an Operation

The Custom operation type which is available exclusively in application services provides application developers with the most extensive options to create their own coding. This operation type permits all types of transformations, checks, calls, manipulations, in short everything that the developer desires and what is necessitated by the application.

CUSTOM operation

> The flexibility for application developers of being able to add their own coding in application services results in opportunities as well as risks. On the one hand there is a high degree of freedom regarding the form of the code. On the other hand this coding must be maintained and debugged, and you are confined to one platform.
>
> The latter must be considered insofar as it can be expected that the functionalities of the modeler will be expanded in the next version of CAF, enabling you to model business process logic with function libraries and formula wizards and based on metadata. This metadata-based coding will then make it possible to not only generate for Java platforms but also for others such as ABAP or .NET.

The BW Extractor type generates a method which enables the extraction of data from the persistence of the Entity Services used. By using this method, the extraction-relevant changes to be described in the chapter on BW are also performed at the same time.

BW Extractor

The use of the operation types also affects the possible input parameters and the return type. You will find a complete list of all dependencies in the appendix.

Application services should be modeled according to the principles of a service-oriented architecture so that they are reusable, manageable and task-specific. Such services can also be more easily maintained and assigned to individual developers when the project scope grows. As the design tools of the CAF considerably accelerate and simplify the creation of services, it becomes easier to move away from services that are very generic and difficult to understand.

Modeling tip

In other words, instead of a very large service, it is better to create several small application services divided into useful units.

By the way, the (technical) name of an application service can be changed at a later stage, as is the case for an Entity Service as well. In addition, the modeler also provides the functionality to create JavaDocs for each operation.

3.6.3 Coding Examples

In the following section you will find some concrete examples as they were used for the xFlights scenario. Naturally, coding can vary depending on the attributes and data types used.

Create The coding for operation `createPerson()` to be placed between the marks `//@@custom code start` and `//@@custom code end` looks as follows:

```
PersonServiceLocal local = this.getPersonService();
retValue = local.create();
retValue.setFirstName(firstName);
retValue.setLastName(lastName);
local.update(retValue);
```

This coding first generates an instance of the object `PersonServiceLocal`, creates a data record, and then changes the two fields `FirstName` and `LastName`. The data type for both of these fields would be obvious in the method header.

Delete The coding for operation `deletePerson()` to be placed between the marks `//@@custom code start` and `//@@custom code end` looks as follows:

```
PersonServiceLocal local = this.getPersonService();
local.delete(person);
```

As in the previous example, an instance of the object `PersonServiceLocal` is generated, and then the `person` object is transferred as an argument to the `delete()` method.

FindBy The coding for operation `findByLastName()` to be placed between the marks `//@@custom code start` and `//@@custom code end` looks as follows:

```
PersonServiceLocal local = this.getPersonService();
retValue = (java.util.List)local.findByLastName(new Query
Filter(lastName));
```

In order to be able to use the `QueryFilter` object to be transferred, the library `com.sap.caf.rt.bol.util.QueryFilter` must be imported. For proprietary imports, there is a separate mark in the application service coding where a developer can add these. Section 3.5 contains a more detailed description on the `QueryFilter` object.

3.6.4 CORE Services

In the CORE project already mentioned above there are also several application services.

ClassificationApplicationService

This service calls the Entity Service **CategoryService** and is used by the UI pattern **Classification** in order to create file structures. This service differentiates between files and folders. Categories are thus assigned to the Entity Service type and folders are assigned to instances.

CurrencyConversion

This service is used internally in order to execute currency conversions.

DocContent

In order to attach a document to a data record the Entity Service attribute is used. By calling a specific dialog a user can select the document (e.g. from the local hard disk), specify a name and other information on the document and finally save it. In the course of this action the document is stored in SAP Knowledge Management.

The document thus consists of header information and content. Loading the header information is carried out via the **Document** Entity Service; the application service **DocContent** loads the actual document. In the dialog that uses the **Attachment** UI pattern this functionality is already integrated. The application developer does not need to carry out any further steps.

The **DocContent** application service should therefore rather be considered as a service used internally by CAF itself. It can however also be referenced directly by the application developer.

UnitConversion

This service is used internally in order to convert units of measurement.

3.6.5 Generation, Build, Deployment and Testing

The generation, build and deployment is not different from the processes already mentioned in Section 3.5.5, as the entire project is integrated with all services and metadata in this step anyway.

For testing, the same procedure applies as the one described for the Entity Services in Section 3.5.6.

3.7 User Interface

While all the previous sections described the services and their modeling in detail, we will focus on the user interface. User interfaces create the connection between logic and persistence on the one hand and the user on the other hand. In the past, the experiences of the users with the SAP User Interfaces were often ambivalent.

In recent years SAP has striven to change this, and to provide application developers with a technology designed to eliminate at least the technical difficulties with using some UIs. Recommendations and instructions (the so-called methodology), along with legal regulations may well lead to a better result here for different user groups.

Excursus: Fresh User Interfaces

The first large project that undertook a redesign of the user interfaces within SAP was the Enjoy project started at the end of the 1990s. In collaboration with Frog Design (a company founded by Germans in California, and the name "FROG" stands for "Federal Republic of Germany"), SAP screens were given a new look.

Since then, there have been many smaller and larger UI initiatives that have produced Web Dynpro and a better separation of the originally overloaded functionality of the BAPIs used by the UIs, as well as a comprehensive catalog of tips and tricks for developing user interfaces. You can find more on the history and results at *www.sapdesign-guild.org*.

3.7.1 Web Dynpro

The UI used by CAF is based on the Web Dynpro. Web Dynpro is a powerful UI framework developed by SAP that permits the creation of application interfaces based on metadata. Coding is generated on this basis, as is the case for the other parts of the CAF. In contrast to earlier UI tools, the Web Dynpro UI Modelers also minimize programming effort for application developers in creating user interfaces, enabling navigation between individual screens and connection between user interfaces and the underlying data sources.

Web Dynpro provides two different approaches of creating interfaces. These are the Pattern and Web Dynpro foundation interfaces. While the Web Dynpro foundation means that an application developer has complete freedom to create a UI with any layout and any functionality, patterns for specific reusable interface templates were developed. The two approaches can be connected with each other, i.e. patterns can be embedded into Web Dynpro foundation interfaces and patterns can also be built using Web Dynpro foundation technology.

Two development approaches

3.7.2 Patterns

In today's applications, it is easy to see which input screens were programmed by which developers. Despite a standardized design, the user-friendliness, labeling and alignment of UI elements is different for the transactions even if they perform similar tasks. For example, the transaction to maintain customer data, material or employee master records are technically speaking nothing other than maintaining header and detail data with different content. The transaction screens are however often so different in their appearance and behavior that a user without training would find it hard to use them.

The patterns are supposed to remedy this drawback. In the context of the CAF world this means that the master data for "Customer," "Material," or "Employee" must correspond to Entity Services. These can be differentiated mainly by their attributes and properties. Calling the CRUD methods, however, is the same for all of them. This means it is possible to use a generic UI to maintain this data which builds up depending on the selected Entity Service during runtime. This generic UI is what we refer to as "pattern."

It will therefore not surprise you that UI patterns are recommended for creating UIs.

Modeling tip

For instance the UI pattern **ObjectEditor** is available to maintain data in Entity Services. It is suitable for creating, changing, deleting and searching for data records.

To a certain extent UI patterns are configurable. To do this, every UI pattern possess a configuration view. During configuration you not only specify the services and methods which are obligatory for every pattern (both entity and application services), but also set the fields to be displayed according to the UI pattern, their sorting, display type, labeling, additional integration of other UI patterns, or Web Dynpro Foundation UIs in other display elements of the UI.

Configuration

SAP supplies approximately a dozen UI patterns with the runtime installation of the CAF. These can be used by existing and newly developed SAP xApps. The patterns are available in two types of variants: as components and as pages. Components are UI patterns which are integrated into other patterns and Web Dynpro foundations but can not be called individually.

Pages on the other hand represent independent UIs. By using the following list of all patterns supplied and the specification of whether they are pages or components, the situation will become clearer.

Attachments (Component)

The CORE project provides the **Document** Entity Service, which can be used to check files in and out in SAP Knowledge Management. If **Document** is used as an Entity Service attribute in another Entity Service, for each document for which an Entity Service is checked in, the relation is automatically saved as well.

In order to check such files in or out or to search for them, the UI pattern **Attachment** is used.

Figure 3.22 Attachment Pattern

NewAttachment (Component)

Using this pattern directories and files can be selected from storage in SAP Knowledge Management. The pattern itself is a UI component and is used in the Attachment pattern.

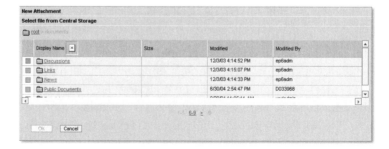

Figure 3.23 New Attachment Pattern

AttachImage (Component)

This pattern can be differentiated from the other Attachment patterns, as only image files to instances can be displayed and attached with it.

Selecting graphics

Classification Assignment (Component)

The Classification Assignment UI pattern (see Figure 3.24) is used for the classification of data records. This UI pattern uses the Entity Services **Category** and **CategoryValueSet**.

Classifying data records

Collaboration (Component)

This pattern is used for discussions on object instances. This means discussion threads can be attached to the individual data records.

Collaboration

ObjectEditor (Page)

One of the most frequently used UI patterns is the **ObjectEditor** (see Figure 3.25). It is used if data records are to be added, changed, or deleted. Because the data models are usually complex, this UI pattern enables you to integrate up to eight tabstrips that in turn contain additional UI patterns or Web Dynpro foundation UIs. Most of the times this means that during runtime, the header information of the object is entered in the upper half of the UI and the detailed information for the tabstrip is entered in the lower half.

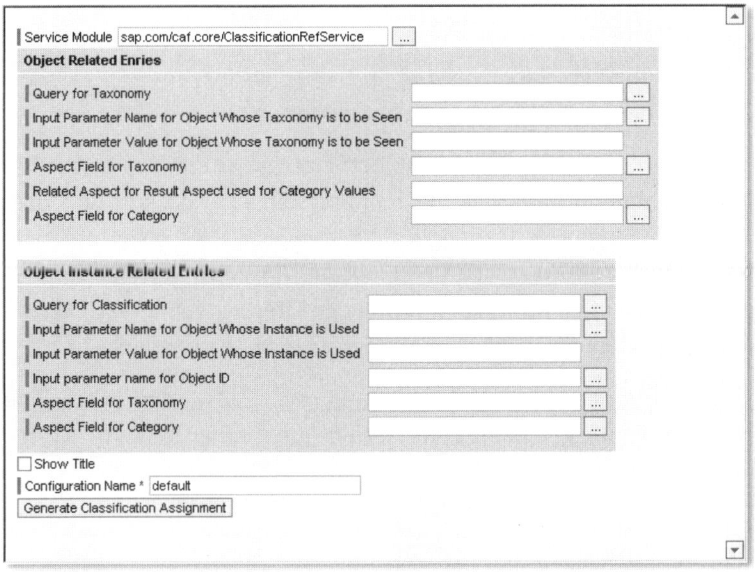

Manipulating data records

Figure 3.24 Classification Assignment Pattern

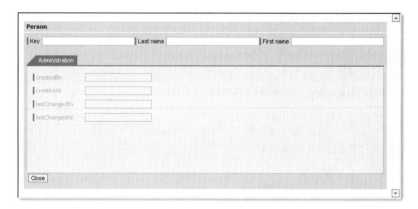

Figure 3.25 ObjectEditor Pattern

ObjectSelector (Page)

The UI pattern **ObjectSelector** (see Figure 3.26) is suitable for searching for data, displaying it and carrying out other actions. It consists of two parts, a search field and a display part. In the search field, there are fields for search criteria that help locate the desired data records. This part is itself a UI pattern, namely **SearchBar**.

The result list **ObjectList** (also a specific pattern) shows the hits found. The list can be configured insofar as the number, type and sorting of the fields can be determined as well as the actions that can be executed by clicking on one of the fields.

To be more precise, two partial configurations are created in this UI pattern (one for the **SearchBar** and one for the results list) as well as a combination of both again as an actual configuration.

In addition, when configuring the **ObjectSelector** pattern, you can define whether an additional application should be started by clicking on a data record in the result list. The application can be a Web Dynpro or any other type of application. Separate applications can be specified for creating a new data record or calling the change screen. If it is a Web Dynpro application, the configuration to be used can also be provided.

During runtime, the application is opened in a new window by clicking on the corresponding column in the results line. In the URL two or three parameters can then be seen:

1. **app.parameter1**
   Refers to the GUID of the data record.

2. **app.parameter2**

Refers to the mode. E stands for Edit (changing an existing data record) and N for New (creating a new data record).

3. **app.configName**

In Web Dynpro applications, the name of the configuration to be called is specified in this manner.

These three parameters are, for instance, interpreted by the UI pattern **ObjectEditor** as specified and the corresponding data record is displayed in the relevant configuration. The developer need not worry about assembling the URL.

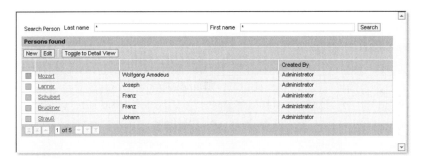

Figure 3.26 ObjectSelector Pattern

ObjectBrowser (Component)

With this pattern, data records can be searched for in an Entity Service in order to link them for instance with the data records of another or the same Entity Service.

Searching for data records

SearchBar (Component)

The **SearchBar** is not used separately but always in connection with the UI pattern **ObjectSelector**. The search criteria and their sequence are defined with the **SearchBar**.

Defining search criteria and sequences

ObjectList (Component)

As already mentioned with regard to the ObjectSelector pattern, the results list **ObjectList** shows the hits found. The list can be configured so as to determine the number, type, and sorting of the fields, as well as the actions that can be executed by clicking on one of the fields.

Displaying data records

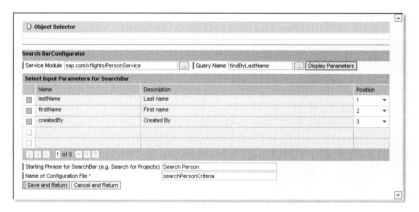

Figure 3.27 SearchBar Pattern

Navigation (Page)

Navigation

The **Navigation** pattern is suitable for navigation between two user interfaces and forwarding the context. The navigation targets that can be defined in the configuration are located on the left-hand side, while the application interfaces can be found on the right.

FlexTree (Page)

Hierarchical lists

The **FlexTree** pattern can be used to display lists in a hierarchical form and the data per column in different forms (see Figure 3.28). The data in the individual columns can be displayed not only as plain text but also as hyperlinks, signal lamps, etc. In addition, you can use several application services as data sources. And apart from that the columns and rows can be exchanged in a **FlexTree** pattern during runtime.

HistoryLog (Component)

Displaying comments

In the pattern **HistoryLog** (see Figure 3.29) all comments that are entered for an Entity Service are displayed in chronological order. Thus discussions and remarks can be displayed quickly without having to search in Entity Services themselves.

RelationTab (Component)

Maintaining relations

This pattern can be used to maintain relations between entities. An example of this is the relation between an instance of the **Customer** object and an instance of the **Sales person** object.

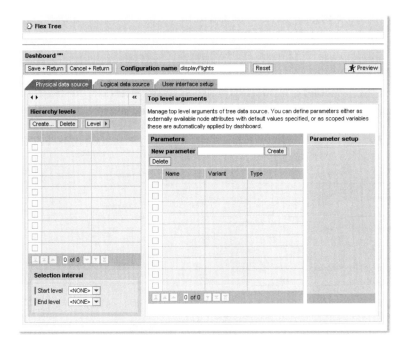

Figure 3.28 FlexTree Pattern

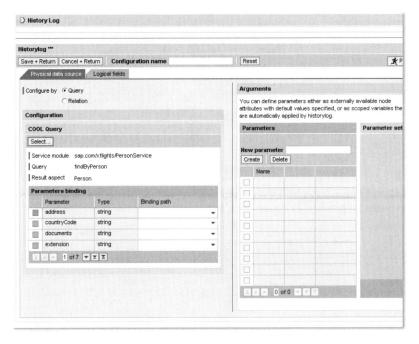

Figure 3.29 HistoryLog Pattern

In the tabstrip **Logical field**, macros can be used in order to display variants of physical data. You can find more on this in the section on macros.

User Assignment (Component)

Assigning roles This pattern enables you to assign roles to users. Users can be searched for according to different criteria such as e-mail address or name.

The pattern is a UI component which calls the UME in order obtain user data.

Figure 3.30 User Assignment Pattern

PropertyEditor (Component)

Creating an input screen You can use this pattern to generate simple input screens with a sequence of captions and fields. The configuration enables you to specify the caption, the selection of fields, the field types, the sequence and much more. This pattern is then used for instance on the tabstrips in the **ObjectEditor** in order to be able to enter detail information for the master record.

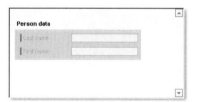

Figure 3.31 PropertyEditor Pattern

Configuration

Each UI pattern can be called by a URL. If the configuration dialog of a UI pattern is to be displayed, an additional syllable "Config" is added to the URL in the patterns supplied by SAP in the standard version. Example:

URL for the UI pattern **ObjectEditor** (replace *<host>* by the respective server name and *<port>* by the respective port number of the server):

*http://<host>:<port>/webdynpro/dispatcher/sap.com/caf~UI~ptn~
objecteditor/ObjectEditor*

URL

URL for the configuration dialog of the UI pattern **ObjectEditor**:

*http://<host>:<port>/webdynpro/dispatcher/sap.com/caf~UI~ptn~
objecteditor/ObjectEditorConfig*

The first services to be specified in the configuration dialogs are those, to be used by the UI. Each service can provide one or several operations. According to which type of operation or structure is being provided, you can speak of an *aspect* or a *query*. For clarity in the CAF it is of major importance, that—simply speaking—aspects corresponds to the entities or data structures respectively, while the FindBy operations of an entity or application service are referred to as queries.

Depending on the UI pattern, you can also specify field sequences, the display type of the fields, captions, layout, and embedded UI components etc. in the configuration. These settings are saved in a configuration file that can be given any name. For each UI pattern any number of configurations can be created.

During runtime, the name of the configuration file is simply added to the URL of the UI pattern as the parameter *app.configName,* and the UI is structured correspondingly. Then the URL for a configuration file with the name "EditPerson" looks as follows:

*http://<host>:<port>/webdynpro/dispatcher/sap.com/caf~UI~ptn~
objecteditor/ObjectEditor?app.configName=EditPerson*

The call of the configuration file in the configuration dialog has the following syntax:

*http://<host>:<port>/webdynpro/dispatcher/sap.com/caf~UI~ptn~
objecteditor/ObjectEditorConfig?app.configName=EditPerson*

The process to search for these configuration files and to transport these from one system into another is described in Section 3.12.3.

A central point of entry into the configurations of all patterns is provided by the configuration browser. You can launch it by using the following link:

http://<host>:<port>/webdynpro/dispatcher/sap.com/caf~UI~
configbrowser/ConfigBrowser

Restrictions

The following restrictions for UI patterns apply in the current version of CAF:

1. Attributes of an Entity Service that are defined as key or mandatory input fields are not highlighted in the UI pattern. The user is only notified about this fact by an error message, when those fields are filled when creating records.

2. In the UI patterns only the Java data type, but not the Java dictionary data type is displayed. This means that the information contained in the Java dictionary data type concerning length (e.g. short text with 50 characters with Java data type string) or format (e.g. for date or amount) is not available in the UI pattern and can therefore not be checked.

Macros

Macros are used in the **FlexTree** and **HistoryLog** patterns in order to display variants of physical data. The term *variants* can refer to the formatting of date and time, the display of complete URLs and so forth.

In total, the current CAF version provides the following macros:

▶ `@switch`
Compares the value of a mapped, physical field value with the logical field name.

▶ `@format`
Formats a field aspect.

▶ `@level`
Returns the name of the level.

▶ `@component_mime`
Returns the absolute path of a URL to the component mime type.

▶ `@app_mime`
Returns the absolute path of a URL to the application mime type.

▶ `@dc_mime`
Returns the absolute path of a URL to the development component mime type.

▶ `@sap_mime`
Returns the absolute path of a URL to the default screen.

Creating a Custom UI Pattern

Because the creation of patterns is still subject to major changes in the Web Dynpro technology, it is not possible at present to provide an introduction to this subject. We would therefore like you to refer to the SAP website, where in the future you will find a tutorial and documentation on this topic.

3.7.3   Web Dynpro Foundations

UI patterns are a fast and flexible way of creating user interfaces for applications. Due to their configurability, they enable the user to quickly perform adjustments. UI patterns however only cover a part of all the required types of input screens. Therefore Web Dynpro foundation UIs must be used.

The term Web Dynpro foundation describes the creation of UIs that can have any appearance and by using any UI elements with Web Dynpro. Provided it is not developed differently, a Web Dynpro foundation UI cannot be configured. Changes to it must be carried out by a developer in the Web Dynpro perspective.

Web Dynpro foundations require a *model* in order to be able to connect with services. A model can be created or imported and contains the structures of the services. These structures are required so the methods and input and output parameters can be mapped to the functions and fields of the UIs.

Model

In the CAF project, a Web Dynpro project is generated as a separate project whereby a typed Web Dynpro model is generated according to the structure of the services. This project only contains the models themselves but no other Web Dynpro components. This Web Dynpro project can then be referenced by the actual Web Dynpro project and the model can be used.

Integrating a UI Pattern

UI patterns that exist as components can be integrated into Web Dynpro foundations because they are exposed to the outside as a public part. In some patterns, other patterns were embedded, as is the case with the **ObjectSelector** where the UI pattern **SearchBar** is included.

Variant 1
The Web Dynpro foundation project must reference the following public parts here:

▶ `Caf/UI/ptn/common` — PublicPartRef CommonInterfaces

▶ `Caf/UI/ptn/common` — PublicPartRef com.sap.caf.ui.utils

Then a reference to the interface `caf/UI/ptn/common` must be set in the component.

In order to use the pattern, it is initialized in the coding:

```
IWDComponentUsage usage;
usage = wdThis.WdGet<Component referencename>
  ComponentUsage();
usage.createComponent(compName, devCompName);
```

In order to be able to access parameters the following coding can be used:

```
wdThis.wdGet<component reference name>.wdGetAPI().
 getContext().getRootNode().getCurrentElement().
 setAttributeValue("configName", <value>);

wdThis.wdGet.initialize();
```

Variant 2
The second variant is new and doesn't need any coding at all. All you have to do is to select the type **Web Dynpro Component** in the public parts as the component used. This provides the UI pattern component.

3.7.4 xFlights Example

In our example we have now defined the Entity Services and the application services. The input screens based on this use UI patterns and foundations. The screens described in the following sections are called by the user roles in the application.

Traveler

Travel profile
Basically, there are three input screens available to the traveler. The first of these is the maintenance of his travel profile with the preferences for air-

line, smoker/non-smoker etc. This input screen uses the UI pattern **ObjectEditor** with several tabstrips.

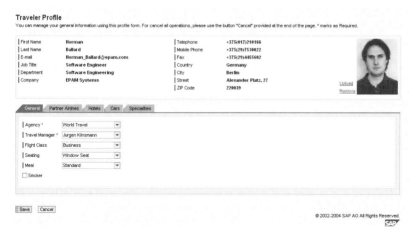

Figure 3.32 Travel Profile—UI Pattern ObjectEditor

The second step is to enter the traveler request (see Figure 3.33). This is a Web Dynpro foundation.

Traveler request

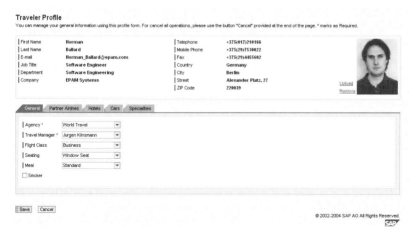

Figure 3.33 Traveler Request—Web Dynpro Foundation

The last UI for the traveler displays the flight connections (see Figure 3.34). In this UI, several patterns are unified in one screen. These patterns are the **FlexTree** to enter and display the desired flights and the **History-Log**, which displays the current changes to the flights by the persons involved (travel agent, manager and traveler).

Flight connection

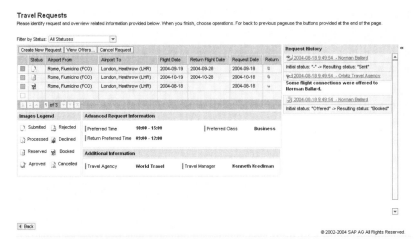

Travel Requests
Please identify request and overview related information provided below. When you finish, choose operations. For back to previous pageuse the buttons provided at the end of the page.

Filter by Status: All Statuses

Create New Request | View Offers... | Cancel Request

	Status	Airport From	Airport To	Flight Date	Return Flight Date	Request Date	Return
☐	🔲	Rome, Fiumicino (FCO)	London, Heathrow (LHR)	2004-09-19	2004-09-28	2004-09-18	✈
☐	🔲	Rome, Fiumicino (FCO)	London, Heathrow (LHR)	2004-10-19	2004-10-28	2004-10-18	✈
☐	🔲	Rome, Fiumicino (FCO)	London, Heathrow (LHR)	2004-08-18		2004-08-18	✈

◄◄ ◄ ◄ 1 of 3 ► ► ►►

Request History «

🔲 2004-08-18 9:49:54 - Norman Ballard
Initial status: "-" -> Resulting status: "Sent"

🔲 2004-08-18 9:49:54 - Orbitz Travel Agency
Some flight connections were offered to Norman Ballard.

🔲 2004-08-18 9:49:54 - Norman Ballard
Initial status: "Offered" -> Resulting status: "Booked"

Images Legend		Advanced Request Information	
🔲 Submitted 🔲 Rejected		Preferred Time	**10:00 - 15:00**	Preferred Class	**Business**
🔲 Processed 🔲 Declined		Return Preferred Time	**09:00 - 12:00**		
🔲 Reserved 🔲 Booked		**Additional Information**			
🔲 Approved 🔲 Cancelled		Travel Agency	**World Travel**	Travel Manager	**Kenneth Krediman**

◄ Back

© 2002-2004 SAP AG All Rights Reserved.

Figure 3.34 Flight Connections—UI Patterns FlexTree and HistoryLog

The travel agent

Flight connections The travel agent sees the traveler requests in the "Flight connections" UI already mentioned above. This UI, however, provides an additional view that uses the UI pattern **FlexTree** twice (see Figure 3.35). In the first **FlexTree**, you can see the flight itself, in the second one the individual connections of the entire flight.

Flights Connections
Please identify connections for this request. For cancel all operations and return to previous page please use the button "Cancel" provided at the end of the page. * marks as Required.
Departure on Monday, 20.09.2004, Business Class   From: Fiumicino (FCO), Italy   To: Heathrow (LHR), Great Britain

			From	To	Departure	Arrival	Duration	Stops »
☐	▼	◉	✈ Rome, Fiumicino (FCO)	London, Heathrow (LHR)	04:05	09:30	5:25	2
☐			• Rome, Fiumicino (FCO)	Milan, Malpensa (MXP)	04:05	05:00	0:55	0
☐			• Milan, Malpensa (MXP)	Berlin, Berlin-Tegel (TXL)	05:35	07:00	1:25	0
☐			• Berlin, Berlin-Tegel (TXL)	London, Heathrow (LHR)	07:30	09:30	2:00	0
☐	►	◉	✈ Rome, Fiumicino (FCO)	London, Heathrow (LHR)	04:05	09:10	5:05	2
☐								

◄◄ ◄ ◄ 1 of 5 ► ► ►►

Return on Friday, 24.09.2004   From: Heathrow (LHR), Great Britain   To: Fiumicino (FCO), Italy

			From	To	Departure	Arrival	Duration	Stops »
☐	►	◉	✈ London, Heathrow (LHR)	Rome, Fiumicino (FCO)	04:05	19:30	15:20	2
☐								
☐								
☐								
☐								

◄◄ ◄ ◄ 1 of 1 ► ► ►►

Booking Detail... | Cancel

© 2002-2004 SAP AG All Rights Reserved.

Figure 3.35 Flight Connections—UI Pattern FlexTree

Booking The view in the "Flight connections" UI also displays what status a flight connection is currently at, i.e.: if a traveler has accepted the suggested flight connection. Accepted flight connections can finally be booked by the travel agent and the confirmation e-mail can be sent to the manager and the traveler.

Figure 3.36 Booking—Web Dynpro Foundation

There were specific reasons for selecting the various UI patterns in this application. It is equally conceivable that instead of the **FlexTree** pattern, the **ObjectSelector** pattern is used. For the traveler request, it is also possible that an interactive form be used which corresponds to the paper version of such a form.

3.7.5 Special UI Elements

Selection Lists—CustomEnumType

The Entity Service **CustomEnumTypes** is used to display configurable selection lists displayed, for example, as selection fields in the UI. These selection lists are not generated in the modeler and then deployed on the server but are generated on the server itself. However, they can be serialized, saved locally, and re-imported in XML. In addition, there is also the option of supplying such enumerations. The CAF also supports the extraction of enumerations in a BW system.

Enumerations are created as follows:

1. Create a simple type in the dictionary of the String type and assign this type to an attribute in the Entity Service Modeler. This attribute is to display a selection list.

2. The name of the type—not the attribute—should be structured as follows: <vendor>.<application>.customtypes.<Name>

Creating enumerations

3. Create a CustomEnumType of the same name on the server and maintain the selection options.

At runtime, the system will detect that this attribute is not based on a simple data type but rather on an enumeration. This means a selection list is generated in the UI.

Maintaining enumeration types

The maintenance of the enumeration types is carried out through a Web Dynpro UI with the **TypeEditor** (see Figure 3.37).

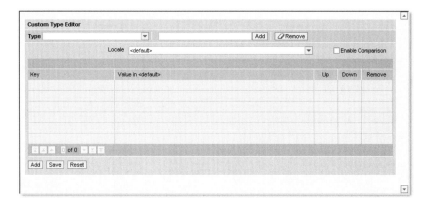

Figure 3.37 TypeEditor

Downloading data

The data of an enumeration can be downloaded locally. To do this, the **Restore** UI is available (see Figure 3.38).

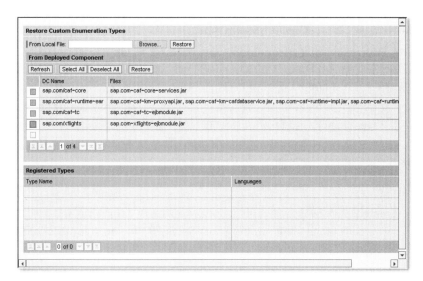

Figure 3.38 Restore UI for Types

Uploading data from a local persistence or from the server occurs with the **Backup** UI (see Figure 3.39).

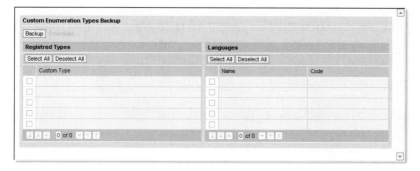

Figure 3.39 Backup UI for Types

Loading from the server is then necessary if the data is supplied together with an application. This means that the data is available on the server, but it cannot yet be accessed by the application.

If a more flexible and two-level categorization of a data record is to be carried out, you should use another option. In this case you should use the Entity Service **Category** as an attribute (see Section 3.5.3.).

F4 Help

In Web Dynpro, the interface IWDOVS exists that can transfer input and output parameters as well as search methods to a model. If this interface is linked to a field an input help with a search template based on a service will be generated.

F1 Help

The F1 help, i.e. the link to a help document is currently only available in those patterns that are defined as pages (i.e. not in the components). The links to the help refer to the SAP Knowledge Management.

Excel UI Reporting Component

This component is already integrated in some patterns such as the **Flex-Tree** and is also available to the Web Dynpro foundations. By using this component, data from the application can be saved locally as text or CSV files. Similar to the other component patterns, this one is referenced in the design time, and a query is specified as a data source for the export. This component also enables you to set filters and it provides a preview.

The name of the component is `sap.com~caf~UI~ptn~reporting` and is used for instance in the report UI for the authorization display.

In the CAF, an API is also available which provides the reverse path, namely loading data from an Excel file into an xApp. However this integration must be coded, which is why we only mention the component name here for the sake of completeness: `sap.com~caf~runtime~exceldataimport~impl`.

3.8 Process Modeler

3.8.1 Introduction

Since the individual components of an application have been discussed in the previous sections, the next step is to integrate these into a process. Processes work at several levels.

Logical sequence of UIs First of all they represent a logical sequence of user interfaces and actions. In order to carry out a specific task, data is entered and analyzed by the user. User interfaces and actions are the individual units of a process, and they are themselves logical and complete. Several user interfaces and actions can in turn be combined in such a unit. If you place such logical units in sequence, and subsequent units depend on previous ones, you will get an initial impression of a process.

Based on this type of data being entered or analyzed, other user interfaces can be called or actions can be triggered which can run simultaneously or with a delay in the background. Typically, simultaneous actions are short-term, delayed actions requiring either more runtime and/or computer capacity. They are therefore executed at later times, or they must wait for the result of another action as they receive their output as an input.

Collaborative aspects Some of these actions are executed through the collaboration of several users. Processes must therefore also support collaborative aspects. This incorporates different activities, from sending e-mails to internal and external user groups, to setting up and using discussion forums, to forwarding process steps to colleagues.

Ideally, the sequence of process steps or their enhancement by collaborative functions can be adapted by the users themselves, according to the specific requirements, without having to refer to a developer each time.

Based on this description, you can understand what kind of requirements a process modeling tool has to meet. For the CAF this tool is called *Guided Procedures*.

3.8.2 Guided Procedures

Guided Procedures (GP) is a status-management-based tool that enables the integration of actions and collaborative functionality into a process. Actions call user interfaces or background steps. A process is divided into phases which in turn are divided into steps. A process step corresponds to a closed logical unit, can be carried out sequentially or in parallel to another process step, and can be a compulsory or optional step.

The status of every action can be transmitted to the Guided Procedure Framework and can be forwarded to subsequent actions. The status states whether a process step or a process phase is open, is being processed, or has already been completed. This information is important in starting actions that depend on this step or in activating subsequent steps or phases.

The status of a process step

In addition to the status, the context of every action of the Guided Procedure is also transferred. Depending on the implementation, the context contains the key of the processed data records, the user data, and any type of other data. Forwarding the context to the Guided Procedure Framework allows subsequent actions and user interfaces to be populated so that the same context can be further processed.

Context

In order to use Guided Procedures, the corresponding libraries must first be installed. If the CAF core has already been installed all you need to do is to add the CAFGP and CAFMP libraries (for the modeler and picker). If no CAF core has been installed yet, the CAFUM library is also required for the UME. Clearly, a CAF developer must install this library both in the development and runtime environments. After carrying out some of the configuration steps according to the documentation, you can start developing.

Prerequisites

Actions

Actions are the central element to start background steps or call user interfaces. Actions connect processes with applications and link their input and output parameters with each other. You can call three different types of user interfaces. These are:

- ▶ Web Dynpro
- ▶ Interactive Form
- ▶ URLs

Web services can also be called from actions.

User Interface

Special Guided Procedure interfaces must be implemented in order to notify the Guided Procedure Framework of the Java-based user interfaces and actions,. These interfaces enable the status and context transfer.

Web Dynpro foundation   For UIs based on the Web Dynpro foundation for instance, the Guided Procedures Action Interface is available (`com.sap.caf.gp.ui.inter-faces.action.IAction`). This interface provides several methods that in effect contain the context (configuration, input and output parameters). If an application implements this interface, its input and output parameters can be assigned to the corresponding Guided Procedures context.

Web Dynpro pattern   In the previous sections the use of the UI patterns was strongly recommended. In these patterns, the Guided Procedures Action Interface is only partially integrated.

Interactive forms   Interactive forms are user interfaces, very similar in appearance to print forms. Their advantage lies in the fact that on the one hand they make it easier for users to change from print forms to the electronic versions, and on the other hand data can be directly saved electronically, thus avoiding an further intermediate step for data entry. Interactive forms can be used for linear data entry and display and can also be used asynchronously (offline).

A disadvantage that must be mentioned here, however, is that only linear data entry is supported with such a UI. The context of such a user interface, as is the case for Web Dynpro applications that implement the interface of the Guided Procedures Action Interface, can be mapped to the context of the Guided Procedures templates.

Modeling tip   Interactive forms should only be used in exceptional cases. They are particularly useful if simple and linear entries are involved, and if a large number of users should be enabled to change from using the print version to the electronic version without having to carry out intensive training.

Process Templates

If all the required applications are available in the form of actions and user interfaces, then the actual procedure to form the process begins. The transactions are integrated in a process template. In the browser-based tool, steps and phases are added, transactions are integrated, contexts are mapped, collaborative elements are included, roles are assigned, start values are set and so forth.

A template created in such a way can then be supplied. As soon as the template has been published, it cannot be changed but can only be copied, or a new version can be created and this can be changed. The reason for this limitation is the longevity of processes once started. Under certain circumstances, they can last for several years. If the template for such a process was changed subsequently it could lead to inconsistencies in the statuses of the process steps and phases. By the way, a copied template contains no information on the original it was derived from.

As Guided Procedures provides an almost entirely browser-based development interface, the creation of a template can typically also be carried out by a user with the corresponding authorizations (and knowledge). The presence of a developer is not necessary. This provides a greater flexibility and allows new processes of a similar type to be quickly adopted.

In the process templates, in addition to the metadata, the texts are stored in an XLF file, which can be translated.

Picker

The picker is a search and selection tool. When templates and actions are being created, the picker supports the search and selection of the following resources:

▶ Actions
▶ Process templates
▶ Process context parameters
▶ Users and roles
▶ Process roles

The picker can also be used within an action by Web Dynpro applications that implement the Guided Procedures Action Interface.

3.9　Business Intelligence Integration

Nowadays, it is no longer sufficient to create applications which have no links to high-performance analytical systems. In recent years, data warehouses and data mining tools have assumed a prominent position beside transactional systems such as the classical ERP systems, CRM or SCM. Transactional systems are mainly optimized for entering data while analytical systems are mainly optimized towards the evaluation of data.

Modern business applications are very strongly integrated with analyses and evaluations, which to all intents and purposes can account for 50 % of the actual solution. For the users, it becomes increasingly less recognizable from which system the displayed data originates. And for the work of a developer, this knowledge is not important at all.

The following descriptions refer to the xApp integration of the data warehouse, SAP BW.

3.9.1　Types of Integration

Analytical systems are connected in several ways with the transactional application.

Extraction

▶ **Extraction of data from a transactional or analytical system into an analytical system**
This involves copying, transforming, and enriching data from a persistence for transactional or analytical purposes into a persistence for analytical operations, using extractors and transformation rules. Extractors are the program code which reads the data from the source persistence, links it and already transforms it partially. The transformation adjusts the data to the data maintenance in the data warehouse, for instance by standardizing the data formats or by using the master data key. Data prepared in such a way is stored in specific data storage facilities in the data warehouse that are optimized for analysis requirements.

This effectively means that the extractors for master data, texts, hierarchies and transaction data must be developed in order to load data into the data warehouse. These extractors should support delta and lock mechanisms and, if necessary, should unify data from several tables and views or "glean" data from different structures.

Display

▶ **Display of analysis and transactions in the same window pane**
In modern roll-based applications, the boundary between the analytical and transactional parts is becoming increasingly blurred. In an ideal

scenario, a user should no longer be able to recognize from which system the data displayed on the screen is coming.

The application can display the data from the analytical report and the transaction on one page, as it normally occurs in the SAP Enterprise Portal with iViews and Business Pages. Another variant is the data that is called during runtime from an SAP BW interface such as the OLAP BAPIs or the SDK, and is displayed in a common window pane together with the transactional data.

► **Retraction of data from the analytical system into the transactional application**

The result of an analysis or statistical evaluation is used as a starting point for transactional tasks. For this reason, a retraction, in other words a "re-extraction," of data from the analytical system to the transactional system is necessary in certain scenarios. The data itself doesn't necessarily have to be written into the transactional system. It can also be requested dynamically from the analytical system.

A well-known example of retraction is the implementation of an ABC analysis of customers with a data-mining tool. The customer master records in transactional systems are then adapted and divided into A (highly profitable), B (profitable) and C (less profitable to unprofitable) customers. Then customers marked A can be selected for a campaign.

Retraction

► **Navigation between the report and the application and vice-versa**

The blurred boundary between transactional and analytical systems already mentioned above means in practice that you can navigate flexibly between the analysis and the transaction. Based on aggregated data in a report for instance, filters are set gradually and drilldowns are carried out in order to change data from the result after several navigation steps. This activitiy automatically takes you from the analytical application to the transaction. SAP systems provide different variants here which will be more closely described in Section 3.9.5.

Navigation

3.9.2 Extraction

The Business Information Warehouse provides the BW service API for the ABAP world, which can be imported as an add-on in the ABAP systems. The BW service API contains tools to create extractors, carry out tests and implement different types of delta mechanisms. These tools enable the extraction of data from the transactional system, without threatening the data consistency because of changes during extraction, and without locking data storages for the transaction during the extraction process.

BW service API

Another challenge we have to face when working with the CAF is the extraction of data from typically distributed persistence of a CAF-based application. Theoretically, it would be possible to extract data from the remotely connected system through the CAF. However, this would lead to confusion if the back-end systems are not extracted directly but through an intermediate system. It is therefore advisable to extract the data from an external system directly by using the extractors provided there.

ABAP-specific The BW service API is provided only to the ABAP world but not to the Java stack used by the CAF. Therefore, in the following sections we will describe which options are available to the CAF developer in order to balance out this restricted functionality.

Universal Data Connect and BW Service API

The data from a CAF-based application is stored on the Java platform of SAP NetWeaver '04. In order to extract this data into the BW, you must establish a connection from the ABAP platform of the BW to the Java platform of the application. To do this, SAP provides the *Universal Data Connect* (UD Connect). In addition to XMLA, ODBO and SAP Query, UD Connect uses the Java Database Connectivity (JDBC) from Sun, which is the standard interface for connections to relational database management systems. JDBC drivers are now available for 170 different data sources.

A fifth variant called "CAF" was created for CAF-based applications to enable Java API requests from UD Connect. For this reason, an operation of the "BW extractor" type must be created in the application service. In the CAF persistence, it is made sure that deleted data records are extracted during extraction as well as the conversions of diverse attributes, such as user GUID in the data types which the SAP BW can use.

Applications created with the BI Java Software Development Kit (BI Java SDK) can now use the JDBC integrated in the BI JDBC Connector. This enables SAP BW to access these data sources. In the current case this means that the following libraries must be installed on the SAP J2EE server in order to be able to access the database of the Java stack:

▶ BI JDBC Connector Library (already installed with SAP BW 3.5)

▶ UD Connect Library

▶ JDBC driver for the respective database

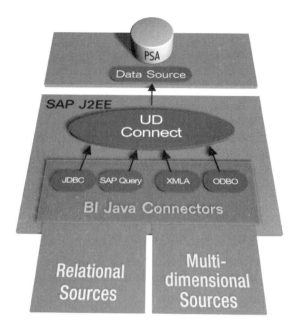

Figure 3.40 Universal Data Connect

If these libraries are installed and configured, extraction from the tables or via the views can be started.

Extractions can actually be carried out, but for applications usually more is expected than just a simple extraction from individual tables. The following points must therefore be taken into consideration:

▶ Locking concept

▶ Data field lengths

▶ Delta load mechanisms

▶ Complex extraction logic

In an application created with CAF, entities are saved in several tables in the database. In order to avoid data inconsistencies that can emerge in these table due to changes to data records during the data extraction, the relevant tables must either be locked or other mechanisms must be applied.

Locking concept

For this reason, the Enqueue Server is used. This provides several APIs that can be used to provide individual data records or entire tables with a lock flag. This lock is not exactly identical to a database lock, as it is ineffective unless an application developer includes it in the extractor coding.

While database locks are always queried without the interference of developers, the program coding must explicitly call the APIs of the enqueue server in certain cases. It must also request data records that might be locked or tables and then carry out the corresponding actions. In the CAF, the JDO ensures that the locks of the enqueue server are queried and actions are carried out correspondingly.

By using process chains that call the actual extraction process from a start program which locks the structures to be extracted in the Java stack, and an end program which in turn unlocks the extracted structures, the requirement for consistent data to be loaded is met. On the Java stack, another class is necessary. This is supplied with the CAF runtime. This class is located between the enqueue server and the lock call from the SAP BW in order to maintain a session. If the session was completed, the enqueue server would otherwise automatically reset the lock. ABAP sample coding which sets these locks is supplied with the documentation.

This solution has the following advantages and disadvantages:

▶ Advantages

   ▷ Data can be loaded consistently.

   ▷ UD Connect is used for extraction.

   ▷ Delta mechanisms of the BW service API can be used.

▶ Disadvantages

   ▷ Due to the locks set, the application cannot update any new data or change existing data.

   ▷ On the SAP side (not relevant for customer projects): The data sources generated by UD Connect cannot be provided with SAP BW 3.5.[9]

   ▷ On the SAP side (not relevant for customer projects): For the same reason as above, process chains can also not be supplied but must be built up in a separate implementation project.

Data field lengths InfoObjects in SAP BW are the basic modules for InfoCubes, ODS objects and reports in the BW. InfoObjects are restricted to 60 characters in their field length. This means that these requirements must be taken into con-

---

9 Background information: The generated data sources have the prefix "6" which cannot be supplied in version D. This version is the version of BW objects generated by SAP. The objects created and changed by users are generated as version A, but they can be transferred. You can find more information on versioning in Section 3.12.7.

sideration from the beginning when building the application and only data types should be used that comply with this requirement. Otherwise, a transformation must be carried out at the time of extraction.

For applications with large data volumes, it is logical that the entire content of the underlying tables is not loaded into the BW each time, but rather only the changed and new data records. This process is referred to as a *delta load*. It avoids long load times and locks on the database.

Delta load mechanism

At the beginning of every first-time load process, there is an initial load which extracts all data records contained in tables into the BW. All subsequent load processes are then delta loads.

Depending on the exact structure of the transaction, the use of an enqueue server and a delta queue, the type of delta mechanism and the type of the data target are determined. You can find more information on the individual delta load mechanisms in the SAP BI Reference Guide.

In this case, more complex extraction logic must be mapped on the BW side in the ABAP stack. The BW provides options to do this at the following points:

Complex extraction logic

1. Extractor

2. Start routine

3. Transfer rule

4. Update rule

Web Service Entry of the Delta Queue

One variant which results from the combination with the SAP Exchange Infrastructure (XI) is the use of messages sent from the CAF application through XI to the BW during the time of the update. In the Web service entrance to the Delta queue, the data records wait to be picked up by the BW. The necessary initial load could then be carried out upfront using the variant with UD Connect.

▶ Advantages

  ▷ Delta processes for all updates

  ▷ No locks

▶ Disadvantages

  ▷ Installation of the SAP Exchange Infrastructure is necessary.

DataStaging BAPIs

The DataStaging BAPIs provide the option of calling an API on the Java or any other stack from the BW. This API must be started as a service on the database or application server. On the BW side this service is published and registered as a non-SAP source system or third-party system.

▶ Advantages

  ▷ Data can be loaded consistently.

  ▷ Extraction logic can be stored in the API.

  ▷ Tried-and-tested technology.

▶ Disadvantages

  ▷ The CAF provides no generic API.

  ▷ Complex development is required in order to make this API sufficiently flexible and stable[10].

  ▷ Delta mechanism must be implemented in the API.

3.9.3 Display

OLAP BAPI/SDK

While the previous sections on the integration of SAP BW with the CAF predominantly dealt with the extraction of data from the CAF into SAP BW, the OLAP BAPI (Online Analytical Processing) and the Software Development Kit (SDK) built around it enable you to use data from the BW in other applications. This involves a generic interface which provides data from the data providers of the BW and the corresponding metadata and context for the individual result values by setting parameters on the call. This is referred to as a multidimensional result set.

This interface enables the dynamic integration of data from the BW into the xApp, and also the extraction of data into the persistence of the calling application. The latter case is referred to as retraction. In general, and for performance reasons, this interface is not suitable for mass data requests.

You can find more information on the OLAP BAPI/SDK in the SAP BI Reference Guide. Examples and additional links can be found on the SAP Developer Network (SDN) at *http://sdn.sap.com/*.

---

10 For example, you have to access the metadata of the data structure to permit changes to the application without having to change the API as well. The calling BW service must be queried for the structure of the data source to provide the result in a corresponding structure. Apart from this, additional extraction and transformation logic must be integrated into the API and so forth.

3.9.4 Retraction

Retraction means the extraction of data from the BW into a transactional application. To do this, the application requires APIs that can be supplied with data by the BW. Technologies for reading out data from the BW are for example the OLAP BAPI/SDK already mentioned and the Open Hub.

3.9.5 Navigation

A flexible navigation should be possible between reports from the analytical application and the input screens from the transactional application. By navigation, we mean a seamless integration of display and input between different levels of detail and aggregation of the application data.

Example: The xFlights scenario begins with an analysis of the passenger data at the flight level where the number of passengers per flight number is displayed for information purposes. In the next navigation step, you expand the view to include the names of all passengers. If you have found the passenger for whom you want to change the data, you select this passenger and the change screen opens. It is not important for the user that in the first navigation steps they received data from an analytical system and in the last step they are working on data in the transactional system.

This navigation and also the opposite navigation direction can be executed in different ways with SAP-proprietary technologies. The most well-known is the report-report interface, although this is provided for navigation between ABAP systems. To navigate between ABAP and Java systems, the following options are available.

Report-report interface

Web API

The BW provides the Web API to call and parameterize its Web reports. The appearance of reports (Web reports) created as HTML pages by BW, the filters used, and the navigation status can all be manipulated using parameters.

By adding a few values in the URL of the example above, a specific flight can be filtered, a breakdown of the passenger data into a hierarchy according to origin can be given, and the exchange of the results axes can be done—all at the same time.

In this way a precisely set analytical report can be called from a transactional application. The navigational directions which are possible in this context are:

Navigation directions

- From BW to BW
- From (x)App to BW

You can find more information on the subject of Web API in the relevant documents in SAP Service Marketplace by using the *BW* link.

Table Interface

If you want to do the opposite and call an input screen from an xApp, you can use the table interface to do so. Provided that the Java application can be called and possibly even be parameterized via a URL, the table interface provides the option of calling the Java application by making changes or adding hyperlinks in the multi-dimensional result set of the Web report. As the ABAP table interface classes are called before the HTML coding for the Web report is generated, the appearance and behavior of the Web report can therefore be adapted in any way you like. The navigational directions that are possible in this context are:

- From BW to BW
- From BW to (x)App

Drag&Relate

This extremely handy feature of the SAP Enterprise Portal enables navigation between iViews and the data records and systems, by dragging a data record and dropping it at a specific destination. For example, a traveler can be moved to an iView called "Flight data" where all flight data for this traveler is displayed.

Disadvantage The disadvantage of this variant lies in the fact that usually only one data record at a time can be transferred to the target iView. In addition, the users do not always know right away how to use the application. The navigational directions that are possible in this context are:

- From BW to BW
- From (x)App to BW
- From (x)App to (x)App

Portal-side Eventing

Communication between iViews The SAP Enterprise Portal permits client-side eventing. That means that several iViews in the portal can communicate with each other. In order to exchange data between Web dynpros and BW reports this technology can be used. The navigational directions that are possible in this context are:

- ▶ From BW to BW
- ▶ From (x)App to BW
- ▶ From (x)App to (x)App

For this reason several prerequisites must be met:

Prerequisites

- ▶ The iViews involved must run in the same domain.
- ▶ The iView sending the information must be able to send an event (`WDPortalEventing.fire`).
- ▶ The iView receiving such information must subscribe to an event (`WDPortalEventing.subscribe`).

Eventing is not included in the UI patterns of the CAF and is therefore only possible in the Web Dynpro foundation. In contrast to Drag&Relate it is simply possible here to transfer several data records to another iView. You can find a detailed eventing example in the SAP Enterprise Portal Reference Guide.

3.9.6 Guided Procedures

Data from the Guided Procedures which appear relevant for evaluation in the BW is primarily the duration and status of the process steps and phases. Guided Procedures therefore provide an API to extract this data.

3.10 Knowledge Management Integration

The SAP Knowledge Management (KM), which is supplied with the SAP Enterprise Portal is integrated in several ways by the CAF, i.e. by the following objects which have already been introduced in the previous sections:

- ▶ Entity Service **Document**
- ▶ Application Service **DocumentContent**
- ▶ UI Pattern **Attachment**

With these objects, documents can be stored, viewed and changed in the KM as attachments to instances.

The KM also provides other functionalities that are relevant for searching metadata and data records. These functionalities involve indexing and searching for texts of any type which goes beyond the scope of a normal database search.

Indexing and searching

3.10.1 TREX

This functionality is provided by the TREX ("full Text Retrieval and Infor-mation Extraction"). By using the *Repository Managers,* you can search and index different persistences. There are repository managers for file directories, databases and so on.

For the CAF, a repository manager is available that runs in KM and can access the metadata texts and the data records of the CAF. An index of the texts is created in KM and is updated automatically when changes occur.

As the result of a search, a hierarchy is provided whose top level is repre-sented by the Entity Service and which comprises the instances as nodes, i.e. the individual data records. The search methods are implemented as separate operations in the Entity Service. Different additional methods that use the KM search functionality can be generated by setting the **SAP NetWeaver Knowledge Management** property. These methods include the following:

▶ `searchIdxForSimilar(IBusinessObject object, int maxRe-sult)`

▶ `searchidxForBOInRelatedDoc(String v)`

▶ `findByKMPropertySearch(Map mapAttributeNameToFilter, Map mapCategoryNameToFilter)`

Using QueryEntries, these generic operations can be freely configured with regard to the filter values for attributes and content as well as to the logical operators and the search method. An example could be the search for the name Catherine with all its different spellings. The field "first name" (attribute) is to be searched for "Katherine" (content) with all its variants, such as "Catharine," "Katherine," and "Cathryn" (fuzzy search), but not for "Catherine" (logical operator).

In order for such a search to run effectively the data and metadata must first be indexed. This can be done in the **IndexAdmin** UI (see Figure 3.41).

In contrast to a pure database search (see Section 3.5.3), the TREX search provides the advantage that an extended wildcard search (the search with placeholders) is possible. Similarly, a search for text components with varying upper case and lower case spelling is no problem.

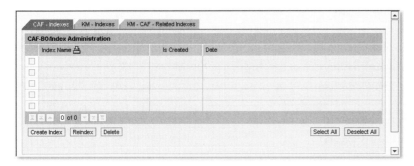

Figure 3.41 IndexAdmin UI

3.10.2 Discussion

The discussion is available as an Entity Service.

3.10.3 Notification & Subscription

If a change is made to the instance of an Entity Service, services that would be impacted by this change should be notified. Such a notification should be sent to all registered subscribers.

In the generated coding for the Entity Services, calls for the **Notification** service are included in the methods `ejbCreate`, `ejbStore` and `ejbRemove`. In the case of an instance change the SAP Knowledge Management Notification service processes an XML-based process template and sends this to the subscribers with the message about the change.

Notification service

The **Subscription** service saves the subscription information either in a database or as an XML file and differentiates between two types of subscriptions: the "deployed" and the "registered" subscription. The **Notification** service itself only knows the registered subscription. In order to manage subscriptions a UI is available.

Subscription service

3.11 Additional Integrations

3.11.1 Exchange Infrastructure

In simple terms the SAP Exchange Infrastructure (XI) is a system that facilitates the communication between different systems. Individual systems don't need to know much about other systems any longer, they only have to be aware of XI as this is where you send your data. It transforms the data and forwards it to the corresponding target systems. This can happen both synchronously and asynchronously.

In order for XI to be able to communicate with the systems, it not only needs the Connector Framework but it must also know which services are available, and what are the methods and fields of these services. XI stores this information in a separate service repository. In XI, these services can be mapped to each other and transformation rules can be defined. The CAF can communicate with the services via XI. For the CAF, the services on the XI are nothing else than Web services and can thus be imported as external services.

> Integration of the Enterprise Service Repository (ESR) is planned for the next version of SAP NetWeaver. This is a repository that will be used by both the CAF and the SAP XI in order to store and call services.

3.11.2 Replication und Synchronization

SAP NetWeaver and hence also the CAF currently don't possess the generic scope to replicate and synchronize data.

3.12 Supply and Maintenance

3.12.1 Configuration

The central entry to the configuration and to other tools for a CAF-based application is accessible using the following URL:

http://<host>:<port>/caf/Config

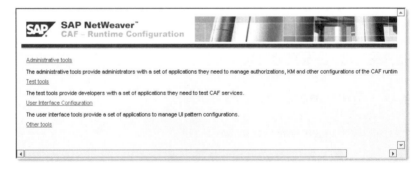

Figure 3.42 Central Entry to all Configuration Screens and Management Tools

3.12.2 Java Development Infrastructure

The SAP Java Development Infrastructure (JDI) basically consists of SAP NetWeaver Developer Studio, the Design Time Repository, the Component Build Server, and the Change Management Service. Due to the combination of these components Java projects can be developed, built and deployed as distributed projects. In addition there are also versioning, merge and test functionalities available. The merge functionality is of importance insofar as it provides a basis to combine customer changes with SAP changes.

Design Time Repository

The Design Time Repository (DTR) is the SAP solution for central management and versioning of sources in a distributed development. The DTR is a central system which developers can log onto with SAP NetWeaver Developer Studio. If during the creation of a project it is marked as DTR-relevant by selecting the corresponding development component (DC), the underlying files will be written to an activity for each change and each new object. An activity thus keeps account of which files were changed and informs the DTR of this. An activity can then be released at any time by the developer, which means that all files based on the activity are checked-in to the DTR and are thus uploaded. This means the files are visible and available for all other developers who are working on the same project. The DTR can be used to synchronize all the files that are located in the DTR and on the local system of the developer.

If the files are checked in, all developers involved in the project can change the files. A change then automatically causes a corresponding remark in the DTR so that other developers cannot make changes to the file until it has been checked in again by the developer who is currently making these changes. This avoids conflicts caused by simultaneous changes to the same file.

From a technical point of view, all files that have been synchronized by the DTR on a local host are set to "read only." If you now want to change a file, SAP NetWeaver Developer Studio realizes this and sets the file to "changeable" and at the same time calls the dialog for this activity.

If the DTR should not be available (due to network problems, hardware defects, system crash—although the latter does not happen with SAP systems), the "read-only" property can also be changed manually. As a developer, however, you must be aware that you have to take the full responsibility for errors that might occur then.

Management and versioning

Two perspectives are available in Developer Studio to use the DTR: the Design Time Repository and the Development Components Perspectives. In general, the developer uses the second perspective.

Comparison to ABAP
The DTR counterpart in the ABAP world is the transport system. In this context, an activity corresponds to the transport or the transport task. The checking-in of an activity is thus comparable to the release of the transport or the transport task and the subsequent import and activation.

CAF metadata project must be checked out
If the Design Time Repository for CAF projects is used, you must ensure above all that the metadata project is completely checked out every time from the DTR. This project contains all XML files with the metadata that describe the services. As changes to one service cause changes to several of these XML files, the files must be changeable. If they are not, the changes are not completely saved and the project becomes inconsistent and fails.

Component Build Server

The Component Build Server (CBS) creates runtime objects such as the Java archives from the objects checked into the DTR by using a build. These builds are generated incrementally by considering the dependent components. The archives thus generated can then be deployed on the J2EE server.

For a CAF project, this means that the project metadata, the dictionary files, and classes that are checked in to the DTR can be built centrally.

Change Management Service

The Change Management Service (CMS) adopts the result of the CBS and installs, distributes and deploys it.

3.12.3 Projects

Technically speaking, a project consists of one or several directories on one or several computers in which all metadata, classes and other files for the objects are stored. One or several developers work with these projects and generate the objects.

CA

For a composite application or an xApp project a *composite application project* is created. This takes place in the Composite Application Services Perspective of SAP NetWeaver Developer Studio. In the navigation display of the project, all the services created in the project are displayed.

Due to the CAF architecture and the nature of the data created and generated, when creating a CA project there are actually six projects with different "natures" generated in the background. The term "nature" refers to the type of a project. This type is represented by different additionally created files, directory structures or functionalities generated during the build. In Eclipse, the nature of a project is specified in the *.project* file; a project can possess several natures. This file is located in the root directory of the project.

Natures

In the case of the CAF the following project natures are available:

1. Dictionary
2. Metadata
3. EJB
4. Enterprise
5. Web Dynpro
6. UME permissions

This complexity is concealed in the CAS perspective, but it can be uncovered by using other navigation views or perspectives. The project types were already described in Section 3.3.3. We will just go into detail once more on the Web Dynpro.

Web Dynpro

UI patterns are supplied with the CAF installation. What are missing are the configuration files for the respective application. For this reason, the repository browser is available. It provides a simple search for configurations and their downloads and uploads. The repository browser is called for searching and downloading using the screen displayed in Figure 3.43.

Repository browser

The tool displayed in Figure 3.44 is used for the upload.

This tool is above all suitable for a simple and fast transport of configuration files. If an application is to be delivered from the development department to a customer, this process is only partly sufficient. The recommended way is to use a Web Dynpro project. Here, in the *src\configuration* path a new folder called *Config* is created, followed by an additional folder with the complete name of the model class.

This project is then checked in to the DTR, supplied and installed. In this context, the configuration files are stored in the correct repository on the J2EE server.

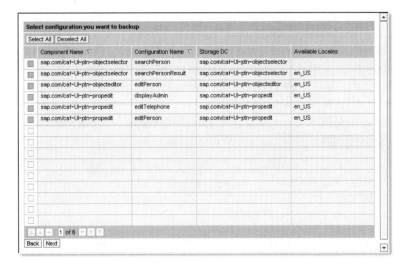

Figure 3.43 Repository Backup

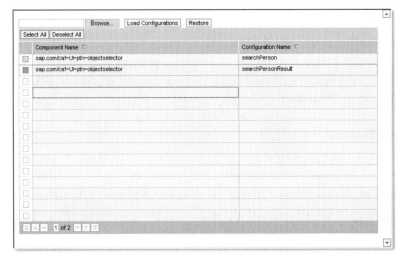

Figure 3.44 Repository Restore

Example

If the model class in the Web Dynpro project is located in the path **Web Dynpro · Models** and the name of the application is **ModelRelationshipsTab · Model Classes · myConfiguration**, then the folder name appears as follows: *com.sap.xpd.relationship.myConfiguration*

The complete path would then be:

src\configuration\Config\com.sap.xpd.relationship.myConfiguration\myConfiguration

It is advisable to keep the names and paths as short as possible.

Modeling tip

3.12.4 Testing and Monitoring

The CAF Services use the APIs of the Java Application Response Time Monitoring (JARM) that provide information on performance, status etc. of a service. The monitoring tool can be called in the Visual Administrator of the J2EE server.

3.12.5 Debugging

There are several debugging options in the CAF:

▶ **Setting program stops**
Setting program stops is carried out in the J2EE perspective. There the folder for the CAF Development Component is opened in the J2EE DC Explorer. In the **ejbModule** folder, the corresponding **MyProgram-Name-ServiceBean.java** class is opened and the program stop is set in the code editor.

▶ **Switching on the debugging mode**
By right-clicking on the selection in the J2EE Engine you can select **Server enable debugging of process** and thus view the debug port.

▶ **Starting the debugging session**
In the J2EE perspective, **Run · Debug.. · Remote Java Application** is selected from the menu. By right-clicking, you can select **New** in the menu which opens. Select the project and specify the server and port of the J2EE Engine. Then you select the **Apply** and **Debug** buttons.

If you now start and use the application, the program stops at the locations where the program stops have been set.

3.12.6 Documentation and Help

If the application is created with CAF, you need documentation that contains the installation, functional scope for the end users, and technical information for a developer or consultant. The F1 help is available in the Web Dynpro user interfaces. The technical documentation should contain a description of the services, UI patterns and Web Dynpro foundations, Guided Procedures templates and all other relevant components used.

3.12.7 Internationalization

The metadata model which the CAF services are based on does not support any multilingual capability in the current release. However, at the Web Dynpro level, and in this specific case, at the patterns level, you not only have the option of assigning different texts to the fields than those supplied through services, but also the option of generating multilingual capability.

Service customization

The *Service Customization* tool enables the creation of texts for each entity and application service in the UI. The texts are stored in a language file with the file ending .xlf. The file name contains the language identifier. The file is then checked in to the DTR like any other project file and can then be released there for further translation. Figure 3.45 illustrates this tool.

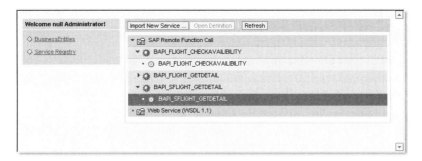

Figure 3.45 Service Customization

Each user in the SAP Enterprise Portal has specified his or her "locale." Among other things this variable determines which language or date and number formats are displayed. If there is a corresponding translation for the user's locale it will automatically be displayed. If not, the default language of the system appears.

3.12.8 Upgrade and Versioning

The SAP xApps and composite applications based on CAF and supplied by SAP are generally supplied without the source code and without the relevant project files. Changes to the services are thus only possible at the predefined locations with configuration dialogs.

For all other applications developed with the CAF for which the source files were also supplied, there is the option to execute changes. It must be possible to merge these with the manufacturer's upgrades. This task is performed by the Change Management Service of the SAP Java Development Infrastructure.

The type of the parts supplied with an application created with CAF will be different in the future. It is planned that only the metadata will be supplied, and the customer will carry out the generation, build and deployment. This means you will be able to carry out adaptations to the standard version according to customer-specific factors.

In SAP BW, the merge functions due to a versioning concept that divides the metadata of the Business Content in A, D and M versions. A stands for active, D for delivered and M for modified. SAP only supplies metadata in version D. These cannot be changed by the customers. As soon as customers activate the Business Content, i.e. as soon as they transfer it from version D to version A, they have created their own version. If customer-side modifications are made to Business Content, a version M is temporarily created which only becomes version A when it is activated.

Comparison to BW

If SAP now supplies an enhanced version of Business Content, in the customer system the D version will first of all be overwritten. Once D is transferred to A merge of both versions is performed by the BW. According to the type and extent of the change, this process can sometimes cause problems.

The CAF currently doesn't recognize such a versioning. However, an upgrade is possible by merging modified and delivered metadata as well as through the CMS.

3.13 Modeling Guidelines

When constructing the xFlights scenario described in this book, different modeling aspects have already been described. This section once again provides a summarized description of the effects of all modeling variants on persistence, performance, enhanceability, integration scope, extractability, and re-useability. We will also explore the clarity of the design and the effects it can have as an application is created and used by people. If the design and user guidance of an application are difficult to understand, there is not much chance that the application will be enhanced and used, and it can also only be maintained with much effort.

Another factor to weigh in deciding in favor of a specific design or type of modeling is whether the application is developed by a company for its own use, by a software provider on behalf of a company, or by a software provider as a standard application.

Decisions on the design based on finances, scarce resources, or simply lack of information will be neglected here.

3.13.1 Data Types

Packages For a CAF project, the following four packages with data types are available by default:

▶ com.sap.caf.base

▶ com.sap.caf.core

▶ com.sap.caf.runtime

▶ com.sap.dictionary.predefined.currency

Modeling tip The most important package is the second one in the above list, i.e. the package com.sap.caf.core. It contains most of the data types and should be your first choice. Data types are primarily required when creating simple and complex attributes. When selecting a data type, you should not only consider the application itself but also the restrictions caused by the integration with other systems. For instance, the BW contains the restriction of having only 60 characters per field. Data types which are longer can then only be loaded into the BW in a restricted form or with additional transformation effort. The same goes for data types which are not "flat" but multidimensional such as objects, arrays and the like.

com.sap.caf.base

The data types in the package com.sap.caf.base are reserved for use in external services. They correspond to the Java simple types and should not be used by the application developer in a CAF project.

com.sap.caf.core

The almost 30 data types of this package should be used preferentially. They were predefined by SAP and comprise the most important data types, which during the development of several SAP xApps were identified as the most frequently used ones.

Restrictions The following data types from this package are not suitable for integration with the BW:

▶ businessObject

▶ bytearray

- ▶ rid
- ▶ xLongText

com.sap.caf.runtime

This package also contains data types (and more) that can only be used by the generated code. They should not be used by the application developer in a CAF project.

com.sap.dictionary.predefined.currency

As the name suggests, data types relevant to the currency are available here. Similar to the data types from the package `com.sap.caf.base` they should also not be used by the developer for a CAF project.

Project-specific Packages

If in a development project you find out that the data types available in the standard packages are not sufficient, you can create your own data types. To do this, we recommend you use the dictionary project of the CAF project. By selecting the dictionary perspective any data type can be created. It is also not advisable to change standard data types.

Data types from different packages can be used without a problem in any combination in the project as long as they are also deployed. This is usually the case for the four standard packages and the project-specific package.

Modeling tip

Specific Data Types

For an attribute with a data type connected with a currency, a currency field is created in the table in addition to the value field. When using Entity Services, both fields are output as one. For each attribute an additional field is created.

Currency

The currency conversion itself can be ensured by using the corresponding external services.

We can see here the advantage of such an Enterprise Services Architecture: The CAF itself uses external services which can be flexibly integrated into the application and can even be exchanged against other services.

| Unit | Like currency fields, an additional field is also created in the table for attributes with a data type which is linked with a unit. This is also provided by the Entity Service to a calling service. |

A unit conversion itself can be ensured by using the corresponding external services.

3.13.2 Entity Services

| Attributes | *Simple attributes* are used if the attribute should not be divided into additional sub-attributes and cannot exist independently from the referenced master data record. |

Complex attributes are used if the attribute is to be divided into additional sub-attributes and cannot exist independently from the referenced master data record.

Entity Service attributes are used if the attribute is to be divided into additional sub-attributes and can exist independently from the referenced master data record.

3.13.3 Application Services

Application services should be modeled according to the principles of a service-oriented architecture so that they are re-useable, manageable and task-specific.

| Small, useful units | The principle involved here is one we stated earlier, but that bears repeating. It is better to create several small application services that are divided into useful units than to create a very large service. |

3.13.4 User Interface

Whenever there is the opportunity to use UI patterns these should be used. This makes it easier for the users to use new UIs.

There is an entire range of publications available concerning guidelines for the correct use and structure of user interfaces. At this point, we would once again like to refer you to the website *www.sapdesignguild.org,* as it represents an invaluable source of inspiration and tips.

For those generally interested in visualizing data we would recommend Edward Tufte's books (www.edwardtufte.com). These should be standard works for all UI designers.

3.13.5 Naming and Other Conventions

Similar to the ABAP world, the Java world also knows certain conventions concerning naming and the writing of classes, interfaces, methods, and variables. Classes generally begin with uppercase letters followed by lowercase letters. Methods and parameters generally begin with lowercase letters followed by lowercase letters. If the name of the method or the variable is made up of several words, these begin with uppercase letters within the words (internal capital).

This convention affects the use of the modelers in the CAF as classes are created in the same way as methods and variables.

> **Example**
>
> The **Person** Entity Service is written as Person, the first letter being upper case. From this information the class name is derived. A search method that is supposed to search for last names can for instance be called with `findByLastName`. It begins with lower-case letters and contains an upper-case letter at the beginning of each new word of which it is composed.

The term "search method" gives us another clue. In order to standardize names and facilitate their incorporation in the coding, it is recommended to always place the "findBy" prefix at the beginning of the search methods in Entity Services.

Methods in application services as is the norm in Java must carry the corresponding functions in their names. If it is a write method, a verb such as "get" should be used as a prefix and if something is being checked, then for instance "check" should be used.

The same goes for variables. In the Java world it is however unusual (contrary to areas of .NET) to include the data type of the variables in names.

> **Example**
>
> Instead of `blnFlightAvailable` the variable should, for example, look like this: `flightAvailable`.
>
> Constants that are always to be written in uppercase letters and with individual words separated by an underscore "_" are an exception in this context. For example: `MAX_PRICE`.

Packages also follow the usual Java naming conventions with top-level domain, domain name, and then the sub packages. The package for our xFlights example could look as follows: `com.sap.xflights`.

There are many publications available on the Internet as well as on the book market that deal with the subject of naming conventions in much more detail. Check out this link for example:

http://java.sun.com/docs/codeconv/html/CodeConventions.doc8.html

4   Implementation Examples

From theory to practice. You will learn in detail about SAP xApp Product Definition and SAP xApp Cost and Quotation Management as elements of the SAP xApp portfolio. A comprehensive overview leads you from the respective business requirements to modeling to implementation, using the Composite Application Framework (CAF).

4.1   SAP xApp Product Definition (SAP xPD)

4.1.1   Introduction

Product and service innovation has become a critical success factor in almost all industry sectors. Many companies are striving to reorient their processes towards efficient innovation, and IT solutions play an essential role. Why and how does SAP xPD, which was developed as an SAP xApp by using the CAF contribute to the future of innovation?

What challenges do companies face today in terms of the product-and-service innovation process? Where is there scope for improvement? How do companies want to use this? These considerations form the basis for the requirements of a possible IT solution. On the basis of the attributes described in Chapter 1, *SAP xApps—Basic Principles*, we will clarify why an xApp solution is particularly suitable for redesigning the innovation process.

The second part of the chapter describes the SAP xPD solution. The business processes, with important activities, objects and actors, are explained. The implementation with the CAF then will be illustrated with some examples.

Finally, we will briefly look at the use and configuration of the software in the company.

From now on, we will use the term "product" not only for new products and product enhancements in a narrow sense, but rather also for services and specific offers, which increase companies' sales and profits. **Product**

Which part in the product-innovation process does SAP xPD aim at? In general the product-innovation process incorporates all phases and activities of the product lifecycle, from the idea to the marketing and the con- **Product-innovation process** stant improvements to existing products. In a holistic approach, success measurement is relevant for all phases of the product lifecycle.

The focus for the IT solution SAP xPD is the product-definition process. For SAP, xPD forms a part of the entire solution of the product-innovation process.

Product definition process Product definition refers to early phases of a new product's lifecycle. This process includes all phases from the conception of the ideas to the decision to develop the product and to introduce it to the market. In Figure 4.1. the product lifecycle is generically illustrated. The early phases of the product definition have been highlighted.

Figure 4.1 Product Definition as a Part of the Product Lifecycle

At the beginning of the process, many ideas must be developed. Then the most promising ideas must be identified, and then refined so that the most promising and feasible ones make it to the next round. In practice, this means a multilevel selection process in which the product idea is further developed into a concept and the feasibility is examined according to different criteria. The concept selection can be carried out in one or several steps. In each step the concept takes on more concrete form. At the same time the feasibility is more thoroughly examined. In addition, each level requires a greater use of resources than the preceding level. The results of this process are a business plan and the decision if this concept will be developed or not. Of course, the information from this process is to be used as a basis for the next phase.

In an ideal scenario, the success of the market introduction should be compared to the forecasts from the definition process. The evaluation can then lead to an adaptation of the definition process.

4.1.2   Business Case

Companies have always developed new products and brought them to market in order to ensure their existence and growth. However, in recent years the importance of product innovations has grown immensely. In some industries, such as consumer goods and technology, the ability to develop new products more successfully and quickly has become a major competitive advantage.

Trends

The following list is a summary of the essential trends with regard to product innovations:

▶ **Shorter product lifecycles**
Caused by the high speed of scientific-technical progress and the changes in society, the demand for products often decreases within a very short space of time. In addition, the number of products launched in the last two decades has multiplied. This trend will continue.

▶ **Changes due to globalization**
A consequence of globalization is increased competition. Innovations are often a possible differentiating factor for a company to remain competitive. At the same time new markets open up, toward which companies must target their products.

In addition, structures in the value-creation chain are subject to change. Therefore, participants in the product-innovation process also may change, for example by addition of external partners or teams in a company. Change has therefore become an inseparable part of the processes within companies.

▶ **"The customer is king"**
Consumers and customers can freely select from an ever-growing number of competing offers. The successful anticipation and meeting of customer requirements in the tension field of fellow competitors thus becomes crucial for product innovations.

Situation of the companies

Research has shown that companies react in different ways to these challenges. Two essential indicators provide the call to action:

▶ **Absence of market success**
The success rate for product introductions has gone down in recent years. This means that the introduction of new products has not yielded the expected profit in relation to the investments.

▶ **Time-to-market too long**
Many companies are unhappy with the time that goes by between the idea and the introduction of the new product. For companies a delayed market introduction means a reduced profit due to the loss of market shares.

The same research and feedback from customers also show the most important reasons for these difficulties:

▶ **Insufficient "homework" in the early definition phase**
A study by Cooper and Kleinschmidt[1] shows that one of the main reasons why new products fail to be successful is that companies don't do their "homework" sufficiently. This means that in many companies the decisions in early phases are not made according to systematic criteria or they are based on incomplete information. This leads to increased costs and a reduced success rate for the entire innovation process.

▶ **Lack of collaboration between "functional silos"**
Product innovation is the result of cross-functional cooperation. The traditional functional organizational structure is specifically constraining in the product-innovation process. If experts from the related areas such as production are not included in an early phase of the process, implementation problems are often identified too late. This leads to lost time and increased costs due to the need for adaption at a later stage.

▶ **Unclear and unstandardized decision-making**
A recurring task in the product-innovation process is to decide on whether or not a new product should be developed. However the criteria in many companies are not always clearly defined or they are not transparent for everyone involved. Different functional areas and even different individuals make decisions differently. In addition to an insufficiently implemented holistic company strategy, there is no way to analyze the product-innovation process. Information is not available from the perspective of this process.

▶ **Incomplete use of idea sources**
The starting point for successful products are good ideas. However, these cannot be ordered on demand. In many companies, some idea centers and traditional "procurement paths" have been established. These can consist of employees from the marketing department, the development department, or from external sources such as partners or focus groups with potential customers. However, research has confirmed that, even so, not all relevant sources are used or, if they are used, then not to their full extent.

---

1   Robert G. Cooper: *Winning at New Products: Accelerating the Process from Idea to Launch*. Perseus Publishing; 3rd edition (June 5, 2001).

► **Problems on the level of the supporting IT solutions**

In addition to structural and system-related problems in the product-innovation process, there are problems at the level of the supporting IT solutions that reduce the efficiency of the entire process.

Many IT solutions were structured to support the individual functions along the value-creation chain. This often meant that specialized IT solutions arose for the functional area but these only supported information exchange to a limited extent, especially when it came to the interaction between the respective functions. Thus integration gaps along the innovation process led to losses of information.

In addition, although collaboration between the functions is supported by constantly improving communication tools such as e-mail, online conferences etc, access to process-relevant information has become increasingly difficult for employees from different functional areas.

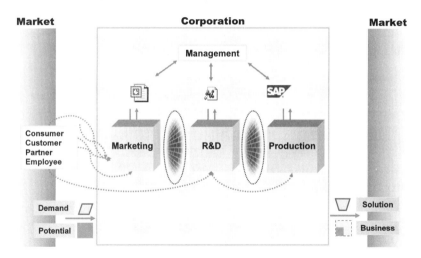

Figure 4.2 Product Innovation Today

Figure 4.2 illustrates the innovation process as it can often be seen today. Information on market requirements arrives through a few different channels in the company. Management must make decisions based on different and separate IT systems. How do companies want to shape the product-innovation process in the future?

The product-innovation process is a key in reaching strategic company goals for the management of many companies. Management is forced to re-evaluate this process and its meaning and to implement a corresponding success design. One of the most important concepts is to orient the

Stage Gate process

product-innovation process toward a Stage Gate™ process, such as the one described by Cooper and Kleinschmidt[2].

In this context, the process is divided into individual stages along the product lifecycle. Each stage is characterized by tasks that drive the new product concept towards market introduction and should produce information relevant to decision-making. At the end of the stage, a decision is made whether the product concept has qualified for the next stage or is stopped. Companies increasingly design their process according to individual decision criteria and aim to run this process for each product innovation. This means decisions can also be aligned to the company strategy and can be made transparent within the entire company. At the beginning, a few qualitative criteria are evaluated such as possible customer acceptance, general feasibility, and the compliance with the company strategy. Later on, quantifiable criteria is focused on, such as the market potential or detailed feasibility analyses on the technical and operational implementation.

Requirements to changed process design

What are now the essential requirements to a modified process design?

▶ **Holistic view of the entire product lifecycle**
The individual stages are strongly dependent on each other. A basic setting of the criteria for success and failure is reflected in the product-definition phase. On the other hand, experience with the later phases in the decision-making process becomes integrated in the early stages.

▶ **Parallel cooperation of the involved functions**
As soon as possible and throughout the process, the individuals concerned from different company functions, such as consumers, customers, developers, marketing experts and production experts, should cooperate on a new product concept.

▶ **Transparent and standardized decision process**
The criteria for selecting a new product are defined according to the company strategy and proven experience. All those involved in the product-innovation process should use this criteria as a guiding light.

Requirements for supporting IT solutions

For the establishment of new processes, a company's own IT solutions can be used as long as it makes sense to do so. IT solutions for supporting the product-innovation process efficiently must meet the following requirements:

---

2 Robert G. Cooper: *Winning at New Products: Accelerating the Process from Idea to Launch*. Perseus Publishing; 3rd edition (June 5, 2001).

▶ **New process management**
It must be possible to support the mapping of a Stage Gate process throughout the entuire product lifecycle. This means that information, user interactions and workflows must be re-assembled in the context of the product innovation. An ultimate goal would be real-time management information on the status of the innovation investments and the effectiveness of the innovation process itself.

▶ **Flexible process management**
On the way to establishing the product-definition process according to tried-and-tested criteria, a best practice will gradually develop. Nonetheless, changing external conditions will make adaptations necessary. Adaptations in the process must be implemented quickly and made easy for the users.

▶ **Flexible integration in existing applications**
Product innovation occurs in the context of existing processes and structures. This means an IT solution cannot start from scratch but should rather make use of established systems For example, customer entries are good sources of new ideas, and existing products are a starting point for further developments.

Another aspect is the integration with analytical systems. The company must be able to evaluate an entire process must be possible such as a portfolio management of all products on the market and all products in the innovation pipeline.

▶ **Supporting the collaboration of cross-functional teams**
Participants come from different functional areas that all have to do with the future product or its development. Each participant must be able to access the information relevant for his or her specific task. Ideally an IT system should speak the jargon of those involved or it should enable an effective communication channel that is easy to use.

▶ **Integrating structured data with unstructured information**
In the product-innovation process, an efficient communication often occurs through the exchange of documents. These documents must be processed at the same time as "hard" data, for instance in the form of key figures.

Figure 4.3 illustrates the product-innovation process as it could look in the future with the support of composite applications.

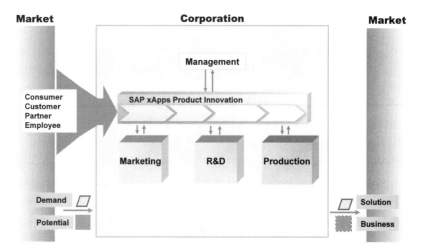

Figure 4.3 Product Innovation in the Future

In addition to these general design criteria, the IT solutions must support individual operational activities in this process. For the product definition, these are in particular the following activities:

▶ **Idea management**
Activities to accept, evaluate, and judge new ideas as well as to analyze and consolidate several ideas.

▶ **Conception**
Information acquisition for a new product concept in order to make a well-informed decision on its further development.

These activities are described in detail in the following sections.

Based on the criteria for an xApp that were referred to in Chapter 1, *SAP xApps—Basic Principles*, and the requirements mentioned in this chapter, it becomes clear why SAP xPD was developed as an xApp.

Like other companies, SAP has recognized the need for solutions to support the product-innovation process. As a matter of fact, there are IT solutions available that support the individual areas of the process. There are established enterprise resource planning (ERP) solutions for the later stages (mySAP ERP), and project management solutions and solutions for the development phase (mySAP PLM, SAP cProjects). For the early phases such as idea management there are "best-of-breed" solutions available as well. In the past, SAP itself would not have been able to provide any specialized solution for this early phase. SAP xPD now provides specific support for this stage.

In fact, there is not as yet any application on the market which can provide a continuous view of the product-innovation process. SAP xPD is therefore not exclusively oriented to the early project phase. In addition, companies should be enabled to take a first step in the direction of Enterprise Services Architecture (ESA) for the product-innovation process. This approach has the aim of supporting a continuous product-innovation process across existing applications. Today, with the use of SAP NetWeaver components, partially merged views and the integration of information for the product-innovation process is possible.

SAP sees great potential in this approach especially in the drive to stand out from the competition.

The IT solution must support optimum flexibility in the innovation process. Changes are necessary at the different levels and must be implemented quickly. That includes the process configuration, the user interfaces (UIs), and also changes in the application logic.

Criteria determined by the characteristics of the business process

The cross-functional character of the process must be realized. In the product-innovation process, for those involved, the view of their functional area has prevailed until today. In the future, these different actors should collaborate from the perspective of the entire process.

The product-innovation process is an extensive process. Numerous systems support companies here. These systems will continue to exist and can be used by a comprehensive application. That means that different pieces of information in these different systems must be related to each other from the perspective of product innovation.

Criteria determined by the type and origin of the information

This does not only involve displaying and manipulating existing information from another context, a job for which a portal might be sufficient. In the case of product definition new objects are required and existing ones are enhanced. These changes must be implemented in specific components in the Enterprise Services layer of the xApp.

Similarly important is the combined handling of structured data and documents in the product-innovation process. For these reasons SAP decided on creating an xApp.

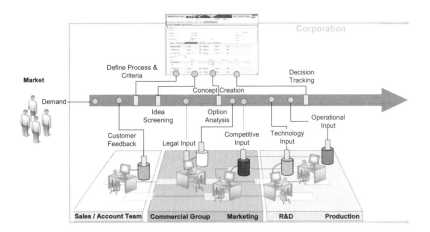

Figure 4.4 SAP xPD as a Composite Application

4.1.3   SAP xPD as a Solution

As mentioned in the introduction, the solution described here should illustrate the implementation of an xApp with the help of the CAF. In the function examples, reference is made to the implementation with CAF. The guiding principle should be the product-definition process itself. A concrete scenario with screen shots will make this clearer.

Idea Generation Phase

Idea   The idea-generation phase mainly serves to collect a large number of new ideas and to consolidate and pre-select them. By "idea," we mean a rough solution to the problem of satisfying a potential market requirement.

In practice, different scenarios for idea generation are used. They can mainly be differentiated by their source, i.e. the creative mind, and by the individual activities to further develop the idea. A typical scenario would be targeted idea workshops in focus groups, from which a handful of favorites make it to the next round. Another scenario is based on ad-hoc ideas from customers, suppliers, the competition, or employees.

In practice, the different ideas are often distributed in space and time. Sometimes valuable sources remain unused. As a result, too few ideas are included in the process and good ideas are completely neglected.

SAP xPD aims to integrate and stimulate the different sources, and to enable access to the results for all those receiving ideas within the company at any time. In concrete terms, this could mean that the favorites from an idea workshop can be easily included in the idea pool, employees are provided with a motivating platform for idea transfer, or customer feedback is transformed and integrated in the selection process. The consumers of ideas, such as product managers, are then enabled to successfully identify or even actively receive the most promising suggestions from this pool. Figure 4.5. displays an overview of the activities and roles to be supported in the idea-generation phase.

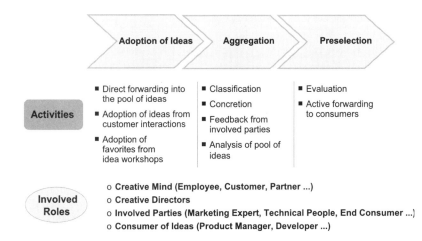

Figure 4.5 Idea-Generation Process

As the chapter progresses, the concrete scenario of an ad-hoc employee idea is used in order to illustrate important SAP xPD functionalities, the object model, and the user interface.

In our first example, a technology company develops and produces robots for households. An employee of the company, Sophie Smart has the idea of developing a Sunday egg robot. She enters this idea in the suggestions page on the Intranet and classifies it accordingly. The idea is directed to Ritu, who is responsible for ideas. She receives a message by e-mail. In the idea editor, Ritu checks if similar ideas already exist. As the idea is new and is most suitable for product manager Frank's product line, the idea is forwarded to him. Frank sees a potential for the idea and has it checked further in his team. The scenario is illustrated in Figure 4.6 using an ARIS process model.

Sample scenario

For the scenarios in which idea givers would like to directly enter an idea in the idea pool, an interface must be provided. This interface can differ according to the role of the idea provider. Therefore, SAP xPD provides the option of configuring several idea entry interfaces and making it accessible to the corresponding roles. This can be done online in the sys-

Idea entry interface

tem or offline by sending a form. Another possible method is the mass entry of ideas, for instance from an Excel table that originated as a result of an idea workshop. Figure 4.7 shows an example of such an interface.

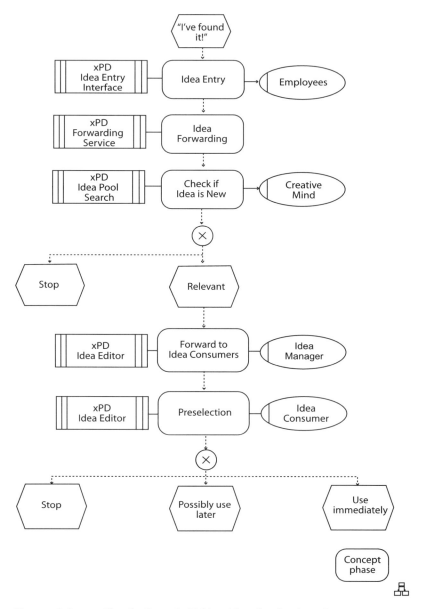

Figure 4.6 Process Flow for Scenario "Ad-hoc Idea of an Employee"

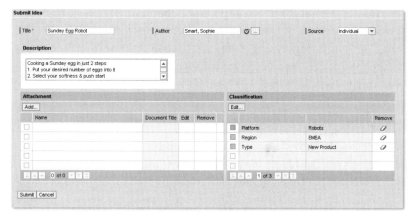

Figure 4.7 Interface for Entering Ideas from Employees

xApps offer the following advantages in this phase:

▶ Flexibility due to the configurability of the user interface

▶ The integration of other systems by providing a Web service for idea entry. External sources can enter ideas in the idea pool through the Web-service interface. Thus forms can be used whose content is sent through a Web service to the pool. The development on the basis of the CAF would make it possible here to easily provide the application services for the idea as Web services for other applications.

A central point of the system is the option to classify ideas. It is only in this way that you can ensure that a clear picture can be created out of a huge mass of information available to the decision-makers. The added value of classification lies in the options of transferring ideas correspondingly or carrying out an efficient search across the entire pool. In the idea process, the classification is often carried out in steps. The individual categories and their values are customer-specific. In SAP xPD they are therefore configured by the customers.

Classification

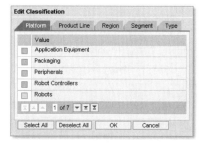

Figure 4.8 Interface for Classification

The essential advantage of the xApp lies in the flexibility provided by the underlying modeling of the classification categories through the CAF Core Entity Services **Category** and **CategoryValueSet** (see Section 3.5.3) and its description in the user interface through the UI pattern **Classification-Assignment** (see Section 3.7.2). Categories can be added to objects at any time. To do this, you don't need to carry out a modification in the user interface or in the application.

Transfer to the creative directors and idea consumers
The best way to provide both those responsible for ideas and idea consumers with new and good ideas is to forward them directly to these individuals. The responsible persons can be established for any sets of classification characteristics so that the system informs the relevant people through suitable channels. SAP xPD provides different options, such as e-mail, an overview of "ideas to be processed," or a note in the "collection point" for workflow information.

In this phase, the advantage provided by the xApp can be seen in the use of existing services from the SAP NetWeaver platform. These are implemented through Knowledge Management Integration provided by the CAF. By using the notification service of the collaboration component, the user is informed through the usual channels. And the existing infrastructure of a company can still be used.

Substantiating in the idea editor
An idea is changed during its development process. A corresponding interface in SAP xPD, the idea editor (see Figure 4.9), provides the option of accessing all the aspects of the idea online and change it if necessary. Changes are thus made accessible to everybody. Access rights for the individual users can be different and can be specifically assigned in SAP xPD.

The advantage in this phase lies primarily in the flexibility afforded by configuring the user interface. The idea editor is based on the UI pattern **ObjectEditor** (see Section 3.7.2). The fields in the header information are configurable. The selection list displayed in the figure can be accessed through the use of the entity service **CustomEnumTypes** (see Section 3.7.5) for the idea status.

Feedback from those involved in the process
An important source of idea information is the flow of useful comments, feedback or questions on the idea uttered by those involved in the collaboration process. In practice, the "journal" has proven itself as the most popular form due to its simplicity and the possibility to quickly enter comments. The CAF provides the **HistoryLog** pattern (see Section 3.7.2) in order to implement this type of commenting and discussion simply. For the existing version of SAP xPD, the implementation of the journal was still used as an attribute.

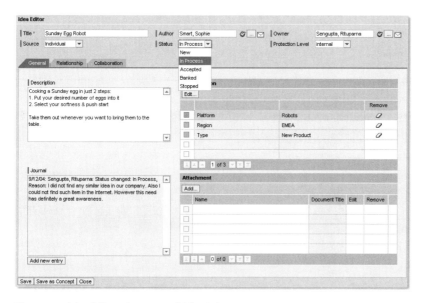

Figure 4.9 Idea Editor, Access to all Idea Information

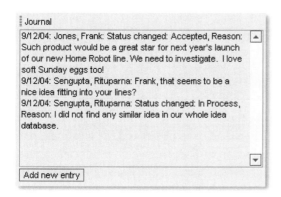

Figure 4.10 The Journal in SAP xPD

In addition, for each idea, further sophisticated collaborative services are available, such as a discussion forum, which like the notification function is reached through the Knowledge Management Integration provided by the CAF.

A central idea pool then promises additional value if those involved can retrieve relevant ideas for their tasks and put these to further use or compare them to a new idea. Furthermore, a good idea pool analysis can, for instance, enable the finding of trends and patterns. A basic prerequisite is a powerful search engine which incorporates all information modules of

Idea pool analysis

an idea, including the attached documents on the idea. For this reason, in SAP xPD, the SAP NetWeaver component SAP Knowledge Management is used with the search engine TREX.

Furthermore, a user interface adapted to the search requirements is essential. Those carrying out searches might pursue a specific search strategy, depending on their goal. In SAP xPD therefore, several different user interfaces can be configured and used in the relevant context.

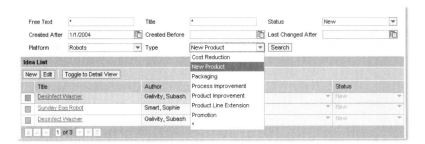

Figure 4.11 Example of a Search Template for the Idea Search; The Free Text Search Also Includes Attached Documents.

The xApp provides two advantages regarding the idea pool analysis:

▶ **Combination of Structured and Unstructured Information.**
Here, one of the most advanced concepts of the CAF comes to the fore: By using the CAF Repository Manager in connection with SAP Knowledge Management, it is possible to perform a simultaneous search through the structured data of an object and the information in attached documents (see Section 3.10.1). The search result can contain both documents and the businss objects themselves (e.g. ideas). The user can in effect "google" through documents and business objects in the company (though a suitable SAP term would be "to TREX.").

▶ **Flexibility through the Configuration of the User Interface**
During implementation, the UI pattern **SearchBar** was used.

Suitable object model The object model must be able to provide the information for the described activities. In addition it must be sufficiently flexible to meet the customer-specific requirements. The idea is a relatively simple object which mainly consists of idea information such as some attributes and attachments, and process information such as the people involved and the status. Furthermore, the classification and the relationship to other objects are important.

The customer-specific characteristics of the individual attributes are key aspects. Table 4.1 contains an overview of the possible customer specifics.

Information	Customer specifics	Examples
General idea information	None	Title, description
Specific idea information	Number of attributes	Individual evaluation per customer
Attachments	None	Picture, weblink, presentation
Classification	Number of categories and range of values	Application area, target group
People involved	Own roles	Authors, those responsible for ideas
Status	Range of values	New, accepted
Relationship to other objects	Number of different objects, meaning of the relationship	Similar ideas, Concepts in which the idea is used

Table 4.1 Customer-Specific Attributes

Figure 4.12 displays a diagram of the implementation in SAP xPD with the CAF. The idea is the central entity service in the idea generation phase. The modeling of core services from other NetWeaver components and external services is specifically emphasized here. With regard to the ideas, core services from other NetWeaver components refer to documents and collaboration services from Knowledge Management Integration. External services are provided by other applications.

Implementation with the CAF

The classification was modeled using the core services **Category** and **CategoryValueSet**. All other attributes within the idea are modeled as simple attributes.

What is the benefit of using the CAF for implementing such an object model?

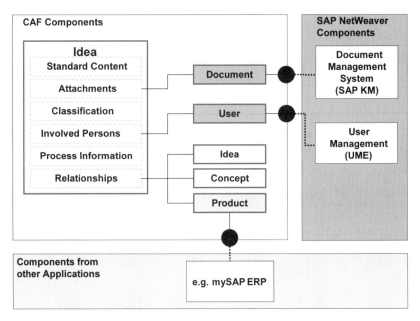

Figure 4.12 Object Model of the Idea

Short implemen-
tation time
First, the development environment of the CAF enables the object to be modeled in a similar way to that shown in the illustration without writing a single line of code. This is not especially relevant for companies at the moment, as SAP xPD can be supplied completely modeled. However, it will be possible for application developers in the future to implement enhancements easily, using the development environment.

Companies already benefit indirectly in the form of a relatively short implementation time for new requirements in SAP xPD.

Relationships
between objects
The relationship to other objects has an important business-related background in the innovation process. For example, a company would like to be able to find out why a concept and later a product emerges from a specific idea. Which decisions lead to success or failure during the process? Another example concerns an idea for a product enhancement. Here, you would like to receive more detailed information on the product and its current sales figures. Much of this information already exists within companies, but in a different context.

It would be desirable if the IT solution for the product-innovation process could provide information from relationships in the necessary context. For example, in the case of an idea for a product enhancement, it would be ideal to get additional product information and the current sales figures in addition to information on the product name. It is obvious that from the combination of context, type of relation and the objects involved, an endless number of variants could emerge. Real added value, however, is only ensured by some of them. An example is the increased efficiency of information acquisition and transfer, another example would be the improved decision-making process through the immediate availability of coherent information. Which contexts in the innovation process promise the highest added value depends greatly on the particular company.

The CAF helps to implement such contexts easily:

1. By using the CAF Service Modeler, business objects can be easily related to each other (e.g. a product to the idea). In this context, the relationship is independent of the specific technical implementation of the relevant objects.

2. In the next step, the type of the relationship is stored ("Idea is an enhancement to product").

3. In the third step, context-related services must be provided ("Display detailed information on the product"). In the CAF, *Application Services* are used (see Section 3.6) to map such relationships. Examples in the standard version are the relationships between the objects along the innovation process "Idea is related to idea," "Idea is used in concept," and "Project belongs to the concept." Further relationships are incorporated gradually in the standard version of SAP xPD.

In Figure 4.13, the relationship between "Related ideas" and the service "Search for similar ideas" is displayed. The user interface in this case enables you to navigate to the other idea. The advantages provided by the SAP xApp in this phase can mainly be found in the following areas:

▶ **Flexibility due to easy modeling of the objects.**
The modeling of the required business objects is comprehensible and feasible for business users.

▶ **Access to existing information in external systems.**
The concept of the Enterprise Services Architetures enables you to use existing information and services for your own application. The existing integration architecture of SAP NetWeaver enables you to do this.

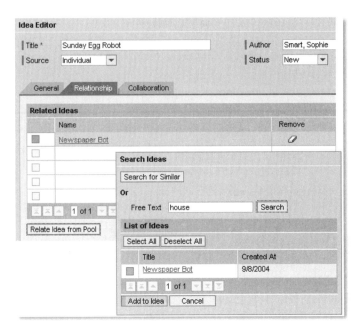

Figure 4.13 Related Ideas and the Service "Search for Similar Ideas"

Conception Phase

The phase of idea generation is concluded with the decision to further pursue an idea. Now the conception phase begins. In this phase, the business case is developed and the feasibility is checked. Several steps are often carried out here, each one ending with a stop/continue decision. This corresponds to the Stage Gate method mentioned earlier in this chapter.

Supporting activities

SAP xPD enables you to first map a Stage Gate process. At this point, the involved people learn what kind of information can be expected. This information can be easily stored while working on the concept. Decisions are thus documented in a transparent manner. In addition, project management tasks such as the organization of teams, tasks and dates are supported simply. An overview of the activities and roles supported during the design is shown in Figure 4.14.

Before we explore the components of SAP xPD in further detail, we want to get back to our example of the Sunday-egg robot.

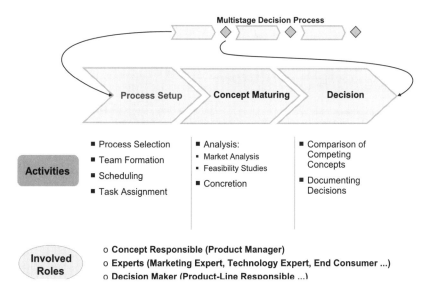

Figure 4.14 Conception Process

Frank, the product manager, wants to process a concept from the idea of a Sunday-egg robot and have the team evaluate it. If revenues of more than $3 million can be expected in the first year, the product will be included in the new product line. A group of experts for marketing, technology, and business planning examines the feasibility. In the first phase, a marketing description, the "concept brief" and a business evaluation are created, and these provide key figures for the preliminary decision. Later on, a market research study is carried out, the technical feasibility of a possible solution is examined, and a business plan is created. Then the decision regarding the start of the development is made. The first phase is displayed as an ARIS process model in Figure 4.15.

Sample scenario

A few essential principles were set in the design with SAP xPD which can successfully support a concept.

In SAP xPD, it is possible to configure Stage Gate processes according to which a concept can be developed in several steps. Different processes can be predefined here. These can be selected during the creation of a new concept by those responsible for the concept. This is necessary because different concept types run through different decision processes. A new product requires different decisions than, for instance, a product enhancement.

Flexible process desing

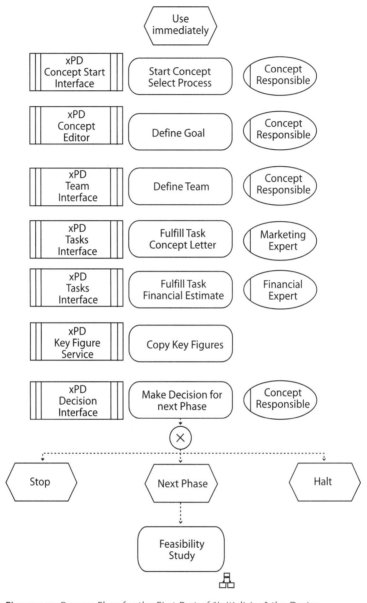

Figure 4.15 Process Flow for the First Part of "Initializing" the Design

A process template determines how many phases are required, which tasks are set per phase, and which information and key figures are necessary for each decision. At the same time, the template specifies the roles involved in the process. Information can be stored in the form of documents. In the process template examples, document templates or links can be stored in order to support the users in the creation phase.

When creating a concept, the process template is selected in SAP xPD as well as some basic information (see Figure 4.16).

The advantage of the xApp lies in the flexible process design available by using Guided Procedures. These define the principles for the process templates and for processing the process at runtime (see *Process Modeler* in Section 3.8).

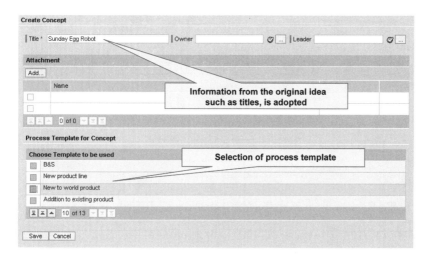

Figure 4.16 Creating a Concept and Selecting a Suitable Process Template

The cross-functional character of the product-definition process demands the parallel collaboration of different roles. Product definition can involve participants who are less familiar with the company applications. The user interface must be comprehensible to each role player in the process.

Simplicity of use

SAP xPD focuses on the relevant information for decision-making and business cases at the early stages of a product development. This means that these are also the focus of the users. The user interface is designed correspondingly. All users know which information is expected of them according to their roles and how the actual concept appears.

The main access to the concept information takes place via the Concept Editor. This editor is based on the same pattern as the idea editor. However, it is aligned to the concept. In addition it contains access to:

Concept Editor

▶ Process information (phases, team, schedule)

▶ Business-relevant key figures

▶ Information for the decision ("deliverables")

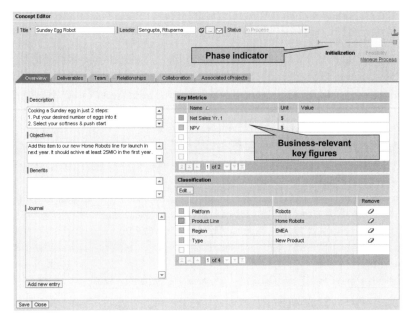

Figure 4.17 Concept Editor for Access to all Concept Information

The processing of a concept requires basic project-management functions for the teamwork. This includes managing the team, the schedule, and specific responsibilities, status, and deadlines for tasks (see Figures 4.18 through 4.20).

Figure 4.18 Simple Management of the Team in the Concept Editor

Figure 4.19 Simple Management of the Schedule for the Conception Steps

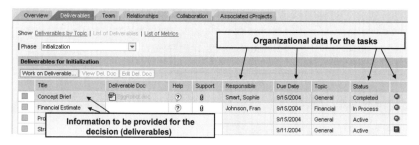

Figure 4.20 Access to Organizational Data for the Tasks

The core activity during the conception phase is the collection of information relevant to making decisions. Different aspects must be examined here, such as market, strategy, technology, or commerce. This requires a broad range of information sources, acquisition paths, and analytical methods that cannot be managed by a single IT solution. However, the aim of all activities is to map a business case. Its structure and modules are clear.

Support in delivering decision-relevant information

This is where SAP xPD comes into play: It mirrors the business case, for instance in the form of key figures. Information, which in turn confirms the details of the key figures, can be added as documents in the context. During the concept formation, the people involved have the task of contributing their parts to the business case.

In order to model the information described, the entity service **Concept** was introduced. In contrast to an idea, a concept also has a 0..1 relationship to the entity service **Process**. Guided Procedures are used for the process. This provides the concept with a team, actions and phases. The Stage Gate process is modeled in this way.

Furthermore. a concept has a 0..n relationship to the entity services **Key figure** and **Key figure value**. The key figure value has a 1..1 relationship to the key figure. This makes it possible to define customer-specific key figures instantly for a concept on the customers' side.

Specific business tasks are supported by specific actions in SAP xPD during the conception phase. That means that SAP xPD can provide the users with specific system support in carrying out business tasks. This support was modeled using actions from Guided Procedures.

Tasks in SAP xPD and the relationship with actions

An example of this would be the standard task "Add business document to be delivered to the concept." The individual steps consist of the provision of support (template or example), the storing of the complete document (e.g. market research analysis) and adding support information on this document (e.g. the report of a market research company). The user is guided through the individual steps in the user interface (see Figure 4.21).

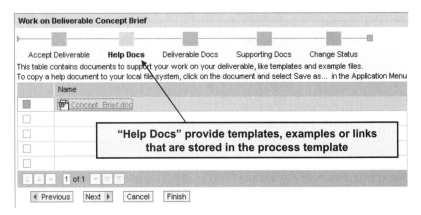

Figure 4.21 Action to Support the Task "Add the Business Document to be Delivered to the Concept"

This already provides added value to a variety of companies. Employees can be notified of a business process change in the innovation process more quickly, because the tasks and help settings for their processing are predefined.

Simple enhancement of the standard version

SAP xPD does not stop here, but rather uses the possibilities of a composite application. You can program and add any further actions you wish to the standard version. Each action that can provide information relevant to the decision can be integrated. Thus, for example, existing bills of material and prices for a product enhancement can be read out and used in a cost estimate for the new product. Such a task could be called "Planning the material costs by using existing products." The result can then be stored in an Excel file or in a planning system like SAP Easy Cost Planning. To complete the action, SAP xPD extracts the data required for the business case.

The direct extraction from MS Excel is already available. An Excel template is used in companies for such tasks as estimating the net present value (NPV) for new products. After the deliverable "financial estimate" has been completed, as in the example, the important key figures are updated in the concept. For this function, the CAF API is used to load data from an Excel file into an xApp.

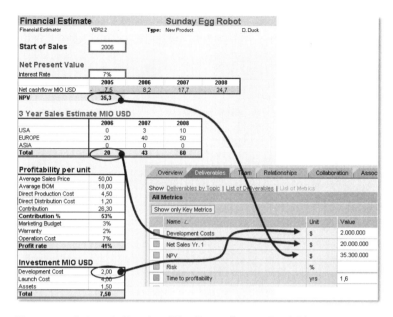

Figure 4.22 Automatic Transfer of Key Figures from an Excel File

The decision whether to pursue the concept further can be based on the information provided, including the key figures. This occurs at the level of the individual concept, but also by comparing it with competing concepts.

Making and documenting decisions

SAP xPD provides analysis "dashboards" that can be used to compare different concepts. Filter criteria enable the selection of the concepts to be compared. The key figures relevant for selection can be configured in the dashboard (see Figure 4.23). The dashboard uses the **FlexTree** pattern of the CAF.

	Title	NPV	Phase	Owner	Creating Date	Discuss	Status	Progress	Projects	remove
■	Newspaper Bot	19,8	Exploration	<undefined>	9/8/2004	0	In Process	25%	0	⃔
■	Sunday Egg Robot	35,3	Initialization	Jones, Frank	9/12/2004	0	In Process	35%	0	⃔
■	Child Watch Robot	43,7	Initialization	Sengupta, Rituparna	9/8/2004	0	Active	0%	0	⃔

New | Edit | Export   Refresh

Figure 4.23 Dashboard to Compare Several Concepts

Another option for multi-concept analysis is evaluation through a portfolio management application or reports in SAP Business Intelligence. SAP xPD provides extractors and a standard integration into the portfolio management SAP xRPM.

In order to document the decision, SAP xPD provides the simple option of storing documents such as meeting memos or a comment along with the decision (see Figure 4.24).

Figure 4.24 Documenting All Previous Decisions

Completing a concept
If a concept has overcome all obstacles, it moves into the design-and-development phase of the product-innovation process. It often happens that at this point a project starts. SAP xPD can transfer the existing information to a project-management system. Interaction with SAP cProjects and the SAP xRPM portfolio management makes a continuous process possible.

The advantage of SAP xApp in this area can be found in the flexible integration into other systems by using the ESA. Information from the concept phase can also be transferred as Web services to a project-management system via RFCs.

User Interfaces

In order to meet customer-specific requirements, the configuration of the user interfaces can be used in SAP xPD. Almost all user interfaces are configurable in SAP xPD, and the use of patterns defines the scope within which this can be done. This scope ensures a standard behavior of the application,. Above all, you can configure which attributes of an object should be displayed. But even the application behavior itself can be influenced. For example, you can configure the behavior of links, mouseovers, or buttons.

The user interface configuration can also be used in order to make the application role-specific regarding its interaction with the portal. Each user-interface configuration can be saved with its own name and can be called as a URL. In the portal, it is possible to integrate every user interface through an iView into its corresponding role-specific content. Thus, for example, for an idea manager, the search function can contain additional search criteria and an enhanced results list, in contrast to an employee who only seldom is involved with ideas.

Implementing SAP xPD in Companies

The goal of companies is to improve the product-innovation process as a core process. For this, SAP xPD provides an optimal point of entry, especially when:

▶ The innovation process should be optimized in companies to become a Stage Gate process.

▶ The early phases of idea generation and conception provide good potential to improve the effectiveness of the entire process.

Due to the architecture and use of SAP NetWeaver components, the company can decide on the scope and speed of the introduction. Three dimensions are particularly relevant here:

Introduction strategies

1. Step-by-step integration of organizational units when using SAP xPD components.

   In order to get to grips more easily with change management, companies that use SAP xPD decided in favor of a gradual introduction. One of the main reasons is that companies often are still in the process definition for a holistic innovation process and must first try out best practices. SAP xPD can be configured in a flexible manner for this and is also very scalable.

2. Enhanced use of the capabilities of SAP Enterprise Portal

   The installation of SAP xPD also entails the implementation of SAP Enterprise Portal. Functionalities of SAP xPD are provided through the portal and based on roles. In addition, contents can be integrated from other applications which are relevant in the context of the product-innovation process. That can for instance involve the access to product information, market information, or other applications in companies (see Figure 4.25).

As already explained above, the access to SAP xPD functionalities can be changed through differently configured user interfaces for different roles.

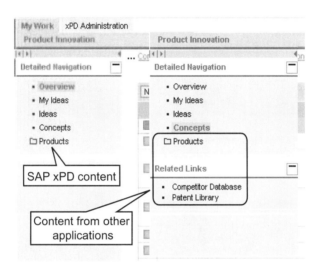

Figure 4.25 Navigation with Jumps to Links, Relevant for the Product-innovation Process Through the Portal

3. Further scenarios for integrating information in SAP xPD with other applications and the integration through the entire process of the product lifecycle.

Due to the design as a composite application, SAP xPD provides a range of options in order to provide specific support for the product-innovation process. Additional components can be programmed and integrated into the process. These are mainly:

▶ Enhancement of object relationships and their use in the context of ideas and concepts, already mentioned earlier in this chapter.

▶ Expansion of supported actions for the conception.

Technical implementation In order for SAP xPD to function, the SAP NetWeaver components SAP Enterprise portal, SAP Knowledge Management, and the SAP Web Application Server (J2EE part) are necessary. In this context, existing portal and knowledge management installations can be used as a basis. If an application server is already available, SAP xPD can be installed on it.

In the case of a complete new installation, all components can be installed on one physical host. Figure 4.26 shows an overview of the components.

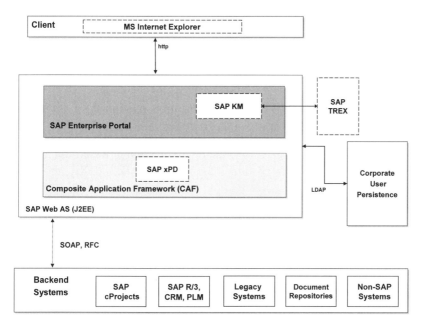

Figure 4.26 Components of an SAP xPD Installation

4.1.4 **Summary**

In previous sections, we demonstrated that SAP xPD, as a composite application, represents a solution path with numerous perspectives for the IT support of the innovation process, whereby the early phases of the product definition in particular are supported.

A high level of flexibility is attained by using the Enterprise Services Architecture. It enables you to compile solution components in a configurable process by using the product innovation. In addition, changes caused by a strict separation of the levels of the user interface, application components, and the executing systems are easily carried out.

The use of the CAF enabled the creation of the application within a very short time frame and the provision of useful services from existing SAP NetWeaver components and external applications.

The boundary between structured data and information in documents becomes especially blurred in the innovation process. By using the CAF with Knowledge Management integration, you not only can combine both types with each other but SAP xPD is the first solution to provide functionality to search across both types of information. For a search request both business objects and documents can be returned.

4.2 SAP xApp Cost and Quotation Management (SAP xCQM)

4.2.1 Introduction

The acquisition of revenue through participation in requests for quotation (RFQs) is a core process in the manufacturing industry.

By means of RFQs, manufacturers are invited to submit a comprehensive offer for production of a product. Depending on the industry, the creation of a quote can be a very complex and time and customer-imposed restraints.

The process of revenue acquisition comprises all parts of a company from sales to production to purchasing and back again. Only if this process chain is continuously supported by a software solution can a profitable result be attained.

Companies therefore search for suitable IT solutions that can cover the process in its entirety. The SAP xApp Cost and Quotation Management (SAP xCQM), which was developed based on the CAF, is intended to continuously supporting this process.

The first part of this section describes the business case for a targeted solution, by describing the business process of revenue acquisition. At the same time, we will describe the business challenges manufacturers face, as well as highlight the internal problems which have to be dealt with.

The second part of the section focuses on the potential for improvement that manufacturers have recognized and want to address, as well as the derived specific requirements for a software solution.

The third part describes the SAP xCQM solution with reference to why the CAF was chosen as a development platform, goals for the application, and how these goals should be reached. In addition to the functional description of the application, the technical implementation is also highlighted, along with the business benefits that the use of SAP xCQM promises.

To conclude, we will take a look at the future development roadmap of the application.

4.2.2 Business Case

Revenue Acquisition—Status Quo

Depending on the industry you use as the basis for consideration, different degrees of the initial product design can be identified. Original Equipment Manufacturers (OEMs) can be responsible for the initial design and increasingly subcontract the actual manufacturing and also sometimes the design of the products to contract manufacturers. This type of production assignment is predominant in the high-tech and automotive industries.

The process of revenue acquisition

In the high-tech industry, for instance, OEMs use RFQs to determine their ideal manufacturing partner. The contract manufacturer receives the design in the form of a bill of material, technical drawings, and often as *Approved Vendor Lists* (AVL). These AVLs contain customer-dictated suppliers per component/part that the contract manufacturer must query in order to collect cost information for these parts.

After receiving the RFQ, usually a qualification process takes place on the part of the contract manufacturer. The aim of this qualification is to find out if participation will lead to a beneficial customer interaction. How a win or loss for the proposal will affect the capacities and overall strategic importance of the customer relationship should be taken into consideration here. In addition you must classify the type of RFQ a contract manufacturer is faced with.

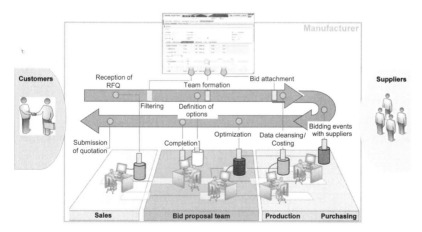

Figure 4.27 The Process of Revenue Acquisition and the Participating Business Areas

Depending on this qualification, resources and time are allocated to the quote creation, a step of highly strategic importance. Existing quote types are for example:

Bid types

- ▶ Quote for a new product/product range
- ▶ Re-quote for existing product ranges
- ▶ Engineering change quotes

A practical example: If during the classification of the RFQ, it can be determined that it is a first-round quote with the aim of qualifying for a further round, you would probably employ less effort and exactness for quote assembly.

Time-critical compiling of a quote …

The time which is required to create a quotation also depends on the type of quote as well as the relevant industry. Industry standards suggest that in the high-tech sector a quote must be created within two to three days, while in the automotive sector a turnaround of two to three weeks is the current yardstick.

If the contract manufacturer decides to take part in the RFQ, a virtual team is generally formed that is tasked with assembling a successful quote in the predefined time frame.

After assignment of the tasks, the actual work begins. This could potentially involve *Data Cleansing* (a particularity of the high-tech area). In this step, an attempt is made to match the customer part numbers posted in a bill of material against the internal part numbers, in order to be able to determine costs from the own actual data records with this key. The matching /assignment of customer part numbers, internal part numbers, and also the supplier part numbers and manufacturer part numbers (MPN) represent a daily challenge for contract manufacturers in the high-tech area. The maintenance of these relationships is highly complex and time-consuming.

Relevant cost information for creating a quote is generally recorded in internal data sources. Depending on the system landscape, however, the time-critical compilation of these costs can be extremely time-consuming and almost impossible, because the quoting systems are often not integrated with the internal data sources to a sufficient extent.

... from different data sources

Potential data sources are:

- ▶ Sales systems (CRM)

- Product Lifecyle Management (PLM) and Product Data Management Systems (PDM) in the production environment
- Procurement and sourcing systems (SRM)

The fast availability of this data is essential. In order to be prepared for incoming RFQs, an attempt is often made to validate the costs of the most commonly used components on a quarterly basis upfront with the relevant suppliers. This process ensures an accelerated creation of a quote using already validated costs.

If cost information is not internally available, or if for given components there should be another sourcing round for external validation, the requests will be channeled through the Procurement department and validated with supply chain in regards to costs and availability. This process is often performed via RFQs. The bids of the suppliers are then included in the cost estimation and the most cost-effective combination is determined.

After determining the material costs, other cost buckets are completed, such as production cost, non-recurring engineering (NRE), and labor costs, taking into account hourly rates for activities, and included in a final quote. If the quote is completed, an approval procedure with the responsible decision-makers in the company may be necessary before it can be submitted to the customers.

Before submitting the quote, sanity checks are usually carried out in order to avoid situations where cost estimates and calculations lead to quotes that cost the manufacturer more money than is actually earned.

Figure 4.28 illustrates the area where the majority of the quotes created should be located, so as not to run the danger of submitting quotes that lead to long-term losses and to ensure that quotes are not priced higher than needed to secure the contract in the first place. **The art of quote creation**

Manufacturers are increasingly responsible for the design, completion, testing, logistics, and often for the after-sales logistics. **New challenges for companies**

OEMs are only to happy to consider outsourcing, as it enables them to supply products more quickly than they could do so themselves, while at the same time it removes the fixed capital from their balance sheets. This means they can focus on their core competencies: research and development, sales, and marketing.

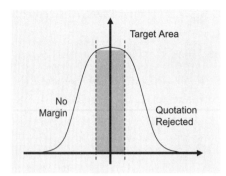

Figure 4.28 Sweet Spot of the Quote Submission

The current quote-creation process for contract manufacturers is characterized by a high degree of labor intensity, a lack of precision in costs determination, and low win rates. In addition, there is a lack of system support and difficult access to relevant data due to a lack of system integration (see Figure 4.29). In order to remain competitive in the quoting process, you must move away from disparate solutions and strive for a software constellation that supports the process in its entirety.

In the automotive industry, tier-1 and tier-2 suppliers find themselves in a tension field that is characterized by mergers, a high degree of staff turnover and reductions, new sourcing methods such as online auctions, globalization, and OEM-driven price reductions. As with the high-tech industry, you will find an increasing number of RFQs (approximately a 28% increase annually). Studies also show that there are discrepancies of up to 25% between actual costs and estimated costs in the quoting process.[3]

> "Sometimes we secure a contract which we regret having won six months later."—project manager, tier-1 automotive supplier

The complexity and duration of the quote creation in the automotive sector is even higher than in the high-tech field. Conversations with potential target customers for the SAP xApp Cost and Quotation Management show that the reuse of historical data is hardly guaranteed as the information is dispersed across a variety of data sources.

Management seldom has the required overview of all the activities in the quote departments to make strategic decisions based on solid data.

---

3 Center of Automotive Research/Altarum Research: *Automotive suppliers and the Revenue Acquisition Process: What's working and what's not?* September 2002. *www.altarum.org*.

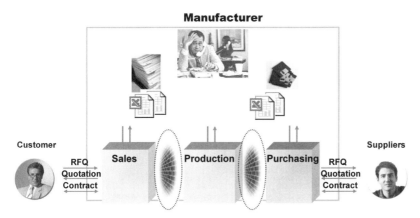

Figure 4.29 Quote-Creation Process for Contract Manufacturers Today

Missed initial submission deadlines are frequently mentioned if you ask for reasons why certain wins were not realized. The current win rate for new business opportunities is at approximately 25%.

Referring to a study quoted above by CAR (Center of Automotive Research), an increase of 2% in the win rate would result in an increase of 5.7% in revenues in a large company, an enormous effect. The same 2% increase in win rate would account for a 9.5% revenue increase for smaller suppliers.

To summarize, you can list the following external and internal challenges when evaluating the current (contract) manufacturing industry:

▶ **Trend towards outsourcing (as described earler)**

▶ **Demand for faster response times on the customer side**
Contract manufacturers are faced with strict time constraints.

▶ **Increased volume of RFQs**
There is an average of up to 3,000 new RFQs per year in the high-tech industry, while the automotive industry shows an average of approximately 500 RFQs. Both industries are expecting increases.

▶ **Increased complexity of the requests**
The increasing use of approved vendor lists in the high-tech industry reduces the option of cost-effective sourcing and leaves less room for margins. Product complexity is increasingas well, while innovation cycles have shortened.

Internal and external challenges for contract manufacturers

- ► **Increasing number of suppliers**
  The increasing number of potential suppliers and their required qualification with regard to quality, ability to supply, and cost is a further challenge for contract manufacturers.

The challenges referred to are systematically examined in the following section and symptoms that are faced along with the process are described. These challenges can only be dealt with if the below-mentioned problems can be solved in their entirety:

Starting points for improvements

- ► **Current extremely low win rate for manufacturers**
  As already mentioned, contract manufacturers work in the high-tech area with win rates of approximately 22 % and automotive suppliers with win rates of approximately 25 %. If you compare these values with actual labor costs in the high-tech area, there is, again according to the company size, approximately $1.2 million US of tied-up capital. In the automotive supplier area, there is up to $11.2 million US of tied-upcapital due to the labor intensity of the quoting process.

- ► **No focus on beneficial RFQs**
  In the attempt to acquire as much revenue as possible, the manufacturers often participate in every RFQ that is received. This leads to a high degree of staff involvement without achieving higher win rates at the same time. Efficient screening before the quote assembly is started, taking into account key performance indicators (KPIs), can help distinguish beneficial RFQs from losing interactions and those that will bring a loss for the company. Manufacturers could allocate labor to those quotes which have a high likelihood of generating profit.

- ► **Process breaks between sales and distribution, production, and purchasing**
  The current existing system landscape of manufacturers does not provide the required continuity that is needed for an efficient quoting process. Disparate systems and desktop applications prevail and lead to information breaks in the process. These must be bridged manually, posing a high risk of errors.

- ► **The reusability of data is not given**
  Access to historical data is often not existent, as different systems are used for the quote submission, and there is no technical alignment between those This is primarily seen in global companies. The lack of synchronization of the data records can lead to unpleasant surprises if historical data cannot be reused and different cost are presented for the same product to the customer.

▶ **No overview of existing records**
The data that must be compiled into the successful assembly of a quote is found in sales systems (customer data, historical bids), in production systems (material costs, labor costs), and procurement systems (contracts, orders, supplier bids). Efficient access to this data proves to be extremely difficult in practice, as the systems are not integrated and aligned, which leads to labor-intensive additional effort.

▶ **Lack of precision in cost determination**
Studies have shown that sometimes massive discrepancies occur between estimated cost and actual cost. These could have been avoided if access to existing records had been improved and more time had been available to validate the quotes.

Contract manufacturers are planning to address the aforementioned problems going forward by implementing better technologies. How will this be done in practice? The following section describes how the implementation can be driven forward.

Which changes must companies carry out—quo vadis?

The individual items in the following list represent the areas for improvement that have been identified in conversations with manufacturers:

▶ Development of a central and standardized quote-creation platform

▶ Focus on beneficial interactions with customers

▶ Increased accuracy and reduced cycle time

▶ Support for virtual teams in a global environment

▶ Integrated approach to the quote creation

▶ Increased internal response capacity

▶ Cost reduction per quote created

▶ Positioning as valuable partner for a customer

All these points influence the success or failure of a quote creation. Manufacturers attempt to implement suitable software solutions that help them to achieve these goals.

Which requirements do IT solutions have to fulfill in order to support companies in this process? The aforementioned company goals can only be reached if a software solution is selected that tackles all the points referred to and addresses them.

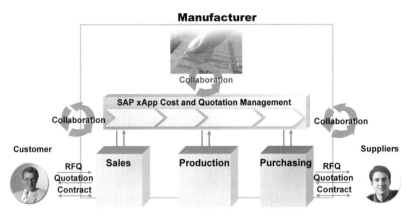

Figure 4.30 Quote-Creation Process for Contract Manufacturers Tomorrow

If you try to derive specific software requirements from the goals listed above, they will manifest as the following demands from a solution:

Requirements of a software

▶ **Efficient access**
Faster access to existing information (current and historical), and as automated as possible.

▶ **Efficient screening**
Provision of efficient screening mechanisms for new incoming RFQs in order to be able to concentrate on the most promising ones.

▶ **Integration of processes**
The cross-functional alignment of sales activities, internal cost determination, and sourcing in close interaction with the supply chain must tbe converted into a continuous process chain on a business as well as on a technical level. You have to be able to control the entire process out of one application.

▶ **Openness**
The software solution must be technically open so that it can be integrated into exisiting applications. Companies would like more effective use of their existing system landscape without having to completely revamp the existing systems for an effective quoting system.

In this context the following application systems are essential:

▷ Sales systems for a continuous chain of interactions with the customer

▷ Production systems for the identification of material, project, production and labor cost

- ▷ Technical systems such as PDM systems to combine technical modifications with the sales and distribution activities

- ▷ Procurement systems to support the required alignment with suppliers such as contracts

▶ **Integration of information**

Linking structured information with unstructured information: A software solution must be capable of providing BOM based cost information based on internal and external costs, to compare them and provide the user with the option of adressing potential conflicts that arise in the cost compilation. Process support must therefore be available for cost processing and in the semantics of the process (end user guidance), because the necessary process steps can vary depending on the type of the quote that is to be created. In addition, role-based access, information visualization and targeted messaging has to be provided.

▶ **Content management**

Fast access and retrieval of relevant documents is required. The instant availability of additional information which can also be captured in documents has to be guaranteed. BOM's, AVL, design documents and others must be accessible in context of the respective data objects and have to be available to the end user at any time.

▶ **Scalability and performance**

A system must be sufficiently high-performing and scalable to cope with the complex structures this process requires.

The use of bills of materials with simultaneous access to internal systems for automatic cost determination is a challenge for the system architecture, and if possible should be addressed with the newest technologies to also provide the corresponding upgradeability.

▶ **Support for collaboration between international and virtual teams**

The global distribution of employees who have to participate in the quote-creation process not only requires a corresponding international approach to software development but also the interaction capabilities needed to provide standardized access to various systems and the targeted integrated process support.

This section has shown what requirements can be derived for software development. The following section will highlight why the CAF was selected as the ideal development environment and how the preceding requirements towards a software solution have been implemented in the SAP xApp Cost and Quotation Management. The section will also be dedicated to the upcoming functional enhancements.

4.2.3   SAP xCQM as a Solution

Customer
demand ...
SAP xApp Cost and Quotation Management (SAP xCQM) tries to address the challenges of the industries and converts into a software solution the requirements that have been voiced in communication with customers.

After in-depth research on whether an existing solution in SAP could meet the requirements described above in their entirety, it was determined that functional support only exists for parts of the process. However, a continuous process-relevant support was not sufficiently realized.

... meets technical
offering
A technical realization based on the CAF was deemed an ideal development approach in order to ensure process continuity throughout all the required areas. The functional scope was developed in several roll-in sessions and workshops with potential pilot customers from the target industries.

Goals

SAP xCQM provides a collaborative work environment for all team members involved in the quote process, in order to assemble quotes in a complex environment in a faster, more efficient and precise manner.

Business benefits
of SAP xCQM
The following business benefits for manufactures can be achieved by deploying the SAP xCQM solution:

▶ **Provision of a companywide, standardized quote-creation platform,**
that enables a better coordination of the quote creation process and provides company-wide transparency

▶ **More precise cost determination in the quote process,**
as internal and external costs can be better determined in an automated fashion. A common platform enables analytical assessment of previous quotes,

▶ **Clear reduction in cycle times**
through better process efficiency

Functional Scope

SAP xCQM currently specializes in the creation of complex quotations based on bills of material, which cannot be handled by classic, automated quote-generation tools and for which pure costing solutions do not provide the relevant process support. For a complex quote creation, an integrated process must be established all the way from sales through production to RFQ interaction with the suppliers and then back in order to improve the current situation for manufacturers.

While initial product versions of SAP xCQM focused on high-tech, automotive, and manufacturing segments during the quote-creation process, further developments in the area of Cost Management (on the side of the OEMs) and additional industrial coverage are planned, such as for the chemical, pharmaceutical, aerospace and defense industry.

Business Process Model

SAP xCQM provides companies with the process support described in the following section. The corresponding process chain is described in this section, and some core process steps will be highlighted that will be described in more detail in the following sections.

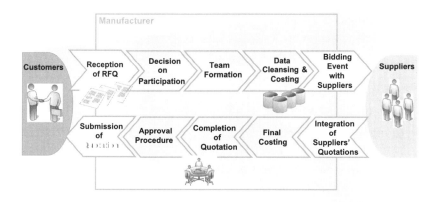

Figure 4.31 Process Support with SAP xCQM

▶ **Screening of incoming RFQs**

SAP xCQM enables sales employees to effectively qualify incoming RFQs and to categorize them according to the corresponding quote type. You can select whether the situation requires dealing with a new customer or a new project, a re-quoting activity, or a technical engineering change. Data concerning probability of profit, expected creation deadline, and expected revenue can also be stored. This captured data provides an excellent basis for effective screening with regards to successful participation in the bidding process, even at an early stage of a customer interaction.

▶ **Team management**

SAP xCQM provides efficient process support for all activities in the area of quote assembly for virtual teams. By providing workflow-based interaction chains and a set of predefined roles that can be assigned to

SAP xCQM
process support

end users in the implementation phase, a smooth and accelerated process flow can be achieved. All roles provided by SAP xCQM will be described in more detail in the following section.

▶ **Management of documents related to the process**
SAP xCQM uses SAP Knowledge Management in order to link the supporting documents of the RFQ, whether it be customer documents or internally supporting documents, to the relevant objects in the quote-creation process and has them accesible at any time upon request.

▶ **Data cleansing**
Mapping between customer name spaces for materials, internal name spaces for materials, and manufacturer part numbers on the side of the suppliers/manufacturer can be carried out based on Web service interfaces, and a corresponding mapping table. This enables an automated cost determination, if a match can be determined between the incoming customer material numbers and the relevant internal material numbers. In the high-tech sector, the MPN can also be used as a key for cost determination by taking into account approved vendor lists, in order to find costs in internal systems.

▶ **Quotation Worksheet (QWS)**
SAP xCQM provides a compelling work environment for cost determination, the *Quotation Worksheet* (QWS) or quote-creation worksheet. This QWS can be flexibly adapted to customer requirements, in dependence of the respective RFQ and provides sufficient structuring options for this matter.

In this environment, the cost breakdown can be defined, and alternative scenarios for different quantity scales and other business considerations can be evaluated. Using the QWS, individual work packages can be assigned and the progress of completion can be monitored.

▶ **The concept of flexible cost buckets**
Individual cost buckets can be directly assigned in the QWS to other employees and the progress can be monitored from here. Cost buckets can be material costs, Labor costs, manufacturing and production costs, NRE costs etc.

The set of costs buckets that is available to the end user is configurable and can be adapted according to the business case of each company using xCQM. Each cost bucket can be even more refined using cost elements.

- ▶ **Cost extraction from multiple data sources**

  SAP xCQM uses the SAP NetWeaver infrastructure in order to read relevant data sources for automated cost determination. This capability to read data includes contracts, standard and moving average prices, purchase orders, supplier quotations, purchasing info records, and historical quotations. Based on the prioritization of these data sources by end user, all these objects can be automatically queried with the relevant quantity information and can be presented to the end user in order to ensure the best possible cost determination.

- ▶ **Sourcing loop with suppliers**

  SAP xCQM provides the option of identifying directly in the cost determination environment those components and subassemblies, that do not yet carry any costs or for which you would like to receive another round validation from the supply chain. The application simultaneously enables triggering of RFQ's for those components and sub-assemblies and incorporating bids from suppliers directly in the application, in order to arrive at the final cost determination.

- ▶ **Approval loops**

  As soon as a quote has been assembled, the proposed values can be transferred into an approval procedure in order to be able to involve all employees who participate in the decision-making process in this critical process step.

- ▶ **Submission and tracking**

  Approved quotes can be submitted to customers, and subsequent interaction with the customers can be captured in SAP xCQM. This involves indication as to whether a revision of the quote is required or, in the ideal case, if an acceptance of the quote by the customer is in sight. For each of these two potential outcomes—whether positive or negative—SAP xCQM provides a range of predefined reason codes that the sales employees can simply select from.

- ▶ **Transparency by analytics**

  Implementation of a companywide quote-creation platform enables analytical evaluation of all data that has been developed along this process. It provides a transparency not available in most companies because disparate systems are used. Thus it can therefore positively influence a company's decision making ability. For instance, you can find out what customer interactions are really profitable, what is the impact of alternative bid scenarios, and much more.

User Interaction

Core roles in SAP xCQM and their interaction

In order to efficiently support the aforementioned core process steps, SAP xCQM currently provides the following roles, which can be correspondingly assigned to end users during an implementation:

▶ **Sales employee (Account Manager)**

This role is of particular importance, as it is intended to support the first person in the company to receive an RFQ and to initiate further steps. Functional support is provided through a compelling Web-based interface in which a sales employee can enter general data about an RFQ received and prioritize it accordingly. The intial screening can also be carried out by this role. Customer documents are linked with the RFQ and an internal project manager (quote team lead) can be appointed.

After a successful quote creation, this role can also be involved in the approval procedure and accounts for the submission and tracking of the customer feedback.

▶ **Project manager (Quote Team Lead)**

As an internal project manager, this person's role is the most important one in terms of overall process control and work distribution. After receiving the work package, he or she can provide the required work environment (one or several quotation worksheets) and can assign individual tasks to be completed. At the same time he or she must ensure that the results are delivered within the predefined timeframe and bundled into a final quote, which can then be transferred into an approval procedure.

▶ **Quote team member**

As a specialist for a given area of responsibility, this member has the task of completing the assigned work packages (completing the assigned cost buckets) accurately within the deadline given in the context of the quote calculation. In SAP xCQM, specialists can be nominated for e.g. the determination of material costs and labor costs.

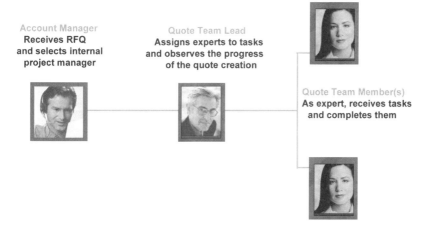

Figure 4.32 Work Distribution between the Core Roles in SAP xCQM

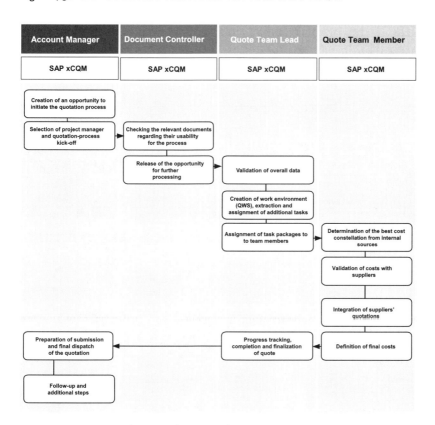

Figure 4.33 Interaction between the Core Roles in SAP xCQM for the Quote Creation (General Overview)

There are also additional roles in SAP xCQM:

▶ **Document Controller**

An employee who has been assigned this role checks files, which were sent by customers or internal sources, and assigns these to the related quote activities. Optionally changes can be performed in order to comply with extraction templates that come with the SAP xCQM application. This control function can ensure that technical or content problems that might emerge during the process, can be captured early on.

▶ **Approver/Reviewer**

The decision-makers responsible for the quote submission within companies can be assigned a reviewer role, in order to be able to approve the quote once it has been created or to request changes.

▶ **Administrator**

As a system administrator this role similarly assumes great importance. Via the administrator cockpit, the initial configuration, connection to backend systems, object selection and control in the connected systems all can be performed.

Each role is presented with relevant information in a specifically designed and targeted environment: the *dashboard* or *cockpit*. For the sales employees' and project managers' roles, a phase-based breakdown is offered which provides a quick overview of the object's current lifecycle phase.

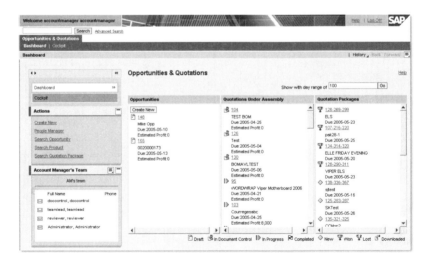

Figure 4.34 The Account Manager Dashboard

In addition to the workflow-based interaction in the SAP xCQM application, email messages can be sent to the respective team members in order to notify them of tasks.

Detailed Description of the SAP xCQM-Supported Process Flow

Incoming RFQs are captured in the SAP xCQM environment by sales employees (account managers), and related customer documents containing additional information are linked with this technical object (opportunity).

In order to understand the following descriptions in context, Figure 4.35 illustrates the object relationships in SAP xCQM.

Opportunity

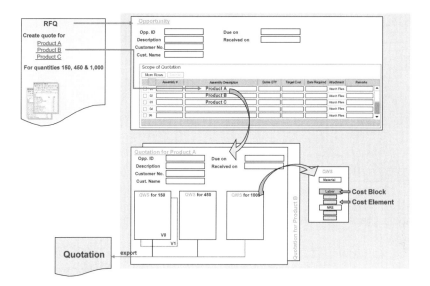

Figure 4.35 Object Relations in SAP xCQM

The user interface provides a set of standard attributes to enter the RFQ data, which can be correspondingly enhanced in the implementation phase. Here the concept of *dynamic attributes* can be used.

At the same time the scope and nature of the RFQ are determined for which one or more quotes are to be created.

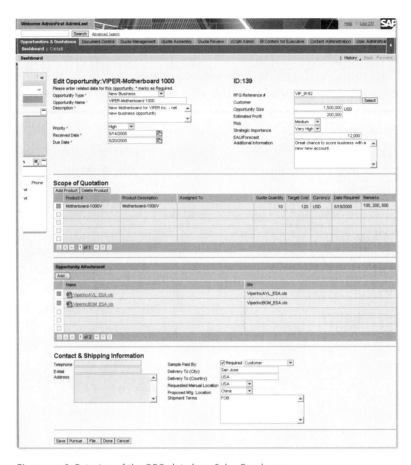

Figure 4.36 Entering of the RFQ data by a Sales Employee

Bid positions   The bid positions (products/quotes) can be transferred as work packages to an internal project manager (quote team lead). After receiving the work packages, the quote team lead can set up the work environment in which quotes can be created.

Quotation Worksheet (QWS)   SAP xCQM provides a very flexible concept for creating quotes: the quotation worksheet (QWS). The internal project manager determines the required cost breakdown, the quantities the quote is to be created for, the data sources for cost extraction, and how the QWS is to be displayed. For example, in order to create a quote for a quantity scale, you can simply create several QWSes with different initial quantities, and the system automatically calculates the applicable costs based on these different quantities. The calculation is carried out according to the quantity scale that is defined in the underlying objects such as contracts, purchase orders etc.

A QWS may contain so-called cost buckets and cost elements which can be used to refine a cost bucket.

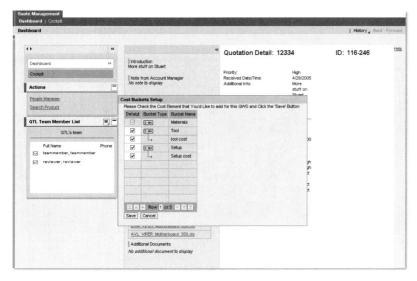

Figure 4.37 Determination of the Cost Breakdown

SAP xCQM provides access to the following objects for a given material/component:

▶ Contracts

▶ Purchase orders

▶ Purchasing info records

▶ Standard and moving average price

▶ Historical quotations

▶ Supplier quotes

As SAP xCQM comes with its own database, previously submitted quotes for a specific material can also be taken into consideration.

Based on extraction templates that SAP xCQM provides, bills of materials and approved vendor lists are read, merged and brought into logical context. At the same time, a Web service calls a mapping environment enabling you to find an internal data record automatically by using a customer part number (if it exists) and to perform costs determination— based on the relevant quantity—with this internal part number in the predefined data sources.

Cost determination

Figure 4.38 Determination of the Cost Sources

If the mapping based on internal part number does not provide results, the manufacturer part number can also be used to query existing data records. The system automatically tries to retrieve a data record that can provide an indication for the cost determination.

The QWS enables you further to evaluate alternative scenarios. For instance, you can create a version based on contractual obligations and for another one create a sourcing loop with the supply chain to get most recent cost. Another application scenario of the QWS is the simultaneous creation of alternative quantity scenarios. In this case, the corresponding quantity scales in the connected backend are read and the relevant costs are displayed for each case. Individual cost buckets can then be assigned to employees (quote team members).

In order to improve the process support for determining material costs, a view concept was developed in alignment with customers. It is divided in four tab strips, with each of these views having an exactly defined scope:

Material costs determination

▶ **Hierarchical bill of materials view (Hierarchical BOM view)**
This view offers a quick overview of the determined costs in the hierarchical context of the underlying bill of materials.

▶ **Exploded bill of materials view (Exploded BOM view)**
This view (see Figure 4.39) provides the main work environment for an employee who is responsible for the determination of material costs. This view enables you to see what costs have been automatically

determined based on the relevant settings and what objects have
delivered these cost estimates. The view also provides conflict resolution capabilities (see below), in case several qualifying costs could be
determined.

▶ **Sourcing prep view**

As described above, you can use the cost determination view to immediately select RFQ relevant components that either do not yet carry
any costs, or for which you would like to receive a renewed validation
from your supply chain, and transfer these RFQ relevant items into a
sourcing bin.

▶ **Sourcing bin**

The sourcing bin is the environment for acutally triggering a RFQ. It is
where you can create targeted packages for individual suppliers and
submit those for completion. The responses can simply be uploaded in
this environment so you have a full overview of all costs before determining the best possible combination for this quote.

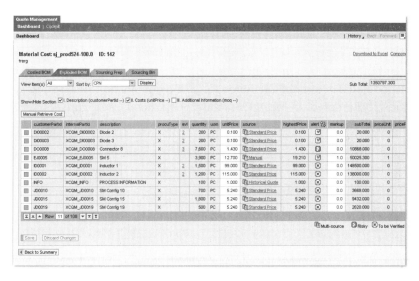

Figure 4.39 Exploded Bill of Materials and Costs Determination

If more than one suitable cost source contains relevant price information,
the system automatically determines the lowest cost, based on the prioritization during the setup. The system also shows the highest cost found.
This allows the company to identify deviations or cost fluctuations
quickly.

Manual cost
determination/
conflict resolution

A graphic indicator is used to show the end user if more than one qualifying option is available.

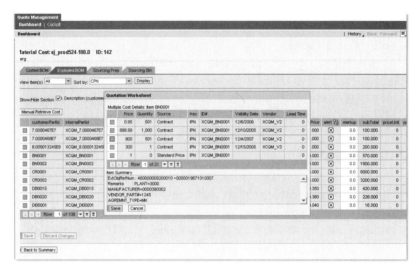

Figure 4.40 Conflict Resolution

The end user can view all the qualifying data records at a glance and can choose the best option. In this context, the work environment provides all additional information required for cost determination such as supply times, minimum order quantities, and stock at hand (see Figure 4.40).

Sourcing
preparation

If there are no costs available for certain components or if the current status of the cost determination is not satisfactory, you can use the *sourcing preparation view* (see Figure 4.41) to select the components which you consider relevant for RFQ processing.

This list of components can then be transferred seamlessly to a sourcing environment in which the components, together with the relevant information, can be downloaded in an offline format (MS Excel, HTML or XML). These sourcing sheets can then be sent to the relevant supplier(s).

Upon receipt of the supplier quotes, these can be directly uploaded into the application in order to evaluate the results within the cost determination environment.

As an alternative, and depending on the company's system landscape, relevant RFQs can also be generated in the mySAP SRM (Supplier Relationship Management) application, and the corresponding supplier responses can be read directly from SRM into xCQM.

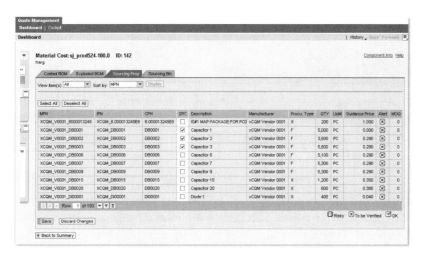

Figure 4.41 The Sourcing Preparation View

The final cost determination is incumbent upon the responsible employee, who can view all the costs at any time in order to accomplish the task. This enables the company to make the best possible decision based on internal costs and externally validated costs.

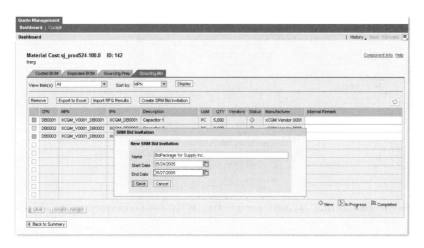

Figure 4.42 Sourcing View and Importing Supplier Quotes

As soon as the determination of the assigned cost buckets is completed, the employee can share his contribution to the overall quote with the project manager. The project manager ensures that all participants will complete their tasks within the predefined time frames and assembles the final quote. After successful compilation of all cost buckets, the quote can be transferred to the responsible decision-makers.

A bid (quote package) may consist of one or more QWS. This is handy, for example, in dealing with different quantity scenarios and the cost impact associated to those.

The responsible decision-makers in companies receive a message that a quote has been assembled and can view this quote in SAP xCQM to either approve it or request changes. If the quote has been approved, the sales employee can submit the quote to the customer and track any further interaction with the customer in SAP xCQM.

Naturally the submission of a quote does not mean the end of the interaction with the customer. SAP xCQM can also be used to support several rounds in a quote-creation process. The quotes already submitted can be referenced at any time and may be used as a basis for creating new quotes.

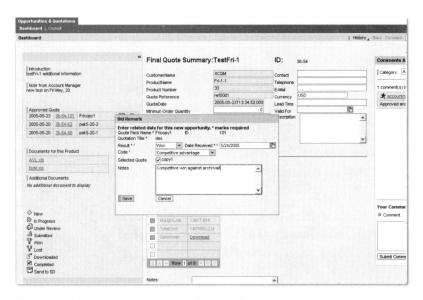

Figure 4.43 Tracking Customer Interaction for a Quote

Why has the CAF been used as a Development Environment?

The above requirements towards a software solution were thoroughly investigated in order to provide as ideal a development environment as possible for the realization and future expandability of this standard solution.

Some of the requirements mentioned above require flexibility, which currently only the CAF can provide:

▶ **Process flexibility to support a continuous process**
The SAP NetWeaver platform with its technical components provides an exceptional development environment to implement the steps relevant to the process, based on the CAF. This capability is also used for standard product development and thus provides companies with the necessary flexibility to model individual scenarios to their requirements.

▶ **Across different enterprise applications**
SAP xCQM is an ideal showcase for design of process-relevant applications based on composite technology. In order to communicate with the systems required for the entire process, these applications can be integrated in the process through the CAF. They can be presented attractively to the end user via an appealing interface (SAP Enterprise Portal and Web Dynpro), without requiring the end user to separately engage in the underlying applications.

▶ **Broad demand in companies with various applications and system landscapes**
The CAF also enables existing applications to be incorporated into the solution and can integrate these software solutions according to the required business process support. The need to integrate sales systems with production systems and sourcing solutions argues strongly for existing IT investments to be incorporated into the entire picture.

In addition to these technical considerations, the existing SAP solution portfolio was scrutinized for contributing software components that needed to be merged into an attractive solution. It was determined that no existing application could cover the requirements in its entirety.

There was no continuous process support realized within the existing SAP solution portfolio, and a composite architecture opened the door for new approaches to use existing SAP applications on the customer side without making them a prerequisite. For this reason, a decision was made to drive the implementation of SAP xApp CQM on the basis of the CAF.

Most of the competitive solutions do not offer the required integration in back-end systems and therefore qualify themselves only to a limited extent for a complete solution that is to provide continuous and future-oriented support for the big picture.

Technical Components

SAP xApp Cost and Quotation Management uses the SAP NetWeaver Stack to provide a solution for the challenges of complex quote creation.

The following section describes which technical components of the SAP NetWeaver infrastructure were used.

▶ **SAP Enterprise Portal**
SAP Enterprise Portal is used for role-based access to relevant information. User interfaces created with Web Dynpro enable a fast understanding and a simple adaption in companies.

▶ **SAP Web Application Server (J2EE)**
SAP xApp CQM is a Java-based application shipped on the SAP Web Application Server (J2EE version).

▶ **SAP Knowledge Management**
SAP Knowledge Management is used for efficient management of documents and quotes to provide for easy retrieval of and permanent access to relevant information. Documents are logically linked to the relevant objects of SAP xCQM and are therefore available throughout the entire process.

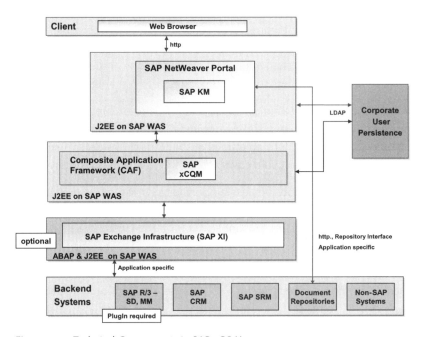

Figure 4.44 Technical Components in SAP xCQM

SAP xCQM is one of the first applications that uses the SAP NetWeaver platform and the SAP CAF to the same extent. We will now describe by way of example how SAP xCQM uses the CAF as a development environment.

Technical Implementation of the Application

We will not describe the implementation in its entirety, but rather concentrate on the corresponding object modeling that was used for the implementation.

All necessary data objects used in SAP xCQM were integrated as business objects in the Entity Service Modeler. With this tool a consolidated data layer of relevant information can be extracted from the connected back-end systems. The object model is declared in the corresponding development component and defines the access to a set of JavaBeans through automatically generated proxy classes.

Object modeling

In order not to completely digress into technical details, and as the technical components have already been described in great detail, we will now describe a few examples for usage of the CAF in the application development of SAP xCQM.

Each role in SAP xCQM is presented with targeted information in form of a cockpit (see Figure 4.45) or dashboard. The visualization of the cockpit is supported through the **FlexTree** pattern which enables you to display hierarchical tables.

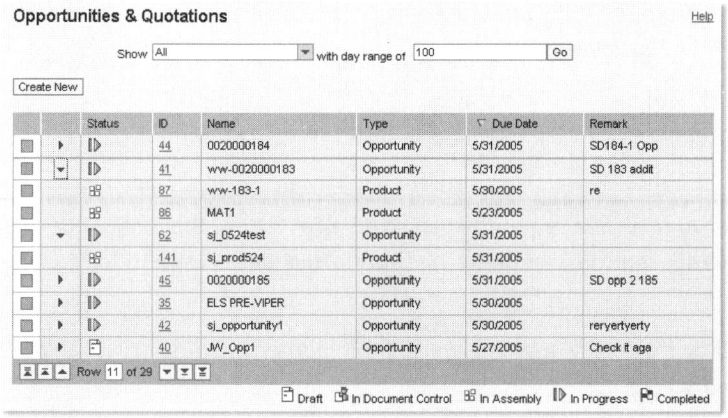

Cockpit example

Opportunities & Quotations   Help

Show [All ▼] with day range of [100] [Go]

[Create New]

		Status	ID	Name	Type	▽ Due Date	Remark
☐	▶	▯▷	44	0020000184	Opportunity	5/31/2005	SD184-1 Opp
☐	▾	▯▷	41	ww-0020000183	Opportunity	5/31/2005	SD 183 addit
☐		🏢	87	ww-183-1	Product	5/30/2005	re
☐		🏢	86	MAT1	Product	5/23/2005	
☐	▾	▯▷	62	sj_0524test	Opportunity	5/31/2005	
☐		🏢	141	sj_prod524	Product	5/31/2005	
☐	▶	▯▷	45	0020000185	Opportunity	5/31/2005	SD opp 2 185
☐	▶	▯▷	35	ELS PRE-VIPER	Opportunity	5/30/2005	
☐	▶	▯▷	42	sj_opportunity1	Opportunity	5/30/2005	reryertyerty
☐	▶	🗎	40	JW_Opp1	Opportunity	5/27/2005	Check it aga

[≖ ≖ ▲] Row [11] of 29 [▾ ≖ ≖]

🗎 Draft   🏢 In Document Control   🏢 In Assembly   ▯▷ In Progress   ▱ Completed

Figure 4.45 The Cockpit

The user interface was developed in Web Dynpro in the SAP NetWeaver Developer Studio. The NetWeaver Enterprise Service Framework and CAF were used as service module providers. Each service module contains one or multiple aspects whose elements correspond to one UI element.

An automated service-generation tool was used in order to generate the relevant basic services, which connect to the object access layer.

Backend integration For automatic costs determination, SAP xCQM requires large volumes of master and transaction data from backend systems. This data is saved for performance reasons in the local SAP xCQM database and is not read each time in real time.

This design decision can be easily understood if you imagine the magnitude of accesses to different data objects for a given bill of material (e.g. all purchase orders, contracts, purchasing info records etc.) in order to reach a simultaneous determination of the most cost-effective as well as highest cost records.

SAP xCQM uses a periodic batch update based on the Java Connector (JCo), to retrieve the most current data records from the backend systems connected. An Enterprise JavaBean (EJB) with a configurable XML file is used in combination with a scheduler servlet.

The XML configuration file enables you to flexibly set the frequency for the delta upload. The relevant SAP backend system requires a plug-in for the JCO access in order to load customer data, units of measurement, and the costs from the relevant data objects. The corresponding development class is /SAPXCQM/PI_APPL.

The back-end systems and relevant data objects (purchase orders, material master etc.) can be specified in the SAP xCQM administration console.

Data model of SAP xCQM In order to meet the requirements of this application, the data model has to be optimized for continuous high-performance access and for enablement of an efficient transfer of information between the data objects.

Entity services The following entity services were implemented in order to enable all required scenarios:

▶ QProject
▶ Quote

- QBucket and QItem
- QuoteRFQExport

An example: In order to enable the flexible combination of a product for which a quote has to be created and the relevant work sheets (QWS) that may be required in this step, the entity service **Quote** contains two functions: The service can be a product instance if the master attribute value is "1,"or it can be a quotation worksheet if the master attribute value is "0." As a product can have several quotation worksheets, all the worksheets which belong to a product bear the same `internalProductID`.

The complete picture of SAP xCQM requires additional entity services, which will not be further detailed at this point.

Documents required for the successful creation of quotes are incorporated into SAP xCQM through the CAF-based document component. For instance, after receiving the RFQ the account manager may load the customer bill of materials and the AVL into the application. For this, the CAF CORE service **Document** is automatically been used, that stores the documents in KM and creates a logical link between the documents and the respective SAP xCQM object. Figure 4.46 shows this component.

Integration with KM

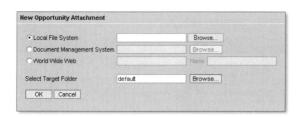

Figure 4.46 CAF Document Component

At numerous points within the business process of the SAP xCQM application, information provided by customers (bill of materials and AVL) or by suppliers in response to RFQs (vendor response) can be read directly into the application, based on Excel formats.

Excel upload

SAP provided an Excel Parsing API for this purpose. In the development phase, a XML schema for the bill of materials and the AVL was deployed, which follows the data model of SAP xCQM. The Excel files are loaded into the SAP xCQM persistence based on extraction templates.

Please note that the relevant CORE service of SAP xCQM expects the data structure of the underlying Excel files to correspond with the schema defined in the XML file. SAP xCQM also provides another program that reads the Excel files and converts them into XML objects, which can then be received by the CORE Service. For this, the SAP XML toolkit Java/XML binding mechanism is used, which facilitates interoperability between the XML documents and the Java objects. Final parsing occurs via the SAP Excel Parsing API.

Excel download The option to transfer data from the xCQM persistence to Excel files at defined points in time (for example for interaction with suppliers) is enabled through the CAF CSV export component.

The CAF export component consists of an UI part and a configuration part.

The user interface for the export screen and the export configuration is a Web Dynpro user interface.

The configuration for the export UIs requires two parameters:

▶ CSVExport Config name
the name to save the configuration in the repository

▶ CSV file name
the name of the file which is to be populated with data

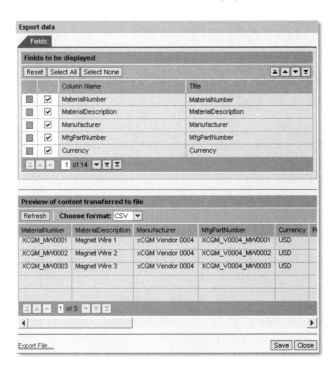

Figure 4.47 The Excel Export Component UI

The user interface is generated at design time and contains all defined data, a WYSIWYG view, the columns that are being downloaded, a link to trigger the download into the CSV file and the option to close the download component.

The aforementioned Excel download component is a so called *reusable component*, which is used in more than one application and can be embedded in other applications without additional programming work. The basic procedure of embedding reusable components in other user interfaces was already described in Chapter 3. Another example is the *People Picker* (see Figure 4.48) that enables you to create virtual teams in complex collaboration scenarios where many parties must interact with each other.

Reusable components

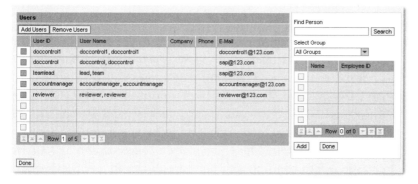

Figure 4.48 The People Picker

In this final section will outline how the SAP xCQM roadmap looks like.

4.2.4 Further Development of SAP xCQM and Outlook

The complexity of the business process covered by SAP xCQM requires close alignment of different activities such as sales, production and/or sourcing, as well as the corresponding objects in the underlying systems that are needed for the individual process steps.

The solutions described below will be integrated effectively into the quotation process. SAP xCQM can be seen here as a central access to the relevant supporting systems in order to provide the end users with the correct information at any time.

In addition to the examples we already mentioned, there are other integration points in the SAP application portfolio:

▶ **SAP Business Intelligence**
Reports for business users and management are milestones for every application. A data warehouse such as SAP BI is particularly suitable for this. Standard reports are being supplied with SAP xCQM.

▶ **Customer Relationship Management (CRM)**
Depending on the system landscape, an existing sell side system such as mySAP CRM can be used as central platform for all interaction with a customer. SAP xCQM provides process support for complex scenarios driven by bills of materials, which cannot be covered by the traditional automatic quote generation capabilities of mySAP CRM. The opportunity- and quote management of mySAP CRM is another integration point here.

▶ **Supplier Relationship Management (SRM)**
For the effective execution of online RFQs with suppliers, there is also an integration to sourcing solutions such as mySAP SRM. Components that are considered sourcing relevant can be sent directly into the sourcing solution, where submission, tracking, and evaluation take place. SAP xCQM can then retrieve and display the received supplier bids. This process allows for an immediate conversion of the supplier interactions into contracts and purchase orders and reduces manual interaction even further.

In addition to these integration points, there will also be other functional enhancements. They will be determined with the early adopters for an exact prioritization in terms of realization.

4.2.5 Summary

In the previous sections, the need for a solution such as SAP xCQM for complex quote creations became evident as we showed that the current process of creating quotes is in most cases not satisfactory. Economical consequences such as the loss of a customer or an incorrect calculation are only two of the most serious effects to be dealt with.

Manufacturers are only too aware of this fact, and are looking for a complete solution that also takes into account existing IT investments to be used for the entire process coverage.

With SAP xCQM, we created a platform based on the latest technology that enables companies to face these challenges in a targeted manner.

The expandability of the solution does not only promise a better standard solution in the future, but also enables new ways to expand the solution in companies that implement it.

CAF, as the underlying development platform, enabled the SAP xCQM development team to create a process-oriented application within the shortest time frame. This application can be seamlessly integrated in an existing customer system landscape and can use its functionalities to a complete extent.

The fast modeling of entity services in CAF, which can then communicate effectively with back-end data, the consequent use of service layers, and the use of components provided by the CAF (such as Excel download components) enabled a new way of application development.

Capacity for fast modeling

Future releases of SAP xCQM will, together with other composite applications, contribute to drive the use of the CAF as a development environment, and thus promote the accelerated future development of other applications from idea to reality.

5   Outlook: Applications and Application Development

The functionality of the first release of the Composite Application Framework (CAF) indicates that we are soon to see a paradigm shift in the development of business applications. Considering the increasing complexity of system landscapes and the ever-more demanding requirements of them, the traditional way of building applications is becoming more and more of an obstacle. This is because, until now, development has depended too heavily on technical and communication skills and on the availability of the persons involved. The classic separation of an application into a transactional and an analytical part is no longer justifiable. The technology now has to be able to seamlessly integrate both parts during development and at runtime.

This requires a subtle and in-depth understanding of business applications as a concept, and also of how and by whom they are developed.

5.1   Development

Previously, the development process for business applications had to be centralized or centrally coordinated, and the development work itself had to be carried out by programmers in a homogeneous system landscape. In this kind of system, changes, extensions, maintenance, and support are assigned to and carried out by the IT department, consulting companies, and maintenance and support departments.

Over the years, technologically and semantically heterogeneous system landscapes and applications have become established. This has occurred for a variety of reasons, including company mergers, technology changes, reorganizations, and changes in basic conditions.

Heterogeneous landscapes

The more heterogeneous and the larger the system landscape and the technologies it uses, the more difficult it is for the people involved to make changes within a timeframe that is acceptable to the users.

Attempts to fulfill requirements in terms of functionality, usability, and speed of modification processes aim primarily to reduce the number of systems and technologies in use. However, this, in turn, is a relatively long, drawn-out process, and changes in basic conditions often cancel out any improvements it brings.

This all places great strain on the resources of IT departments, with the result that those resources are no longer sufficient to fulfill the requests and requirements of the technical departments.

Prioritizing requirements Different priorities are assigned to different requirements. Requirements to do with stability, performance, security, data consistency, and scalability are basic prerequisites and must always be fulfilled. Then there is system integration and functional extensions to applications, both of which have to be implemented quickly ("quickly" in this context means "within a few days"). Usability and personalization are usually at the bottom of the list of priorities. Of course, depending on the difficulty of a problem and the available resources, priorities may be ordered differently.

The applications involved can be roughly divided into the following categories:

1. Backbone applications
2. Applications that support business processes
3. Applications that drive innovation

Depending on the business of an enterprise, there can be variations. While the first two categories deal with maintaining the existence of the enterprise in the short and medium term, the last category is responsible for the enterprise's long-term survival. Let us now look at each category in detail.

Backbone applications Backbone applications directly safeguard the immediate existence of the enterprise. They are therefore indispensable. They literally form the backbone of the enterprise in its daily operations and make it possible to fulfill legal requirements as efficiently as possible; they ensure that salaries and invoices are paid, or balance sheets created. If one of these applications fails, the existence of the enterprise is in danger. Examples are the applications in the HR, CO, and FI areas, which were known in the past as Core[1] applications.

Applications that support business processes Applications that support business processes safeguard the medium-term existence of an enterprise. They are not urgent, but do facilitate the execution and monitoring of processes and, thanks to automation, usually reduce costs. Used correctly, they represent a competitive advantage.

For example, using a project-management system is not necessary for the survival of a project, but it does greatly facilitate the process of efficiently

---

1 Not to be confused with the CORE project.

executing, analyzing and administrating the project. Without the Travel Management system, for instance, employees would still be able to organize business trips, but it would be much more difficult and time-consuming, and thus more cost-intensive overall.

Applications that drive innovation safeguard the existence of an enterprise in the long term. This category includes all applications that collect data of all kinds, often within the framework of projects. The type of data and the need to keep up with changing conditions in competition, society, and technology mean that in many cases, aside from existing applications used in the project, additional, individually adapted applications may be required.

Applications that drive innovation

The structured and, in many cases, unstructured data in this last application category encapsulates the innovative potential of an enterprise, as this data holds information from the many large and small projects in the enterprise, and also from the daily work activities that take place there. The ideas and findings that are collected from a specific group of employees, be it over a shorter or a longer period, indicate the degree of innovation in the enterprise and thus help to secure its long-term success.

5.2   Paradigm Shift

In light of the above, the ability to create applications that drive innovation with the required degree of flexibility and speed is becoming increasingly important. The need to be able to call up this data later in order to maintain the enterprise's competitive edge in terms of information and innovation also presents special challenges.

The analytical character of an application becomes more important, and the integration of tools and interfaces, the shared use of metadata, and transparency for the user are regarded as given. This applies not only to applications that drive innovation, but also to all other business applications. Therefore, the term "business applications" as used from this point on always applies to applications that combine structured, aggregated, and unstructured data for a business process.

Business applications must be capable of being further developed, modified, and, in extreme cases, exchanged. These days, project teams necessarily consist of employees who work in different, often physically separate, departments and who are thrown together for the duration of the project. This fact poses challenges for the business application, as the applications and business processes in question are required only for the duration of the project. This greater emphasis on projects means that the classic business processes will be surrounded by short-term applications that arise quickly from non-central sources.

New kinds of applications

What are these kinds of applications like? First, they come into being in a matter of a few days, seemingly on the spur of the moment, which is why they are referred to as *instant applications*. Not only the application is created in this way, but also any changes to existing applications.

Also, in many cases, applications that are required only for the duration of one project or just a few projects quickly become disposable and are no longer needed. In many cases, only the stored data is required, and the applications themselves are discarded.

The applications and the data they hold are initially required only for the project or specialist department itself. Any possible use for the enterprise as a whole only becomes clear later. However, it is very likely that data from other, usually central, applications will also be required in these applications. *Integration* is very important in this case.

Also, the applications are created or adapted non-centrally; that is, they are not created by the central IT departments and consulting firms. Instead, the people responsible for them are project team members with the relevant skills, or possibly decentralized IT groups that can be assigned flexibly. These applications thus do not correspond to the usually theoretical and idealized design requirements. To put it politely, they are more *practice-oriented*.

For the reasons mentioned above, they are also usually not very extensive, and are thus more like "micro-applications."

Creating an infrastructure for projects is becoming more the job of project teams. This is a job that often includes project-specific business applications. Different projects can produce very different data, and attempts to provide generic applications for this kind of data often fail because of the above-mentioned duration of the development phase and because of how the requirements are prioritized.

Guerrilla applications

To date, this has led to the emergence of "guerrilla applications." These are applications that are created secretly and in an uncontrolled fashion by the technical departments or project teams themselves, but sooner or later fall into the area of responsibility of the IT department. This is a department's worst nightmare, because the applications in question will, in the meantime, have played a certain role in the system landscape and will thus have to be integrated. Despite all efforts to the contrary, there will always be these guerrilla applications.

So what should one do about it? There is only one solution: Forget about the previous paradigm and adopt a new approach. The decentralized teams should be able to create their own specialized applications, and the IT department should support them in this.

What this means for centralized IT departments is that the focus of their work changes; it moves away from producing and operating business applications and towards providing a service. Instead of creating and supporting all applications themselves, or outsourcing development to a small number of contractors, IT departments have to provide decentralized teams with an infrastructure and tools that enable them to create business applications with an adequate scope of functions quickly and as easily as possible. This should be accompanied by standards and methodologies, plus detailed consulting and support for the individual teams. Once a project has ended, the data collected in that project has to be preserved or integrated in a form that allows it to be re-used without the need to keep maintaining the application in question. Integration in this context does not mean that the data is transferred to the data structures of the centralized system; it means that it can be accessed by services and thus the system as a whole remains aware of its existence.

IT department as a service provider

The CAF already includes this approach and allows non-programmers to be involved in application development. Code is generated and systems are integrated based on model data and metadata. We find this approach so compelling that we are certain that the CAF will be used not only to build xApps and Composite Applications, but also—once it attains a certain level of maturity and sufficient functionality—that it will increasingly be used to extend classic applications as well, and possibly even to create new ones.

What is more, it will redefine these classic applications. The CAF will change our understanding of what makes a classic Core application and what it is supposed to provide. We would now like to illustrate this by means of some independent facts.

5.3   Facts

Information from the IT departments of enterprises listed among the Fortune 500 shows that, in many cases, several thousand business applications are in used within an enterprise. A well-known oil company reports

Fortune 500

has 6,000 applications, and a large computer company as many as 12,000. These figures came as a surprise, even to the IT departments themselves.

Only a fraction of these applications had been set up or were being supported centrally. Also, although the centrally maintained applications were mission-critical, they were not innovation-critical, and thus did not create value for the future survival of the enterprise.

Even if we assume that 500 business applications, for example, were created or purchased under the auspices of the IT department, this still begs the question: What exactly was the purpose of the remaining 5,500 or 11,500 applications? Do they correspond to the definition of the term "business application?" Even if, let us say, 50 % of applications do correspond to this definition, and 50 % of the remaining applications are classic applications, there are still 1,375 or 2,875 left unaccounted for. In every case, the number of applications left over is a multiple of those that are supported by the IT departments.

In all likelihood, these are probably mainly macro-based Excel files, Access databases, Lotus Notes applications, and other applications created using similar tools. These tools were selected because they are easy to use, contain lots of templates, and also provide Wizards that assist users in creating their own applications without the need for much programming knowledge. These applications probably do not fit with any ideal design, but seem to fulfill their purpose. The tools make it possible to run an application locally for a small circle of users, but with the disadvantage that the application is therefore usually known only to these users.

Internet There are similar phenomena in other areas too, such as the Internet. The Internet also has backbone applications without which it would collapse, such as domain administration and registrars. Then there are also the applications that are not vital, but very convenient and popular, such as search engines, book dealers, mail providers, online magazines, and so on. Some of these provide applications that use large stocks of information and are of very high quality, which cost huge sums to install and run, and which are owned by companies that may well be worth billions of dollars, as we have seen in the latest IPOs.

There are also the applications that deliver the actual added value; that is, the millions upon millions of small websites that provide content on every possible topic. The technical design of these applications and sites tells us that the person behind each one is in most cases not a programmer, but rather an expert on the topic in question or an enthusiast who also uses other applications in the same area (web logs, guest books, news feeds, and so on). The innovation in this case lies in how the content is prepared and presented. Many of the technologies and know-how we are familiar with are developed in response to the content and requirements of these small websites and the people behind them (as it is often one person and not a company). Many new products, services and business areas are created in this way.

Previously, the tools used for these purposes are based on open standards and were often not much more than simple home-page design tools. Since then, they have been functionally extended and simplify even the most complex development activities, such as connecting to a database, reading RSS feeds for messages, and so on. Non-programmers can thus become website designers and Web application builders, and thus provide important information. The significance of these "private" websites has increased due to their sheer number, and they now represent the real value of the Internet.

In 1997, a development project was started in SAP whose aim was to replace existing reporting systems. This system was also intended to follow a new approach for model-based and metadata-based report development and code generation. Hoards of de-facto developers inside and outside SAP, who had never before written a single line of code, were now suddenly able to produce complex and useful reports and their data repositories, and very quickly too. Today, this system is called SAP Business Intelligence (BI).

SAP Business Intelligence

Within two years, the reports in this new system already exceeded in functionality and number all the old (SAP) systems combined. Today, we know that BI, with 10,000 installations, was and is not only very successful, but also brought about a change in the way we view reporting and its integration into the daily workflow of an employee.

Now, employees in an enterprise were able to create their own reports quickly and easily. Many of these reports are only ad-hoc reports; that is, reports that are only called once and never used again. Of course, there are still the large, central reports and analytical applications, and these are often created by central groups. These applications are now in the minority, however, even though their importance cannot be discounted.

5.4 Overall Picture and Solution

These three examples and everything we discussed above show that we need to change how we think about applications in order to remain competitive. Technical departments will increasingly develop their own applications and integrate existing applications into these new ones. Tools are required that make work easier for both the technical and the IT department.

In our opinion, the CAF, based on SAP NetWeaver, is the tool now best-suited to this new paradigm and one that, to a certain extent, helps define it.

Uses of the CAF There are multiple uses for the CAF: creation of cross-system applications with integration and extension functions for enterprise-critical uses that simplify and facilitate processes; and the construction of "instant" business applications. The target users of such applications are both classic programmers and business-process experts. The capability of the CAF to display complexity and its functional scalability will remain a big challenge. Likewise, the integration of analytical application components and unstructured information—without the fragmentation that still exists at the moment and the obvious divisions into different worlds—is more important than ever.

New applications that use and extend existing applications and map processes are candidates for the CAF. These applications have a life-cycle of several years and are developed and extended over a long period. These have been discussed in this book by means of several examples.

Programmers from the IT departments will continue to be required for this, but they will receive more support from experts in the technical departments, who will relieve them of the (from a technical point of view) less interesting work.

On the other hand, the CAF is also suitable for creating transient applications that have to be created quickly and flexibly by non-programmers for the purposes of an individual project. The development phase in these cases is limited to a few days, and the project duration to only a few weeks or months. These applications fall more into the "instant" category.

The above-mentioned challenges pose the following question: How might it be possible to take the structured and unstructured data from these applications, which are created by project team members who are usually also non-programmers, and make it generally available and capable of being integrated, without having to keep maintaining the applications?

The time and effort required to load data into another (central) system and to maintain it there is often too great or even impossible. There is therefore a need for alternatives that offer low effort plus maximum availability. The Enterprise Services Architecture (ESA) implemented in the CAF is one such alternative. In the CAF, data is made available through services. The services contain the persistence information, business logic, and use the metadata that makes sense of the data. Once the services of the application are known to the future central Enterprise Service Repository, they are available to the whole enterprise.

Low effort—high availability

We thus find ourselves in the same situation as the search-engine operators some years ago. The exponentially increasing number of websites made it impossible to manually catalog all sites. Other solutions were required that provided automatic and intelligent cataloging and indexing. To the surprise of many, complex algorithms were developed that fulfilled these requirements very well. The latest trend is a dual approach in which computers perform a pre-cataloging process, and then human beings carry out partial and additional categorization in order to further improve the quality of the categorization.

For the IT departments in enterprises, this means a shift in the focus of their work. They must shift away from developing and operating applications, and towards coordinating development, providing an infrastructure for decentralized application development in the business departments themselves, and integrating the resulting applications and data. Control over the appearance of applications that drive innovation is largely handed over to the user without adding to the workload of the IT departments.

For those of us who work at SAP, this means that we have to provide IT and business departments with these tools for taking applications apart and putting them together, in order to keep up with this paradigm. And we're working on it at full steam …

A Appendix

A.1 CORE Objects for CAF 1.0

Data Type	Definition	Length	JDBC Type	Description	BW-Compatible
boolean	Integer		INTEGER		x
business-Object	String	256	VARCHAR		–
bytearray	Binary		BLOB		–
char1	String	1	VARCHAR		x
char5	String	5	VARCHAR		x
counter	Integer		INTEGER		x
currency	String	3	VARCHAR		x
date	Date		DATE		x
id	String	36	VARCHAR	Technical ID of Business Object	x
long	Long		BIGINT		x
longText	String	256	VARCHAR	Long text	–
multiUserType	String	256	VARCHAR		–
objLink	String	256	VARCHAR		–
objType	String	256	VARCHAR		–
operator	String	2	VARCHAR	Constraint operator for condition of business rule	x
permission-Level	String	4..11	VARCHAR	Permission levels for access control list	x
rawData	Binary		BLOB	Serialized data	–
readOnlyDate	Date		DATE		x
readOnlyLong-Text	String	256	VARCHAR		–

Table A.1 CORE Data Types

Data Type	Definition	Length	JDBC Type	Description	BW-Compatible
readOnlyTime-stamp	Timestamp		TIMESTAMP		x
refType	Integer		INTEGER		x
recordType	Integer		INTEGER	Record type for BW extraction	x
replication-Mode	String	10	VARCHAR	Replication mode	x
rid	String	256	VARCHAR	Resource ID	–
shortText	String	30	VARCHAR		x
singleUser-Type	String	255	VARCHAR		–
sourceName	String	256	VARCHAR		–
sourceType	String	0..5	VARCHAR		x
status	String	0..10	VARCHAR		x
timestamp	Timestamp		TIMESTAMP		x
title	String	0..60	VARCHAR		x
unit	String	0..3	VARCHAR		x
userId	String	256	VARCHAR		–
value	decimal		DECIMAL		
xLongText	String		CLOB		–

Table A.1 CORE Data Types (cont.)

Data Type	Definition	Length	JDBC Type	Description	BW-Compatible
base64Binary	Binary		BLOB		–
Boolean	Boolean		INTEGER		x
Byte	Short		SMALLINT	x	x
Date	daye		DATE	x	x
Decimal	Decimal		DECIMAL	x	x
Double	Double		DOUBLE	x	x
Float	Float		REAL	x	x

Table A.2 BASE Data Types

Data Type	Definition	Length	JDBC Type	Description	BW-Compatible
Int	Long		BIGINT	x	x
Integer	Integer		INTEGER	x	x
Long	Long		BIGINT	x	x
Short	Short		SMALLINT	x	x
String	String		CLOB	x	x
Time	TIME		TIME	x	x
timestamp	Timestamp		TIMESTAMP	x	x
unsignedByte	Short		SMALLINT	x	x
unsignedInt	Integer		INTEGER	x	x
unsignedLong	Long		BIGINT	x	x
unsignedShort	Short		SMALLINT	x	x

Table A.2 BASE Data Types (cont.)

Service	Description
Category	Category
CategoryValueSet	Values for the individual categories
Document	Document (stored in SAP NetWeaver KM)

Table A.3 CORE Entity Services

Service	Description
DocumentContent	

Table A.4 CORE Application Service

Pattern	Development Component
Attachments	Caf~UI~ptn~attachments
Classification	Caf~UI~ptn~classification
FlexTree	Caf~UI~ptn~dashboard
HistoryLog	Caf~UI~ptn~historylog
KM File Select	Caf~UI~ptn~kmfileselect

Table A.5 CORE UI Pattern

Pattern	Development Component
ObjectBrowser	`Caf~UI~ptn~objectbrowser`
ObjectEditor	`Caf~UI~ptn~objecteditor`
ObjectSelector	`Caf~UI~ptn~objectselector`
SearchBar	`Caf~UI~ptn~searchbar`
UserAssignment	`Caf~UI~ptn~userassignment`

Table A.5 CORE UI Pattern (cont.)

A.2 Operation Types

Operation Types	Input Parameter	Output Parameter
CUSTOM	Any	Any
CREATE	Attributes of the data structure	Reference attributes of the data structure
READ	Key	–
UPDATE	Reference data structure	–
DELETE	Reference data structure	–
FINDBY	Attributes of the data structure	Reference data structure

A.3 User Interface Links

▶ Central point of entry to all configuration screens and administration tools
http://<host>:<port>/caf/Config

▶ UserAdmin
http://<host>:<port>/useradmin

▶ Configuration Browser
http://<host>:<port>/webdynpro/dispatcher/sap.com/caf~UI~ configbrowser/ConfigBrowser

▶ CategoryAdmin
http://<host>:<port>/webdynpro/dispatcher /sap.com/caf~UI~km~admin/CategoriesAdmin

▶ ServiceBrowser
http://<host>:<port>/webdynpro/dispatcher/sap.com/caf~UI~ servicebrowser/ServiceBrowser

▶ **Authorization**

http://<host>:<port>/webdynpro/dispatcher
/sap.com/caf~UI~ptn~authorization/Authorization

▶ **Principal Authorization Report**

http://<host>:<port>/webdynpro/dispatcher
/sap.com/caf~UI~ptn~authorization/PrincipalReport

▶ **Authorization Report**

http://<host>:<port>/webdynpro/dispatcher
/sap.com/caf~UI~ptn~authorization/Report

▶ **Authorization Report Configuration**

http://<host>:<port>/webdynpro/dispatcher
/sap.com/caf~UI~ptn~authorization/ReportConfig

▶ **Attachment Pattern**

http://<host>:<port>/webdynpro/dispatcher
/sap.com/caf~UI~ptn~attachment/Attachment

▶ **Knowledge Management File Select Pattern**

http://<host>:<port>/webdynpro/dispatcher
/sap.com/caf~UI~ptn~kmfileselect/FileSelect

▶ **Classification Assignment Pattern**

http://<host>:<port>/webdynpro/dispatcher/sap.com/caf~UI~ptn~
classification/ClassificationAssignment

▶ **ObjectEditor Pattern**

http://<host>:<port>/webdynpro/dispatcher
/sap.com/caf~UI~ptn~objecteditor/ObjectEditor

▶ **ObjectSelector Pattern**

http://<host>:<port>/webdynpro/dispatcher
/sap.com/caf~UI~ptn~objectselector/ObjectSelector

▶ **ObjectBrowser Pattern**

http://<host>:<port>/webdynpro/dispatcher
/sap.com/caf~UI~ptn~objectbrowser/ObjectBrowser

▶ **SearchBar Pattern**

http://<host>:<port>/webdynpro/dispatcher/sap.com/caf~UI~ptn~
searchbar/SearchBar

▶ **FlexTree Pattern**

http://<host>:<port>/webdynpro/dispatcher/sap.com/caf~UI~ptn~
flextree/Dashboard

► **HistoryLog Pattern**

http://<host>:<port>/webdynpro/dispatcher/sap.com/caf~UI~ptn~
historylog/HistoryLog

► **User-Assignment Pattern**

http://<host>:<port>/webdynpro/dispatcher/sap.com/caf~UI~ptn~
userassignment/UserAssignment

► **PropertyEditor Pattern**

http://<host>:<port>/webdynpro/dispatcher/sap.com/caf~UI~ptn~
propedit/PropEdit

► **TypeEditor**

http://<host>:<port>/webdynpro/dispatcher/sap.com/caf~UI~
typeeditor/TypeEditor

► **Restore UI**

http://<host>:<port>/webdynpro/dispatcher/sap.com/caf~UI~
typeeditor/TypeRestore

► **Restore UI**

http://<host>:<port>/webdynpro/dispatcher/sap.com/caf~UI~
typeeditor/TypeBackup

► **External Service Configuration**

http://<host>:<port>/webdynpro/dispatcher/sap.com/caf~UI~
configuration/ConfigurationApplication

► **IndexAdmin**

http://<host>:<port>/webdynpro/dispatcher
/sap.com/caf~UI~km~admin/IndexAdmin

► **RepositoryBackup**

http://<host>:<port>/webdynpro/dispatcher/sap.com/caf~UI~
repositorybackup/RRBackup

► **RepositoryRestore**

http://<host>:<port>/webdynpro/dispatcher/sap.com/caf~UI~
repositorybackup/RRRestore

► **ServiceCustomization**

http://<host>:<port>/webdynpro/dispatcher/sap.com/caf~UI~
servicecustomization/ServiceCustomization

A.4 Tables

Meta Model Repository	Remarks
BI_MMRL1ASC BI_MMRL1HIER BI_MMRL1INST BI_MMRL1SAV BI_MMRL2ASC BI_MMRL2HIER BI_MMRL2INST BI_MMRL2JCLASS BI_MMRL2SAV BI_MMRNRRANGE BI_MMRNRSIDS	Meta-model repository tables have to be backed up together.

Guided Procedures	Remarks
CAF_GPACTADHOC_D CAF_GPACTAPPS_D CAF_GPACTCONFCT_D CAF_GPACTCONFPUB_D CAF_GPACTCONFVAL_D CAF_GPACTCONF_D CAF_GPACTEXCPT_D CAF_GPACTION_D CAF_GPACTION_T CAF_GPACTRESCT_D CAF_GPACTRESO_D CAF_GPACTRESO_T CAF_GPCONT_ACAT CAF_GPCONT_ACAT_T CAF_GPCONT_CAT CAF_GPCONT_CAT_T CAF_GPCONT_UDR CAF_GPCONT_UDR_T CAF_GPCTXMAP_DT_D CAF_GPCTXMAP_RT_D CAF_GPCTXVAL_DT_D CAF_GPCTXVAL_RT_D CAF_GPEVENTCTX_D CAF_GPEVENTLOG_D CAF_GPEXCEPTION_D CAF_GPEXCEPTION_T CAF_GPEXCEPTMAP_D CAF_GPEXCEPTRESO_D CAF_GPEXCTXRESCT_D CAF_GPINVUSRS_RT_D CAF_GPPETRACK_RT_D CAF_GPPROCEN_DT_D CAF_GPPROCEN_RT_D CAF_GPPROCLOG_DT_D CAF_GPPROCMAP_RT_D CAF_GPPROCPER_DT_D	Guided-procedures tables have to be backed up together.

Guided Procedures	Remarks
CAF_GPPROCPUB_DT_D CAF_GPPROCROL_DT_D CAF_GPPROCROL_RT_D CAF_GPPROCROL_T CAF_GPPROCTAR_DT_D CAF_GPPROC_DT_D CAF_GPPROC_RT_D CAF_GPPROC_RT_T CAF_GPPROC_T CAF_GPSUBPROC_RT CAF_GPTMPLMAP_RT_D	

CAF Runtime	Remarks
CAF_RT_ATTRIBLIST CAF_RT_ATTRIBSET CAF_RT_BO CAF_RT_BO_CAT CAF_RT_CAT_VAL_BO CAF_RT_CONDITIONS CAF_RT_IDX CAF_RT_NUMBERRANGE CAF_RT_PK_GEN CAF_RT_RULEHEADER CAF_RT_SRVMODULE	CAF runtime repository tables have to be backed up together.

User Management	Remarks
CAF_UM_RELGROUPS CAF_UM_RELGR_ACES CAF_UM_RELGR_ATTRS CAF_UM_RELGR_MEMBS CAF_UM_RELGR_TEXTS CAF_UM_RELGR_WORDS	The imported backup copy is not guaranteed to function correctly in the case of backed-up user management tables.

xApps	Remarks
XAP_CAFCORE_CATEGO XAP_CAFCORE_CUSTOM XAP_CAFCORE_VALUES XAP_CA_NUCATEG_L	xApps tables have to be backed up together.

A.5 Property Rules for Attributes

Property\Attributes	Def Key Attribute	Default Attributes	Simple Attributes	Simple Key Attr	Associations	Complex Attrs	Sub Complex
Key	False	False	False	True	False	False	False
Object type	Read only	Read only	Read only	Read only	Read only	Read only	Read only
Cardinality	0..1	0..	If (!langDependent) Modifiable	1..1	Modifiable	Modifiable	0..1
Data type	Read only	Read only	Read only	Read only	N/A	N/A	Read only
DB field	Read only	Read only	Read only	Read only	N/A	N/A	Read only
Description	Read only	Read only	Modifiable	Modifiable	Modifiable	Modifiable	Modifiable
DB table	Read only	Read only	Read only	Read only	Read only	Read only	Read only
Language-dependent	False	False	If (! 0..n && instance of string) True	False	False	False	False
Mandatory	False	False	True	True	True	False	False
Name	Read only	Read only	Modifiable	Modifiable	Modifiable	Modifiable	Modifiable

B   Glossary

Advanced Business Application Programming (ABAP) After Java, ABAP is the second object-oriented programming language of the SAP Web Application Server and its environment for development, application, and the use of mySAP application components.

Application Consists of a number of functions or Web services that are usually made available as one component.

Application Service Business logic is stored in an application service. The entity services, external services and other application services in the application service use the information provided to make decisions. An application service is created using the Application Service Modeler in the CAF Designer.

Application An application is a set of logically related functions and Web services (such as Financial Accounting) that are provided together and are usually used by an end-user by means of a user interface.

Application Programming Interface (API) An API is a set of functions or Web services that are logically very closely related (such as price calculation). An API is intended for use by programmers.

Business Application Programming Interface (BAPI) BAPI is an open SAP interface standard that makes the functionality of all SAP solutions available to all other SAP solutions, and to applications by other providers. All BAPIs can also be addressed as Web services.

Business Package Business Packages contain portal content for specific roles within the enterprise. This personalization ensures a higher level of user

acceptance. Business Packages provide ready-to-use solutions that speed up rollout, optimize shared processes, and increase productivity.

Business Process A series of activities that function beyond the boundaries of individual departments and enterprises. A number of different parties are involved in a business process, and each party carries out specific tasks or has specific roles. All parties interact and cooperate to achieve a common aim. Internet technologies and services, supported by various IT environments and systems, can be used to optimize business processes.

Business Scenario A business scenario consists of one or more thematically related business processes, and, as software, supports activities in or between whole business areas.

Client/Server Architecture A system architecture in which the application is distributed across servers that provide certain services and clients that use these services.

Collaboration Cooperation and communication between employees and systems, including those of business partners, suppliers, and customers, all of whom are working towards a common business goal.

Component Similarly to applications, components are a collection of thematically related functions and Web services. Components can usually be delivered on their own and have their own development cycle.

Composite Application A composite application consists of functions that originate from multiple different sources within a service-oriented architecture. Components can be individual Web services, selected functions from other applications, or whole systems whose tasks are combined in the form of Web services (often legacy systems). As "applications on applications," they are used to implement innovative business processes.

Directory Shared information is stored and made accessible in directories. Usually, directories are intended for read access. In this context, repositories are mainly used for information during the configuration phase.

Electronic Data Interchange (EDI) EDI is a series of standards to do with the electronic exchange of information between companies.

Enterprise Services Enterprise Services are based on the same technology as Web services. They aim to use Web services to fulfill the business requirements of an enterprise by combining them to form re-usable components of an Enterprise Service in a business context.

Enterprise Services Architecture (ESA) The ESA extends the concept of Web and Enterprise Services to form an architecture for business applications. While Web services, in the main, represent only a technical concept, ESA is the basis of extensive and service-based business applications. ESA makes it possible to design a complete solution for a business process that includes existing systems and applications and that speeds up the use of new functionalities. The central component here is the SAP Composite Application Framework. SAP NetWeaver is used to implement an ESA.

Entity Service The job of an entity service is to store and allow access to application data. This data can be located in a local storage location or a back-end such as an R/3 system, or be accessible via a Web service. Every entity service is based on tables, relationships between tables, and program routines for reading, writing, deleting, changing and searching in these tables. An entity service is created using the Entity Service Modeler in the CAF Designer.

Extensible Markup Language (XML) A universal format for structured documents and data on the Internet that is becoming increasingly established as the general document format standard for structured data. For more information, see *http://www.w3c.org/XML.*

External Service External Services are created in the CAF by importing the definition of a remote function call or a Web service. External Services make it possible to access data from other data sources and can be used by entity services and application services.

Hypertext Markup Language (HTML) Standard format for displaying documents in Web browsers.

Hypertext Transfer Protocol (HTTP) The open standard Internet protocol that is used for exchanging documents.

Interface Abstract definition of functions and Web services. Interfaces make it possible for users to access Web services that are compatible with this interface. An interface determines which information and data needs to be provided so that users can use the functions and Web services in question.

Interface Interfaces are abstract definitions of functions and Web services.

Internet Standards Generic, open standards that are used for communication and integration on the Internet. Examples of Internet standards are HTTP, XML, and WSDL.

iView A small program that retrieves data from content sources and displays it in the SAP Enterprise Portal.

Java 2 Enterprise Edition

(J2EE) Defines the standard for developing multi-level, Java-based enterprise applications. This standard was defined in an open initiative (with SAP's involvement) and developed by Sun Microsystems. For more information, see *http://java.sun.com*.

Java Message Service (JMS) JMS is an API for message exchange and gives users unified access to various e-mail, groupware, and workflow systems.

Java Management Extensions

(JMX) JMX is a technology that makes it possible to connect to and manage applications and even hardware in a unified manner.

Java Server Pages (JSP) JSP is a technology that facilitates the development of Web applications by providing commands and mechanisms for easy website creation. JSPs also allow for a separation between content and layout.

Lightweight Directory Access Protocol (LDAP)

Standard protocol for accessing directories. It is usually used to provide organizational data, user data, and other resources, such as files and devices on the Internet or internal enterprise networks.

Microsoft .NET A platform for XML Web services developed by Microsoft. It comprises functions for developing and using Internet-supported applications. For more information, see *http://www.microsoft.com/net*.

Multi-Channel Access The term used to describe an enterprise system that can be connected to via voice, mobile, or radio technology. Multi-Channel Access is implemented by means of the SAP Mobile Infrastructure in SAP NetWeaver.

mySAP Business Suite The mySAP Business Suite is a complete package of open enterprise solutions that interconnects all parties, information, and processes, and thus increases the effectiveness of the business relationships. SAP NetWeaver is the basis of this solution.

Online Analytical Processing

(OLAP) OLAP is used for searching for and displaying data simply and selectively from different perspectives. To enable these kinds of analyses, OLAP data is stored in a multi-dimensional database structure.

Pattern Patterns (such as UI patterns, and Web dynpro patterns) are user interfaces that can be configured to varying degrees. They are defined for a specific use without being tied down to that particular business logic or data storage location. One purpose of patterns is to create and maintain an instance in an object or to search for an instance. The pattern is "tied" to an Entity Service or an Application Service by the configuration, and the user interface is dynamically constructed at runtime.

Release SAP calls its software versions releases.

Remote Function Call (RFC) RFC is a proprietary SAP protocol that is used to call the functions and BAPIs of applications on other computers. SAP provides the protocol in the form of APIs for several operating systems and programming languages.

Repository Metadata and information is stored and made accessible in repositories. In this context, repositories are mainly used for information during the configuration phase.

Role A role is based on the content that a user has to access in order to fulfill his tasks. Roles are specially designed for individual groups of internal or external users and their particular tasks, and for particular information and service requirements.

SAP NetWeaver SAP NetWeaver is the comprehensive integration and application platform that forms the basis of the mySAP solutions and SAP xApps. SAP NetWeaver has thus started the process of implementing the blueprint of the Enterprise Services Architecture, in which SAP's experience of enterprise applications is combined with the flexibility of Web services and open technologies. The result is extensive, service-oriented business solutions. The NetWeaver technology brings together structured and unstructured information. Thus, data sets that were previously isolated in different systems can now be harmonized, thanks to solutions for Business Intelligence, Knowledge Management and SAP Master Data Management. SAP NetWeaver also uses Internet standards such as HTTP, XML, and Web services.

SAP Business Intelligence (SAP BW) SAP BW is a data warehouse that supports strategic and operational enterprise decisions. It connects warehousing technology with pre-configured business content, and provides a comprehensive overview of internal and relevant external data in an enterprise. It contains a large number of pre-defined reporting schemas that are tailored to the special requirements of specific industries and user groups, such as production planners, financial controllers, and human-resources managers.

SAP Business Process Management SAP Business Process Management is used to create and further develop business processes in a dynamic IT environment. The customer can thus monitor the efficiency and effectiveness of these processes. SAP Business Process Management also provides a modeling environment with a unified data model and a unified storage system, and also different views.

SAP Composite Application Framework (CAF) The CAF is based on SAP NetWeaver and makes it possible for developers to create Composite Applications and SAP xApps quickly, thoroughly, and efficiently. It contains all the relevant tools, methods, rules, and modules for modeling composite applications, on the basis of which code is then generated.

SAP Enterprise Portal The SAP Enterprise Portal provides a unified means of access to a wide range of—ideally, all—enterprise information, applications and services that employees, suppliers and business partners require to complete their daily work in the optimal way.

SAP Exchange Infrastructure (SAP XI) SAP XI is the product that carries out message-based integration of all internal and external systems.

SAP Knowledge Management SAP Knowledge Management (KM) comprises the components Content Management (CM) and Search and Classification (TREX). It supports integration, ordered data preparation, and unified administration of unstructured information from different sources. It provides users in the SAP Enterprise Portal with a centralized, role-specific entry point to information and documents that may be physically located in different repositories. Search and classification functions make it possible for portal users to access information that is contained in the connected repositories quickly and easily. SAP Knowledge Management provides application programming interfaces (APIs) that make it possible for programmers to develop extensions and their own functions and to integrate them into the standard system. The possibilities in this regard range from developing repository managers, to developing purpose-built KM functions, to extending the user interface.

SAP Master Data Management This is used for data integration in heterogeneous IT landscapes. It enables master data from across the whole system, including partner information, product templates, product structures, and technical information, to be collected and harmonized.

SAP Mobile Infrastructure SAP Mobile Infrastructure provides a universal platform and ready-to-use scenarios for mobile devices. The central components of this solution include mobile access, mobile applications (access to a wide range of information and processes), and mobile technology. With this solution, it does not matter whether users are online or offline.

SAP Web Application Server The SAP Web Application Server is the scalable and reliable component platform for developing and operating J2EE and ABAP-based Web applications and Web services. It provides tried-and-trusted scalability and performance,

but also supports native Web technologies and open standards such as HTTP, XML and J2EE. The SAP Web Application Server also provides both ABAP and J2EE environments in a shared, integrated infrastructure. It is thus SAP's underlying infrastructure for both new and existing application components.

SAP xApp Cost and Quotation Management (SAP xCQM) SAP xCQM is a solution that enables contract manufacturers to increase the quality and precision of their quotations. Using SAP xCQM can also greatly reduce lead times, giving contract manufacturers more time to concentrate on profit-generating interaction with their customers.

SAP xApp Product Definition (SAP xPD) SAP xPD is a Packaged Composite Application that removes obstacles and inefficient processes in the product development process. It makes it possible to test and rationally assess new ideas, to make provisional evaluations, and to carry out detailed analyses, all of which can then be used in the prototype development process. It also facilitates the re-evaluation and re-working of product concepts on the basis of previous findings.

SAP xApps Based on their service-oriented architecture, SAP xApps extend existing functionalities and combine them into new, cross-function business processes. SAP xApps are composite applications whose purpose is to quickly realize innovations and competitive advantages in the form of independent solutions.

Secure Sockets Layer (SSL) SSL is a standard protocol for secure data exchange on the Internet. It uses both public-key and private-key encryption.

Simple Mail Transfer Protocol (SMTP) SMTP is a standard protocol for e-mail exchange.

Simple Object Access Protocol (SOAP) A simple protocol for information exchange in a decentralized, distributed environment. This XML-based protocol is usually transferred via HTTP. It contains display rules for method calls of objects or function calls, as well as the relevant responses, plus display rules for standardized data types. For more information, see *http://www.w3.org/TR/SOAP*.

Single Sign-On (SSO) A mechanism that means that the user no longer has to enter a password every time he or she logs on to a system. With SSO, the user has to enter a username and password only once, and can then access all systems that are part of the SSO environment.

Universal Description, Discovery and Integration (UDDI) An initiative of leading enterprises for developing an open, platform-independent environment for describing Web services, publishing services and their associated enterprises, and integrating Internet-supported enterprise services. The platform also serves as a company directory. For more information, see *http://www.uddi.org*.

Web Dynpro A new SAP technology for creating user interfaces for Java and ABAP programs. It is run on SAP software and is displayed and used in the end-user's Web browser.

Web Service Independent, modular functions that can be published, searched, and made accessible on a network using open standards. They are the implementation of an interface of a component. A Web service is an executable entity. For an entity whose function is to call and to send, a service functions as a kind of "black box" that requests input and returns a result. Web services provide both internal and cross-enterprise integration functions, regardless of the various communication technologies—synchronous or asynchronous—and independently of the format.

Web Services Description Language (WSDL) Specification for describing Web service interfaces. It also defines message formats. For more information, see *http://www.w3.org/TR/wsdl*.

C   Sources and Further Reading

This part of the appendix contains a list of the sources used in this book as well as some recommended additional literature, subdivided into SAP sources, books and the Internet.

C.1   SAP Sources

The following SAP websites provide freely accessible information on the subjects treated in this book:

help.sap.com
This SAP website provides you with extensive and up-to-date documentation as well as installation and upgrade instructions for all SAP solutions and products.

service.sap.com
The SAP Service Marketplace mainly provides installation, configuration and troubleshooting information for SAP solutions and products.

service.sap.com/partnerportal
The SAP Partner Portal provides all information and contact data for existing and future SAP partners.

uddi.sap.com
This website contains SAP's UDDI Business Register.

www.sap.com
This SAP website provides general information on all products of the SAP solution portfolio as well as white papers and features lists.

www.sap.info/goto/glo/de
The SAP magazine, *SAP INFO*, provides the SAP community with up-to-date information and profound knowledge regarding SAP software. In addition, it contains an extensive glossary.

www.sapdesignguild.org
This website contains guidelines and tips provided by SAP for the appropriate use and design of user interfaces.

www.sdn.sap.com
The SAP Developer Network (SDN) is an online community for SAP developers, consultants and integrators which represents a central meeting place for the collaboration between SAP experts. The SDN pages con-

tain an extensive collection of technical content on SAP-related subjects with a special focus on SAP NetWeaver and SAP xApps.

C.2 Books and Articles

Abrams, Charles (2003): *Service-Oriented Business Applications: Process Revolution or Next-Wave Hype*. Gartner Inc., Presentation at the Web Services & Application Integration Conference 2003, Baltimore.

Cooper, Robert G. (2001): *Winning at New Products: Accelerating the Process from Idea to Launch*. Perseus Publishing, 3rd ed., June 2001.

Donough, Brian (2004): *Worldwide Packaged Composite Applications 2004–2008 Forecast: A First Look at an Emerging Market*. IDC, #31280, Vol. 1, May 2004.

Kinikin, Erin; Ramos, Laura (2004): *Packaged Composite Applications Emerge–Slowly*. Forrester Research, Inc., January 2004.

OVUM (2002): *Web Services for the Enterprise: Opportunities and Challenges*.

Tufte, Edward R. (1992): *The Visual Display of Quantitative Information*. Graphics Press, Cheshire.

Woods, Dan (2003): *Enterprise Services Architecture*. O'Reilly & Associates, Inc., Sebastopol.

Woods, Dan (2003): *Packaged Composite Applications*. O'Reilly & Associates, Inc., Sebastopol.

Woods, Dan; Word, Jeffrey (2004): *SAP NetWeaver for Dummies*. Wiley Publishing, Inc., Hoboken.

C.3 Internet

java.sun.org
Details on the specifications of the Java community process such as J2EE or JNDI.

www.altarum.org
Center of Automotive Research/Altarum Research: "Automotive suppliers and the Revenue Acquisition Process: What's working and what's not?", September 2002.

www.standishgroup.com

The Standish Group's CHAOS 2001 Research.

www.uddi.org

Details on the UDDI specification.

www.w3.org

Specifications for Internet standards such as HTML, XML, SOAP or WSDL.

The Authors

Mario Herger is a doctor of Technical Chemistry and Process Engineering at the Technical College of Vienna and also holds a degree from the Vienna University of Economics and Business Administration. In 1998, he started work at SAP as a developer in the Business Content team of SAP Business Intelligence. In 2002, he became a founder member of the CAF team. He has been a Product Manager with responsibility for CAF since the beginning of 2004.

Jo Weilbach holds an MBA and began his career at SAP as a Senior Consultant in the Portals area. The Sun-certified Java programmer has been active in the Composite Applications area since 2003, and is head of the Implementation Services xApps—EMEA at SAP. He played a major role in the success of the world's first SAP xApps projects, regularly speaks at specialist conferences on the subject of Composite Applications, and has many years' experience of international projects and project management.

Alexander Kupfer holds a degree in Physics as well as a Diploma of Management from Henley Management College. For many years, he was responsible for product innovation at an international consumer goods manufacturing company. He has been a consultant with SAP Deutschland AG & Co. KG since 2001. He works in close collaboration with the product management team for SAP xApps Product Definition (SAP xPD) and is responsible for supporting pilot customers during the development phase of SAP xPD. He has also been responsible for SAP xPD in Business Development at SAP Germany since 2004.

Jürgen Lindner is a graduate in Business Administration and has been working at SAP/SAP Labs LLC since 1998. He has held a number of product management positions in the areas of mySAP Product Lifecycle Management (PLM) and mySAP Supplier Relationship Management (SRM). Since 2003, he has been a Solution Manager with responsibility for SAP xApps Cost and Quotation Management (xCQM).

Index

**A practical guide
to implementing and using
SAP xApp Analytics**

**Easily deploy, configure, and
combine analytic applications
to customize SAP xApp
Analytics for your needs**

408 pp., 2006, 69,95 Euro / US$ 69.95
ISBN 978-1-59229-102-1

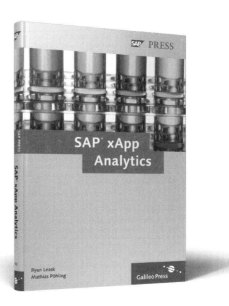

SAP xApp Analytics

www.sap-press.com

Ryan Leask, Mathias Pöhling, Ryan Leask,
Mathias Pöhling

SAP xApp Analytics

A practical guide to implementing and using
SAP xApp Analytics

This book fulfills two goals. First, it gives readers a
look at the technology behind building Analytic
Applications within SAP. Second, it gives a business
perspective as to why xApp Analytics are beneficial.
It addresses how SAP meets industry-specific
challenges with various pre-packaged Analytic
applications. Practical examples and the authors'
experiences while working with Analytics are
valuable resources for readers. Readers will also
obtain insight into the future of xApp Analytics.
Other topics include installation, administration,
transporting, and coverage of the Visual Composer.

omprehensive introduction to
e basic principles and tools of
the Adobe Flex Application
Framework

ActionScript and MXML, data
communication, chart
generation, dynamic screens,
and much more

approx. 300 pp., 69,95 Euro / US$ 69,95
ISBN 978-1-59229-119-9, Feb 2007

Developing SAP Applications with Adobe Flex

www.sap-press.com

A. Lorenz, Dr. G. Schöppe, F. Consbruch, D. Knapp,
F. Sonnenberg

Developing SAP Applications with Adobe Flex

This book provides you with the practical guidance
needed to develop intuitive user interfaces for SAP
NetWeaver Portal, using Adobe's Flex Application
Framework. First, you'll get a concise introduction to
the details on the development environment for Flex
applications: Adobe Flex Builder. Using clearly
structured examples you'll quickly learn to understand the syntax of the Flex programming languages,
ActionScript and MXML. Readers get detailed
coverage of the backend connection to the SAP
system, data communication functions, and learn
how best to generate charts.

Improve your Design Process with "Contextual Design"

182 pp., 2006, 49,95 Euro / US$ 49,95
ISBN 978-1-59229-065-9

Designing
Composite Applications
www.sap-press.com

Jörg Beringer, Karen Holtzblatt

Designing Composite Applications

Driving user productivity and business innovation for next generation business applications

This book helps any serious developer hit the ground running by providing a highly detailed and comprehensive introduction to modern application design, using the SAP Enterprise Services Architecture (ESA) toolset and the methodology of "Contextual Design". Readers will benefit immediately from exclusive insights on design processes based on SAPs Business Process Platform and learn valuable tricks and techniques that can drastically improve user productivity. Anybody involved in the process of enterprise application design and usability/quality management stands to benefit from this book.

Examples of dynamic programming, componentization, integration of applications, navigation, and much more

Essential and practical knowledge about installation, configuration, and administration of the Web Dynpro runtime

497 pp., 2006, 69,95 Euro / US$ 69.95
ISBN 1-59229-077-9

Maximizing
Web Dynpro for Java
www.sap-press.com

B. Ganz, J. Gürtler, T. Lakner

Maximizing Web Dynpro for Java

Standard examples of Web Dynpro applications can leave SAP developers with many questions and severe limitations. This book takes you to the next level with detailed examples that show you exactly what you need to know in order to leverage Web Dynpro applications. From the interaction with the Java Developer Infrastructure (JDI), to the use of Web Dynpro components, to the integration into the portal and the use of its services—this unique book delivers it all. In addition, readers get dozens of tips and tricks on fine-tuning Web Dynpro applications in terms of response time, security, and structure. Expert insights on the configuration and administration of the Web Dynpro runtime environment serve to round out this comprehensive book.

Basic principles, architecture, and configuration

Development of dynamic, reusable UI components

Volumes of sample code and screen captures for help you maximize key tools

360 pp., 2006, 69,95 Euro / US$
ISBN 1-59229-078-7

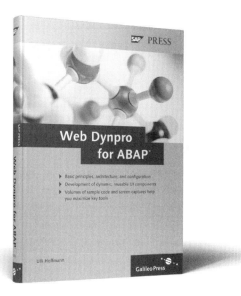

Web Dynpro for ABAP

www.sap-press.com

U. Hoffmann

Web Dynpro for ABAP

Serious developers must stay ahead of the curve by ensuring that they are up-to-date with all of the latest standards. This book illustrates the many benefits that can be realized with component-based UI development using Web Dynpro for ABAP. On the basis of specifically developed sample components, readers are introduced to the architecture of the runtime and development environment and receive highly-detailed descriptions of the different functions and tools that enable you to efficiently implement Web Dynpro technology on the basis of SAP NetWeaver 2004s. Numerous code listings, screen captures, and little-known tricks make this book your indispensable companion for the practical design of modern user interfaces.

Learn to design intuitive business applications with SAP Visual Composer for NetWeaver 2004s

est practices for configuration settings and advice to master the development lifecycle

524 pp., 2007, 69,95 Euro / US$ 69,95
ISBN 978-1-59229-099-4

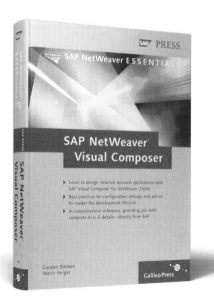

SAP NetWeaver
Visual Composer

www.sap-press.com

C. Bönnen, M. Herger

SAP NetWeaver Visual Composer

Instead of conventional programming and implementation, SAP NetWeaver Visual Composer (VC) enables you to model your processes graphically via drag & drop potentially without ever having to write a single line of code. This book not only shows you how, but also serves as a comprehensive reference, providing you with complete details on all aspects of VC. You learn the ins and outs of the VC architecture—including details on all components and concepts, as well as essential information on model-based development and on the preparation of different types of applications. Readers quickly broaden their knowledge by tapping into practical expert advice on the various aspects of the Development Lifecycle as well as on selected applications, which have been modeled with the VC and are currently delivered by SAP as standard applications.

sights on the architecture and
ools of SAP Web AS Java 6.40

Sample application for Web
Dynpro and SAP NetWeaver
Development Infrastructure

cludes 180-day trial version of
AP Web AS Java 6.40 on DVD

514 pp., 2005, with DVD, 69,95 Euro / US$ 69,95
ISBN 978-1-59229-020-8

Java Programming with the SAP Web Application Server

www.sap-press.com

K. Kessler, P. Tillert, P. Dobrikov

Java Programming with the SAP Web Application Server

Without proper guidance, the development of business oriented Java applications can be challenging. This book introduces you systematically to highly detailed concepts, architecture, and to all components of the SAP Web Application Server Java (Release 6.40), while and equipping you with all that's needed to ensure superior programming. First, benefit from an SAP NetWeaver overview, followed by the authors' guided tour through the SAP NetWeaver Developer Studio. After an excursion into the world of Web services, you then learn about the different facets of Web Dynpro technology, with in-depth details on user interfaces. This information is further bolstered with insights on the SAP NetWeaver Java Development Infrastructure and the architecture of SAP Web AS Java.

Completely new, 3rd edition of the benchmark ABAP resource

New chapters on Web Dynpro, Shared Objects, ABAP & XML, regular expressions, dynamic programming, and more

Up-tp-date for SAP NetWeaver 2004s (ABAP release 7.0)

approx. 1050 pp., 3. edition, with DVD 5
79,95 Euro / US$ 79.95
ISBN 1-59229-079-5, Feb 2007

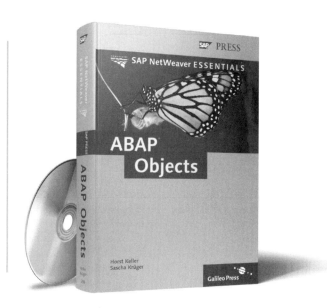

ABAP Objects

www.sap-press.com

H. Keller, S. Krüger

ABAP Objects

ABAP Programming in SAP NetWeaver

This completely revised third edition introduces you to ABAP programming with SAP NetWeaver. All concepts of modern ABAP (up to release 7.0) are covered in detail. New topics include ABAP and Unicode, Shared Objects, exception handling, Web Dynpro for ABAP, Object Services, and of course ABAP and XML. Bonus: All readers will also receive a complimentary copy of the newest Mini SAP System.

Detailed guidance on integrating PHP applications with SAP systems

Expert instructions to install and master the SAPRFC extension module

98 pp., 2006, US$ 85,00
ISBN 1-59229-066-3

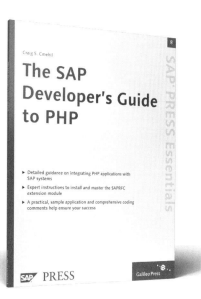

The SAP Developer's Guide to PHP

www.sap-hefte.de

Craig S. Cmehil

The SAP Developer's Guide to PHP

SAP PRESS Essentials 8

With growing interest in the development of low cost development solutions in a corporate environment, PHP is becoming more and more popular. However, the biggest problem for most SAP developers is the need for quick information to help them hit the ground running. This SAP PRESS Essentials guide provides readers with a comprehensive assessment of what is really needed to work with PHP, as well as how the SAP and PHP systems work together. After a short introduction to PHP and its capability characteristics, the SAPRFC extension module for PHP 4 and PHP 5 is explained in detail. Working with a sample application, you will learn how the two systems communicate with one another, and how best to use PHP for your own SAP-related development projects.